LEOPOLD VON RANKE

# The Secret of World History

# LEOPOLD VON RANKE

# THE SECRET OF WORLD HISTORY

## Selected Writings on
## The Art and Science of History

Edited, with translations, by
ROGER WINES

New York
FORDHAM UNIVERSITY PRESS
1981

© Copyright 1981 by FORDHAM UNIVERSITY PRESS
All rights reserved
LC 80–65600
ISBN 0–8232–1050–2  (*clothbound*)
ISBN 0–8232–1051–0  (*paperback*)

Printed in the United States of America

For
A. PAUL LEVACK
Another Great Teacher
of
History

"World history does not present such an accidental tumult, conflict, and succession of dates and peoples as appears at first sight. Nor is the often dubious advancement of civilization its only significance. There are forces, and indeed spiritual, creative forces, life itself, and there are moral energies whose development we can see. We cannot define them or put them into abstractions but they can be glimpsed and perceived. We can develop a sympathy for their existence. They unfold, capture the world, and express themselves in the greatest variety of forms; contend with, contain, and conquer one another. In their interaction and succession, in their life, their decline or resurrection, which then encompasses an ever greater fullness, higher significance, and wider extent, lies the secret of world history."

"The Great Powers"

# CONTENTS

# CHRONOLOGY

| | |
|---|---|
| 1795 | December 21, born in Wiehe, Thuringia, son of Israel Ranke, lawyer. |
| 1814–1817 | Studied theology, classical philology, and history at University of Leipzig. |
| 1818 | Teacher of classics at Friedrichs *Gymnasium*, Frankfurt on Oder. |
| 1824 | Published *History of the Latin and Teutonic Nations*. |
| 1825 | Professor extraordinarius, University of Berlin. |
| 1827–1831 | Research leave: travels to Vienna, Florence, Rome, and Venice; *History of the Ottoman and Spanish Monarchies*. |
| 1828 | *History of Serbia.* |
| 1832–1836 | Editor of *Historisch-Politische Zeitschrift*; essay on "The Great Powers"; the "Political Dialogue." |
| 1834–1836 | *History of the Popes.* |
| 1836 | Inaugural lecture as professor ordinarius at Berlin, on the relationship of history and politics. |
| 1839–1847 | *History of the Reformation in Germany.* |
| 1841 | Appointed Royal Historiographer by King Friedrich Wilhelm IV of Prussia. |
| 1843 | Married Clarissa Graves-Perceval; two sons, one daughter. |
| 1847–1848 | *History of Prussia*; prepared memorials encouraging conservative policies of king in Revolution of 1848. |
| 1852–1861 | *History of France in the Sixteenth and Seventeenth Century.* |
| 1854 | Delivered lectures on The Epochs of Modern History to King Maximilian Joseph of Bavaria. |
| 1859–1868 | *History of England in the Seventeenth Century.* |

| 1865 | Granted title of nobility by King Wilhelm I of Prussia. |
| 1871 | Retired from teaching; studies in German and Prussian history; editing Collected Works. |
| 1881–1886 | Writing *Universal History*; completed posthumously. |
| 1886 | May 23, died in Berlin. |

LEOPOLD VON RANKE

# The Secret of World History

Leopold von Ranke in formal attire and wearing his doctoral gown; his decorations
include the *Pour le Mérite* and the Order of the Black Eagle. This portrait, which
his son presented to Syracuse University, is a "Copy after J. Schrader by H. G.
Herrmann, Berlin, May 29, 1883."

"An historian must be old": von Ranke, late in life, in his library; the books
are today at Syracuse University.

# INTRODUCTION

THE NINETEENTH CENTURY accomplished one of the great revolutions in the history of Western thought. Romanticism and the cold shock of the French Revolution had forced the growth of historical seeds which had lain dormant since the playing out of the Renaissance in the seventeenth century, and European man came to perceive life differently, dropping the habits of Scholasticism and the philosophical system of the Enlightenment. In their place came a growing awareness of the changeability, growth, and development of all things. For Herder and an entire school of subsequent thinkers history was, not a mere set of practical political maxims, but the key to understanding reality. It was in the development of things that their nature was to be perceived. Each age was composed of past heritage; had its unique achievements, values, and constraints; and bequeathed its inheritance to the next. No abstract rational definition could encompass the changing, vital reality. Thus the nations, bearers and shapers of linguistic and social culture, rather than mankind as a whole, ought to be the focus of attention. Behind the nations the transcendent force of Providence utilized men and institutions as causes of change; some thinkers such as Hegel went as far as to identify the divine with the historic process, to make of history the self-realization of God as Reason. Most would have agreed with Friedrich Schlegel's dictum: "The world is, not a system, but a history."

All the great intellectual advances of the first half of the century were touched with this growing sense of the past: geology, evolutionary biology, law and politics, the novel and theology; no area was safe from the stimulus of history. In an age when thought and science became historical, history became scientific. Drawing on the critical skills developed by classical philology, historians made rapid strides in correcting their untruthfulness. Raised to the unwonted position of queen of the sciences, history could no longer remain the preserve of retired generals, politicians, and antiquarians. Historians

became professionals, and usually professors, and the discipline became a basic part of the university curriculum. The search for accurate
documentary sources replaced stirring imagery as the test of excellence.
Under the demands of this new, more scientific history, the archives
of Europe were pried open in an intensifying search by scholars, as
first ancient, then medieval, and finally modern history was sub-
stantially rewritten.[1]

At the very heart of this intellectual revolution was Germany, and,
within that country, no figure was more central than the Berlin
professor Leopold von Ranke. To oft-critical contemporaries he
seemed both an initiator and one of the greatest members of the
movement. "In Ranke," the German philosopher Wilhelm Dilthey
remarked, "all the forces of the nineteenth century come alive." And
Britain's Lord Acton summed up:

> Ranke is the representative of the age which instituted the modern
> study of history. He taught it to be critical, to be colourless, and to
> be new. We meet him at every step, and he has done more for us
> than any other man. . . . some may have surpassed him in political,
> religious, philosophic insight, in vividness of the creative imagina-
> tion, in originality, elevation, and depth of thought; but by the ex-
> tent of important work well executed, by his influence on able men,
> and by the amount of knowledge which mankind receives and em-
> ploys with the stamp of his mind upon it, he stands without a
> rival.[2]

The Collected Works of Ranke run to 54 volumes, with an additional nine volumes of his *Universal History*. Although the latter
testifies to his interest in antiquity and the Middle Ages, the greater
part of his work is in the history of Europe after the Renaissance,
where his main works encompass an amazing range of subjects: the
history of the popes, of the Ottoman and Spanish monarchies, of
England and of France, of the Reformation in Germany, and of
Prussia. The Vienna archivist Arneth saluted him for having given
each nation a masterpiece of its own history. But the quantity of his
work was the least part of it; Ranke stood for a new type of history,
and his example galvanized others to follow. Acton tells us that
"Before Ranke appeared modern history was in the hands of Robert-
son and Roscoe, Coxe and Sismondi, good easy men whose merit consisted in making things more accessible which were quite well known

already." As G. P. Gooch noted, Ranke was not the first to use the archives, but the first to use them well. Ranke's stress on the critical use of original sources forced other writers to abandon dependence on memoirs and contemporary histories, and they followed him with increasing thoroughness into the archives. By the time that Ranke died in 1886 the intensity and accuracy of historical research had been entirely transformed, and no scholar of repute could ignore his standards. In reviewing Ranke's role in that revolutionary century of German historiography. Eduard Fueter concluded: "no one came so near to being the ideal historian. . . . As a political thinker, a scholarly researcher, or a philosopher of history he has been surpassed, but no one was [an historian] like him."[3]

Leopold von Ranke was born in Wiehe, Thuringia, in 1795, the oldest child of the small-town lawyer Israel Ranke, and descendant of a long line of Evangelical pastors who had dwelt in the sleepy villages of Luther's native Saxony. Like most Germans of the Romantic era, Ranke was deeply impressed with his native green valleys and hillsides, with the hazy peak of the Kyffhäuser mountain in the background. In later life he made frequent sentimental visits to the Unstrut valley of his youth, and his letters show that he had never failed to be touched and renewed by its tranquillity.[4]

His early education, pursued at home and at the renowned classical *Gymnasium* at Pforte, firmly grounded him in a Lutheran pietism and the languages of the Graeco-Roman world. While the Holy Roman Empire fell and Napoleon remade the map of Germany and of Europe, the young Leopold was hardly stirred. "We lived," he tells us, "in our studies of the ancient world. . . . The zeal for war which seized the Prussian youth at that time . . . had no place within our walls. We let the great world events whose completion shook the earth take their course without our playing any part in them."[5] By 1814, when Ranke graduated from the *Gymnasium* and enrolled at the University of Leipzig, the political activity of the students was at a peak. He read and admired J. G. Fichte's *Addresses to the German Nation*, but in a curiously detached way did not seriously concern himself with the national movement. In part this detachment, so characteristic of his later work, was due to his being a Saxon, one of the defeated Napoleonic allies, rather than a Prussian. But it seems to have been more a matter of temperament. Ranke never became passionately attached to the cause of German political unification so ardently preached by the liberals. Like Goethe, he was really a cultural nationalist. Nor was his attachment to Prussia very strong in his early years, either after in 1815 the valley of his homeland was annexed from Saxony, or after he himself had obtained a teaching position with the Prussian state. In 1819, when his younger brother Heinrich was dismissed from a Prussian teaching post for being a follower of Friedrich Ludwig Jahn's, the disillusioned Leopold described his feeling for Prussia in negative terms: "it is not really my fatherland; I have no obligations to it."[6] Only much later, in the 1830s, after he had become firmly established in Berlin as a professor with influential political friends and the favor of the government, did Ranke become a warm defender of the Prussian state, which he saw as one of the cornerstones of a stable social order. He remained cool to German unification, and it was not until the late 1870s that he grudgingly came to accept Bismarck's achievement as a necessary bulwark of that order.[7]

During his years at Leipzig theology and classical literature, rather than politics, formed the center of his interests. His original intention to pursue the ancestral career of clergyman was blunted by an increasing unorthodoxy, and he turned to classics, which he studied under the critical eye of Gottfried Hermann. He also worked on the texts of medieval sources with Gustav Adolf Stenzel. The chief intellectual influences of these years seem to have been J. G. Fichte, Friedrich Schlegel, Goethe, and, above all, Thucydides, upon whom he wrote his now-vanished doctoral thesis, "a powerful, great spirit before whom I knelt."[8] He also read Barthold Georg Niebuhr's *Roman History*, "the first German historical work which made an impression on me." Finally, in 1817, the anniversary year of the Reformation, he turned his attention to Luther whose career he described in an unpublished sketch. "The weak popular narrations which then appeared led me to attempt a biography based on a study of the authentic documents." Ranke's student fascination with Luther as a religious leader also led him briefly to the study of Christ as an historical figure, a line of development which might have anticipated the later work of Renan and Strauss, and which continued to interest Ranke into advanced age. In 1873 he recommended to his son Otto that he undertake such a biography, which Ranke had once wanted to compose. Carl Hinrichs' analysis of the parallels between the myth of Prometheus and the portrayal of Christ as an historical figure in Ranke's *Universal History*, as the personality who infuses through his own career a spark of the divine into the life of his epoch, reflects traces of ideas which young Ranke possessed at Leipzig.[9]

But it was classics rather than history which he had chosen to study, and in 1818 he began his career as a teacher of classical literature at the Friedrichs *Gymnasium* in the Prussian town of Frankfurt on Oder.[10] Sedate in the outward aspects of his career as teacher, Ranke's years at Frankfurt were stirred with the intellectual passions revealed in his letters to his brother Heinrich. He moved in the spirit of his generation, seeking to express relationships between the visible world and the divine, however conceived. He sat late at table and in the *Weinstube* with his young colleagues, with his brother, and, even on one occasion, with Jahn himself discussing such matters. His mind expanded.

> The material is unlimited; the man, small in comparison; and the time, short. I have resolved never to waste my time with the writing of books, but to strive for every insight which redeems and enlightens mankind. Since everything springs from God, such insight will depend not on the material but on the eye; as we uncover reality, remove its shell, and bring forth its essence, it happens also that our own existence, inner life, source, and breath reveal the passage of God, or at least His being.[11]

In such excitement his attention gradually turned to the more concrete aim of historical studies, turned in part by his practice of consulting original sources in composing his school lectures. In later life Ranke was to claim that the comparison of Sir Walter Scott's novel *Quentin Durward* with the actual *Mémoires* of Philippe de Commynes sparked his interest in modern history. "I found by comparison that the truth was more interesting and beautiful than the romance. I turned away from the latter and resolved to avoid all invention and imagination in my works and to stick to facts."[12] Early poetical drafts reveal that Ranke toyed with a career in literature, but finally turned to history. "It is certain," he told Heinrich, "that I was born for studies . . . less certain that I was born for the study of history; but I have for once taken it up . . . and will stick to it."[13] Early diary entries and his letters to Heinrich reveal strong religious roots to his choice of vocation. For history had special relevance to young Ranke's search for values. It was the key to Revelation: "in all of history God lives, dwells, and is to be found. Every deed testifies to Him, every moment preaches His name, and above all the great interactions of history."[14] History was for Ranke a "holy hieroglyph," a divine puzzle worthy of a lifetime of decipherment. But in the age of Hegel such expansive visions of Providence led most young thinkers into philosophy. Ranke—like Wilhelm von Humboldt in his 1821 essay "On the Task of the Historian"—was among the few who saw history as an alternative method of comprehending reality.[15]

As he formulated them later in his lectures, Ranke maintained that there were two distinct ways of coming to a knowledge of reality. The first was by traditional deductive philosophy; the second, by history. The latter would proceed from a critical study of sources to the establishment of certain facts, thus offering material to the historian from which his intuition might discern traces of the divine plan. "After criticism, intuition is necessary," he explained. "The result is a sympathetic comprehension of the universe." Despite a common preoccupation with the role of Spirit in history, Ranke came to distinguish his approach clearly from that of Hegel. For Ranke history was not a process in which an immanent deity progressed to self-consciousness, a self-realization of reason. Not only did Ranke reject such a teleology of history, but he also espoused panentheism, maintaining a clear distinction between the Creator and the created world. In a way which we do not clearly understand, God providentially guided His creation; divine ideas infused themselves into historical institutions and personalities which then intervened to change the course of history. Historical development required, he asserted, not only "the breath of God, but also the effort of man." This was indeed in the tradition of the Christian philosophy of history, but Ranke differed from other philosophers of this school by maintaining that only a scrupulous and rigorous study of the sources could establish a history sufficiently accurate to trace the designs of Providence.[16]

His years at Frankfurt on Oder (1818–1824) culminated in his final decision to become an historian of modern Europe and in the writing of his first book, published in 1824: *History of the Latin and Teutonic Nations, 1494–1535.* The work created a stir for several reasons. The oft-cited Introduction declared Ranke's intention to liberate history from its advocacy of contemporary religious or political causes: "History has had assigned to it the office of judging the past and of instructing the present for the benefit of future ages. To such high offices the present work does not presume; it seeks only to show what actually happened [*wie es eigentlich gewesen*]."[17] The appendix to the book made Ranke's reputation as a critical scholar. In it he systematically investigated the sources used by such leading Renaissance writers as Machiavelli and Guicciardini in their histories. He discovered an enormous number of plagiarisms, errors, and distortions, proving finally the impossibility of erecting a sound historical work on such memoirs and contemporary authors without a recourse to primary sources. Finally, he was quite original in perceiving the scope of European history. For Ranke, the interaction of the Latin and Teutonic peoples after the fall of the Roman Empire had created in Europe a unique culture and civilization. He excluded the Slavs as having only a peripheral interest in the process, and allowed each nationality its particular role and contribution, while seeing the whole as greater than the sum of its parts. This vision of Europe as an interacting whole was to become the program for a life's work of detailed study of the major nations, just as the critical appendix presaged his ever-deepening search for more reliable information which would lead him shortly into the dusty archives of Europe.[18]

Ranke prudently arranged to have copies put in the hands of the Prussian minister of education von Altenstein, who in 1825 appointed the *Gymnasium* teacher to an extraordinary professorship at the University of Berlin. He now had the leisure to do research and the necessary libraries at hand. More than that, he found in his city and his colleagues stimuli to an enrichment of his own personality and his perception of politics. Berlin in the 1820s was a small town by modern standards, but already the intellectual capital of Germany. The university established in the reform era by Wilhelm von Humboldt (1810) had attracted the outstanding men in each field—Schleiermacher in theology, Hegel in philosophy, von Savigny in legal history,

and Niebuhr in ancient history—and now young Ranke. Its elite frequently met socially and mingled with high officials of the Prussian
government. It had its own currents of intrigue; at the university
Ranke came under the patronage of von Savigny and placed himself
firmly in the historical school, which opposed the philosophic school
led by Hegel. In social circles, Ranke became an habitué of the salon
of the liberal Karl and Rahel Varnhagen von Ense, where the country
scholar acquired sufficient social polish to stand him in good stead at
the courts of kings. Later, in the '30s, Ranke shifted to a more conservative circle of friends, and in his older years became somewhat
of a recluse. Aside from his lectures and the seminar which he gave
for selected students, Ranke played a relatively inactive part in the
university. His aim was scholarship, and he cast about for his next
subject. The publisher Friedrich Perthes urged him to continue his
work on the Renaissance period, and Ranke agreed to a study in
several volumes of the princes and peoples of the Mediterranean area
in the sixteenth century. About the same time he discovered in the
Berlin library some 47 bound volumes of relations by Venetian ambassadors to their home government, reporting the conditions at the
courts of southern Europe in the sixteenth and seventeenth centuries.
The find had a major effect on his career, revealing to him the sources
necessary to fulfill the ambitious program of his first work.[19] Here
were the original reports of eyewitnesses; there would be many more
like them in the archives of the several states. From such immediate
reports and the papers recording the daily transaction of state business
it would be possible to place history on a new basis of certainty, freed
from dependence on memoirs. "I see the time approaching," he later
wrote,

> when we shall base modern history, no longer on the reports even
> of contemporary historians, except insofar as they were in possession
> of personal and immediate knowledge of facts; and still less on
> work yet more remote from the source; but rather on the narratives
> of eyewitnesses, and on genuine and original documents.[20]

Even his narrative style bears witness to the profound influence which
the Venetian relations had on Ranke. Like their authors he cultivated
the polished description of the court, the quick character sketches of
leading men, the shrewd judgments on the motives and causes of po-

litical deeds and policies. Too, he cultivated the ambassador's cool detachment from the court described, so in accord with his own striving for an impartial and objective portrayal of "what really happened." With the passing years, Ranke's increasing use of such archival sources made his later works greatly superior to his first publications.

The appearance of the *History of the Ottoman and Spanish Monarchies in the Sixteenth and Seventeenth Centuries* in 1827 was the occasion of his being awarded a generous research grant from the Prussian government for study of the sources of sixteenth-century Italian history. His travels took him first to Vienna where he made the close acquaintance of Friedrich von Gentz, the sage adviser of Metternich. Introduced to the Austrian minister, Ranke found the archives open to him, not only those in the Habsburg capital, but the even more valuable holdings of the former republic at Venice. In Vienna his political outlook matured at weekly conversations with Gentz and his circle; Ranke also came in contact with the Serbian literary exile Vuk Stephanovitch, and developed a side-interest in the oppressed Christian nations of the Balkans, which led him to write his little *History of Serbia* (1828). It was a warmly written minor jewel which won Goethe's admiration and Niebuhr's praise as "the best contemporary history which we possess."[21]

But his main work led him over the Alps to Italy, that magnet for German travelers in all centuries. Far from the carnival atmosphere of Goethe's tour, Ranke's was a sober and hard-working visit which extended over nearly two years. Barred from the use of the papal archives as a suspicious Protestant, he gained entrée to the private holdings of the Roman nobility; there he found the papers of former popes, cardinals, and generals. He abandoned his earlier plan for a history of Italy to undertake a more original venture: the history of the popes in the Renaissance and in the Reformation era. Ranke's letters to family and friends in Berlin picture a hard-working scholar with little time for leisure, but imbued with the great joy of discovery. "Let no one," he later wrote, "pity a man who devotes himself to studies apparently so dry, and neglects for them the delights of many a sunny day. It is true that the companions of his solitary hours are but lifeless paper, but they are the remnants of the life of past ages, which gradually assume form and substance to the eye occupied in the study of them." He did circulate within the small German community at Rome, meeting the future king of Prussia, Friedrich Wilhelm IV, with whom he struck up a friendly acquaintance. Reflecting on his Italian years, Ranke confessed that "Never did I learn or think more" than in the year 1830/1831. In the latter year he returned to Germany, laden with notes and manuscripts which would form the basis of years of writing, filled with a new awareness of history and politics, to resume his teaching in Berlin.[22]

His arrival offered an opportunity to the Prussian foreign minister, Count Bernstorff, and other officials who had been seeking a conservative scholar of established reputation to edit a new journal which would combat the liberal political ideas which were current in Germany in the wake of the French and Belgian revolutions of 1830. "So," Ranke tells us, "I became a political journalist—but on the basis of ideas which I had formed from the study of history and my experience in life."[23] The magazine proved to be a commercial and political failure; Ranke was unable to enlist many collaborators or to attract many readers, and in the end had to write most of the important pieces himself. Only four issues appeared between 1833 and 1836 when he concluded the final issue with his "Political Dialogue." Undoubtedly, the experience of wrestling with contemporary issues clarified Ranke's own historical outlook, confirmed him in his monarchical politics, and, incidentally, brought him a substantial raise in salary and a promotion to the professoriate at the university from a grateful Prussian government. His close association with government figures was influential in having him appointed Prussian Royal Historiographer in 1841, and during the revolution of 1848 he composed several position papers urging Friedrich Wilhelm IV to resist the liberals in preserving monarchical rule in Prussia.

Ranke's view of the relationship between history and politics is stated in his professorial Inaugural Lecture (1836), his "Political Dialogue" (1836), and his essay on "The Great Powers" (1833). The first affirmed that a lack of historical perspective could lead to the most extravagant political injustices, while its employment would allow statesmen to discern the inner spirit of their particular state, and guide its development in a way compatible with its nature.[24] In the second he explored the spiritual nature of the state. Far from being an artificial construction based on a contract theory of government, each state, in Ranke's view, was the embodiment of spiritual tendencies and moral energies which determined the character of its citizens and shaped its constitution. Each state was thus unique; it should not copy others but seek to realize its inner idea, which ultimately derived its origin from God. "Instead of those temporary conglomerations which the contract theory of the state presents, like cloud formations, I see them as spiritual substances, original creations of the human mind—one could say, thoughts of God." Whatever divine sanction this seemed to give a particular state, however just, what moral order could be imputed to the ruthless conflict of states which had marked modern European history? [25]

Ranke attempted to answer this in his essay on "The Great Powers." [26] "World history," he declared,

> does not present such an accidental tumult, conflict, and succession of dates and peoples as appears at first sight. . . . There are forces, and indeed spiritual, creative forces, life itself, and there are moral energies whose development we can see. . . . In their interaction and succession, in their life, their decline or resurrection, which then encompasses an ever greater fullness, higher significance, and wider extent, lies the secret of world history.

This is a lofty and moralizing view of war, but Ranke went further. On another occasion he noted: "victory falls wherever the greatest energy, the most vital concentration of forces, lies. What we often describe as material force has in itself a higher significance, for the greatest possible unfolding of the rule of the spirit reveals itself among the most resolute." [27]

The pitfalls of such a spiritualization of power are obvious: a glorification of the state, whose morality cannot be judged either by its citizens, or in relation to any outside standard, and hence a vindication of that state's aggressions against competing states. In the end, for the historian and the citizen, might is equivalent to right. It is true that Ranke believed in the existence of God and of moral ideas which influenced the states, rather than accepting the state as its own self-justification. But with the secularization of German intellectual life in the later-nineteenth century, the Idealist tradition which Ranke shared lost the religious restraints against unrestricted state power, giving way to a sort of biologic determinism which eventually produced Spengler, and even Hitler.[28]

Thus after 1945 the Dutch historian Pieter Geyl assailed Ranke and his followers for producing a fundamental weakness in the German political tradition which left it peculiarly susceptible to totalitarianism. "Behind the radiant Ranke," Werner Stark remarked, "looms the sinister Bismarck." Whatever the long-range effects of historicism—which were considerable—on the German political tradition, it seems only fair to warn against an exaggeration of Ranke's role. We know the extent to which he personally disapproved—albeit usually in his private letters and conversations—of Bismarck's Machiavellian tactics in achieving German unification. To his conservative friend Manteuffel, he complained in 1869 about Bismarck's policies: "We are using the victory to deny the principles upon which we ourselves rest."[29] Though Ranke's published works accepted without criticism a state morality quite at variance with the personal Christian ethic, he was not the only bearer of the historicist tradition. He was part of a broad cultural movement which affected most of his contemporaries, and the glorification of Prussian power and justification of Bismarck's power politics were more the work of his pupil Sybel, of Droysen, and, above all, of the militant Treitschke. For the following generation, the successful existence of Bismarck's Second Reich provided its own converts, whose admiration of Ranke was based on considerations other than his rather mild exaltation of Prussia. Ranke could resolve the tension between spiritual force and power in terms of his own subjective religious beliefs, but not objectively. There remains an unresolved contradiction in the treatment of power in his works which is characteristic of the historicist tradition he did so much to launch.

Ranke's responsibility lies in his establishment of historicism as an intellectually respectable position. He gave validation to the mere outline of Wilhelm von Humboldt's 1821 essay and of his own works of 1836 by producing an impressive series of research studies. In his books Ranke employed not only his critical method, but also his attitude toward power. Moreover, he raised up two generations of students in the historical seminar which he instituted at the University of Berlin, the origin of the modern way of training scholars in history. At his death, Sybel eulogized: "For the critical research and determination of historical facts, Ranke's teaching method had almost epoch-making effects upon Germany." The implications of historicism and especially of its opening of the way to a relativism of all values, because they were historically derived rather than based on an absolute transcendent morality, were also explored in the Berlin lectures of Ranke's colleague Gustav Droysen. Their pupils in turn produced pupils.[30]

As Georg Iggers points out, this historicist outlook thus became part of the attitude of the educated middle class, inoculating German minds against Western natural-law liberalism, which cut the intellectual ground out from under developing German liberalism. In place of the stress on individual liberties and the limitation of state power characteristic of England, France, and the United States, Germany continued to view the state as a self-justifying moral community in which individuals had to participate to achieve personal fulfillment.[31]

We should not overlook the lasting contributions of German historicism: the realization that all human institutions and values have their origins within the historical process; that the nature of things can be understood only in relation to this genetic process; that each individual and each institution are unique and cannot be comprehended fully in any abstract definition or principle; and, finally, that this uniqueness can be studied only through the critical use of historical sources. The stress on the unique by historians following Ranke led to an ever-deepening and narrower specialization. German historical thinkers such as Dilthey, Windelband, and Rickert employed the concept of historicism to define for history a new mode of knowledge distinct from the deductive speculation of philosophy or the inductive search of the natural sciences, both of which sought to attain general laws while history was concerned with the unique and nonrepeatable. To a greater extent in Germany than elsewhere this discouraged the historical study of the typical or recurring elements in human affairs and effectively delayed until after World War II that rapprochement between history and the social sciences which has marked contemporary historical work.[32]

During Ranke's brief engagement with the *Historisch-Politische*

*Zeitschrift,* his *History of the Popes* made its appearance, the work from which he was to gain an international reputation. As the first Protestant to write impartially on the subject, he incurred reproaches of faint-heartedness from some co-religionists while the papacy condemned the work as hostile. Ranke had written the first account of the Catholic Church as an historical phenomenon and had described the interaction of secular and religious concerns in the Counter Reformation. But it was also one of his most vivid works, and the impress of strong personalities such as Ignatius Loyola, or Popes Paul IV and Pius V, can be felt in its narration.[33] He next turned to a project closer to the heart of his countrymen, completing the other half of the story by writing a *History of the Reformation in Germany,* which was published in six volumes (1839–1847). For this undertaking he had unearthed a new source: the 96 volumes of relations by the Frankfurt ambassadors to the German Imperial Diet during the Reformation. Ransacking the princely archives of Germany, he completed a work which many consider his masterpiece. Traces of his early fascination with Luther can be found in his treatment of the Saxon monk. Ranke felt a closer affinity to this than to any of his other subjects, and the warmth of his enthusiasm shows through the narration of events, secular and religious. As in the history of the papacy, he remained the master of political intrigues and conflicts, showing how they had determined the outcome of religious reform in Germany. Sybel praised it as "impregnated with the enthusiasm of a German patriot for the greatest act of the German spirit." It became a great national classic and was probably his most successful literary work.[34]

After his appointment as Prussian Royal Historiographer by Friedrich Wilhelm IV, Ranke produced a series of nine—later enlarged to twelve—books of Prussian history, which carried the history of the Hohenzollern monarchy from the end of the Middle Ages through the period of Frederick the Great. The work made its appearance on the eve of the Revolution of 1848. It proved less publicly satisfying than his *Reformation*; Ranke pictured Prussia primarily as the exemplar of the old Protestant territorial state rather than as the precursor of German unity. He wrote his work, as Hermann Oncken put it, "in the same spirit in which Friedrich Wilhelm IV declined the Im-

perial Crown." Ranke's old-Prussian particularism was sneered at by
the nationalist historian Treitschke, who maintained that Ranke had
no calling for Prussian history.[35]

The 1848 revolution reinforced Ranke's intention to develop further the outline in his essay on "The Great Powers" of the rise of the
monarchical state and the origins of the French Revolution, and he
attempted to bring into view the great historical events which are
based on those same contradictions: the development of the Prussian
state, the formation of French power, and, finally, the history of the
seventeenth century in England. His middle years passed quietly, devoted to long journeys to foreign archives and study hours surrounded
by rooms of books in his aging home on the Luisenstrasse. Rarely did
he take dinner out; more frequently he took the air strolling in the
Berliner Tiergarten.[36] In 1843, when he and the family had given him
up for a celibate, he met and married Clarissa Graves, daughter of a
Dublin lawyer, by whom he had two sons and a daughter.[37] Between
1852 and 1861 he published five volumes on the French monarchy;
and between 1859 and 1868, six on the history of England in the
seventeenth century. These were, in Ranke's words, "not at all histories of France and England, but general European history, world
history . . . in which one epoch encloses another." In terms of archival
research and the power of narration they were his masterpieces; his
sketches of such figures as Charles I and Cardinal Richelieu, his account of the reign of Louis XIV, his understanding of the European
significance of the English Revolution of 1688 not only broke new
ground, but even today afford fresh insight into the period.[38]

He was 70 years old when he completed the research on the *History
of England*. In early 1871 he retired from teaching at Berlin and
devoted the next decade to collecting and editing his complete works.
He also returned to research in German history, turning out studies
on the neglected history of Germany from 1555 to 1618, the career of
Wallenstein, Frederick the Great's *Fürstenbund* of 1785, and smaller
studies of the outbreak of the Seven Years' War and the opening of
the revolutionary wars of 1791–1792. He also edited the memoirs of
the Prussian statesman Hardenberg and the correspondence of King
Friedrich Wilhelm IV with Bunsen.[39]

Ranke was heaped high with honors: granted hereditary nobility in 1865; made a Privy Councillor in 1882, an honorary citizen of Berlin in 1885. Visitors from all over the world sought out the slight man who was revered as the initiator of the historical revolution. In 1884 the infant American Historical Association made him its first (and only) honorary member.[40]

To the amazement of the public, in 1880 the 84-year-old scholar, half-blind and dependent on his devoted assistants for aid in reading and dictation, announced that he would undertake a *Universal History* of mankind! Combing through his old research notes and his draft university lectures, but drawing above all on the insights of a lifetime, the white-haired historian turned out a volume a year, bringing the story from the ancient Egyptians and Hebrews down to the twelfth century before his death on May 23, 1886. His student Alfred Dove completed the *Universal History*, using Ranke's lecture notes to carry the account down to 1453, the point at which his extensive publications on modern history commenced. Ranke's work thereby spanned the entire course of human history. Thus was concluded, in Acton's words, "the most astonishing career in literature."[41]

For the English-speaking reader of today, Ranke is surprisingly inaccessible; indeed, he has become something of a patron saint, more praised than read. Not all his major works have been translated, while almost none of his letters, notes, or essays, so important in getting an informal appraisal of his craft of history, is in English. Many of his books, whether in German or in English, no longer are in print, and the modern reader is less likely to bear up with the four- or six-volume works which are. Thus the purpose of this anthology is to bring attention to some of the riches which a reader might find in a more extended study of Ranke's histories. Its emphasis is on Ranke as an historian, with translations of essays and addresses which lay down his program for research, politics, and the relationship between an historian's values and his work. It also attempts to give some sense of Ranke's literary skill, by including examples of his historical portraiture from his *History of the Popes, History of France*, and *History of the Reformation*. Finally, a selection of letters and brief reflections culled from his works and notes tries to recapture the man, whose own inner development joined with the tendencies of his age to make him a world-historical figure in Ranke's own sense of the word.

A word concerning some ideas frequently used by Ranke might be helpful.[42] Regarded in England and America as the founder of scientific history, Ranke has sometimes been mistakenly identified as a Positivist. He was actually an Idealist standing in close relationship to the Romantic philosophers of history, though differing from them in method. Ranke himself thought such misimpressions amusing. "It is laughable to hear that I am lacking in philosophical and religious interests; it was just these, and these alone, which drove me to history." Though he was not a systematic thinker and declined the role of philosopher, he had come to history from the study of theology and philosophy, was aware of what he was doing in declaring the autonomy of the historical method, and clearly distinguished his own approach from those of both the Enlightenment and Hegel, whom he sometimes superficially resembled.

The key to Ranke's understanding of the historical process lay in his concept of the individual, and the various relationships of the individual to other individuals, to the realm of moral values, and to the historian who studied both. For Ranke, as for most of the Romantics (such as Friedrich Schlegel, Wilhelm von Humboldt, or Karl von Savigny), the concept of individuality, whether applied to a single person or to a nation, implied a discrete being whose nature could be understood only in terms of the process of becoming; the present was inseparably connected with the past and the future; because all individuals were caught up in a differing experience of change, each was unique. "The first germ," Ranke said, "continues to affect the entire growth, consciously or unconsciously." This is quite in the spirit of the Romantics, who saw individuality as indefinable because it included both the rational and the irrational elements of a unique being.

Ranke characteristically uses the concept of the individual in a dual context; the individual is always regarded both for itself, and at the same time for its relationship to other individuals and to a larger whole which he calls the universal. Reading Ranke, one comes across frequent references to this interaction of the individual or particular and the universal (*besonderes* and *allgemeines*). As Meinicke indicated, Ranke applied the concept of individual to describe persons, states, and nations. He used a sort of hierarchy of individuals, each embedded as it were within a higher one, the focus of attention varying as the historian turned to different aspects of a period. The particular is a very concrete object under study.[43]

By universal Ranke usually refers to the sphere of ideas, the sphere in which all historic individuals interact. By universal he can refer to a century, an epoch, to the entire process of world history. Finally, in dealing with persons as individuals, Ranke sometimes distinguishes between the purely private and domestic aspect of their personality and the part in which they played their historic role, that is, entered into interaction with the universal as political or religious leaders, or artists. Ranke thus uses the concepts as verbal tools rather than as strict definitions; they are employed to express a dynamic relationship between the individual and its context. This dynamic relationship occupies Ranke's special attention, and is his most original contribution to the perception of history. As Ernst Simon wrote, the basic historical problem for Ranke was "how the individual could be brought into harmony with the universal."[44]

Ranke used the concepts to express the difference between his own historical method and that of philosophy: "From the particular we can indeed thoughtfully and boldly ascend to the universal; but from the universal, there is no way to the particular." This is the essential idea of historicism. But exactly how was the individual brought into such contact?

Describing the state in his "Political Dialogue" of 1836, Ranke uses the term *realgeistig*. As a panentheist, Ranke did not use *Geist* or spirit in the same sense as did Hegel, whom he had rejected; he distinguished between a realm of ideas or spirit, and the concrete manifestation of these ideas in the historical world. Only the latter was susceptible to historical investigation. History as a science, he said, "would be nothing if it did not take as its real object history as a form of being."[45] His term *realgeistig* was used to stress the dynamic interplay of ideas upon the concrete observable state. Only in such real individuals could the general tendencies, leading ideas, of which he frequently speaks, find expression, and work on the historical process. As Srbik notes, these leading ideas are related more to the notion of *Zeitgeist*, the spirit of the age, than to an Hegelian developing World-Spirit. "We understand," Ranke explained, "by 'leading ideas' nothing other than the dominating tendencies in every century. These tendencies can only be described and not summed up in the final instance in a definition. Otherwise we would be back at the rejected [Hegelian] position."[46] "The universal tendencies alone do not decide the outcome of history," he noted in his *Universal History*; "they always require the great personalities to bring them into play." These ideas affected states as well as persons: he saw Austria as the expression of the Catholic and monarchical idea; Prussia, as the expression of the Protestant and monarchical idea.[47]

For Ranke, then, the ideas behind each person, institution, or century—he once called them "thoughts of God"—could be studied by the historian only at their point of interaction with the individual, a point which he described as the *Moment*. In the *History of England*, for example, he speaks of the confluence: "the greatest thing which a human being can attain is to pursue the universal while pursuing his own affairs. Then the personal existence is exalted into a world-historical moment."[48]

The emphasis on ideas might suggest that Ranke thought that history was a determined process. Yet he expressly rejected that limitation, conceding that although tendencies and contemporaries restricted the freedom of any historical individual, the possibility of free development always remained.

> Freedom stands side by side with necessity. Both rest in what has already been formed and can again be abolished, which is the basis of everything which ascends to new activity. That which has become is related to that which is becoming. But this relationship, too, is not to be understood as arbitrary; rather, it occurs in a certain manner, so and so, not otherwise. It is also an object of knowledge. A long series of events, following one another and accompanying one another, bound together in such a manner, forms a century or an epoch.

As Helmut Diwald pointed out, this necessity for Ranke was not a causal necessity in the ontological sense but belonged to a different, historical sort of existence. Events were not entirely caused by tendencies, nor were they arbitrary—they were "so and so, not otherwise"—as a result of the actions of individuals. "In everything which we experience," the old Ranke noted, "we can perceive—I will not say a necessity—but a logical consequence." In describing the stormy career of Wallenstein in the Thirty Years' War, he reflected:

> How much more powerful, deeper, and encompassing is the general life which fills the centuries in uninterrupted flow than that of the individual who enjoys only a brief span, who seems only to begin things and never to complete them. . . . Significant events occur only in collaboration with the existing homogeneous world elements. Each individual appears almost as a mere child of his age, as the expression of a universal tendency external to him.

But Ranke does not pause here, insisting that individuals do have their contribution "which is entirely their own. They possess an independent life of original force. Although we say that they represent their age, they also intervene decisively with their innate drive in their times." If freedom in history is limited, it is nonetheless real. Though "history consists of a series of events following one another and determining one another," Ranke elsewhere explained, "when I say 'determine' that does not really mean through absolute necessity. What is great is that human freedom is always taken into account; history is performed in scenes of freedom."[49]

The concept of the individual also lies at the root of Ranke's notion of objectivity in history. Historians such as Lord Acton who accept human responsibility and freedom often feel the need to judge the past figures they describe.[50] Ranke expressly rejected this in his preface to his first book in 1824; he felt that such attempts at judgment falsified the understanding of the past. History had to be freed as much as possible from contemporary religious and political struggles and understood on its own terms. It was impossible, he wrote elsewhere,

> to have no opinion about the struggles of power and ideas which are contained in the greatest decisions of history. But the essence of impartiality can still be retained, for it consists only in recognizing that each of the active powers has its own position, and in evaluating them in terms of their own relationships. We must see them for their own selves, appearing before and contending with one another. In these struggles are fulfilled the events and the course of world history. Objectivity is at the same time impartiality.[51]

In his lectures to the Bavarian King Max Joseph, Ranke delivered the famous dictum that "every epoch is immediate to God." There was in point of moral or aesthetic matters no such thing as progress, and each age had to be judged on its own unique terms, not as a precursor of the present.[52]

True, he later conceded that "history will always be rewritten," for it was not possible for an historian to take up pen without "the impulse of the present." But the ethical task of the historian—he compared it to a priestly obligation—was to surmount these obstacles to his objectivity by returning as closely as possible to the original sources of past eras. In his lectures of 1845 he summed up:

> No one could be more convinced than I that historical research requires the strictest method: criticism of the authors, the banning of all fables, the extraction of the pure facts. But I am also convinced that this fact has a spiritual content. For any action is not the outermost limit. The external appearance is not the final thing which we have to discover; there is still something which occurs within. The event occurs only as the result of a spiritually combined series of actions. It is our task to recognize what really happened in the series of facts which German history comprises: their sum. After the labor of criticism, intuition is required.[53]

For Ranke the historian's task remained the pursuit of the entire "Real-Geistiges." He must operate on two levels of thought, that of critically researchable history, and a second stage which Meinecke described as intuitive recognition, by which the historian would perceive the ideal relationships inherent in the relationships of the events which he studied. Secure in his own religious faith, harmonious in his own relationship to the universal, Ranke did not proceed, as Droysen did, to the recognition that the second stage was too purely personal and opened the way to a total relativism of values.[54] In the long run, then, Ranke offered no lasting theory of historical knowledge. What he did demonstrate were the fruitful insights which he personally could achieve in attempting to discern the great tendencies and combinations of history, intuition following research. Ranke was modestly aware of the limitations which he or any historian faced in carrying out his program.

> Everything hangs together—critical study of authentic sources, impartial understanding, objective narration—the goal is the presentation of the whole truth. I put forward an ideal, which people will say is unrealizable. For so it is: the idea is immeasurable, the attain-

ment by its very nature limited. Fortunate, when we take the right path and achieve a result which will withstand later research and criticism.[55]

One such criticism, frequently voiced even by those who respect Ranke's achievement in his chosen field of political history, is that he consistently neglected to take into account the activities of the lower classes and ignored the social and economic factors in history. There were reasons for this: partly because Ranke chose to write about an age of absolutism when the decisions of a few courtiers and monarchs decisively shaped the result of European history; partly because of the rich new finds of primarily political documents which he unearthed in the archives of the European states, a treasury which required decades of work by historians to explore. But it was personal as well; Ranke's own politics were most congenial to the pre-democratic monarchies of the era after 1815. He sympathized with rule from above by legitimate dynasties. "Is it bearable," he complained during the revolutions of 1830, "that we should be governed by apprentices and street urchins?"[56] Critical of liberal reformers for their abstract political schemes, he remained rooted in the existing, historic monarchy, and conceded only that it should gradually accommodate itself to some popular representation. Leading the sheltered and comfortable life of an academic, he was never touched personally by the plight of the masses in the Industrial Revolution, and though he recognized the social tensions of his times, he did not choose to write on any major topics after the period of the French Revolution. He seemed, in fact, to have more sympathy for preceding centuries than for the one in which he himself lived. The dramatic advances in our knowledge of the English seventeenth-century revolutions or the coming of the French Revolution contributed by contemporary scholars using new social and economic sources only indicate how much Ranke missed by his bias, and how necessary it is for the modern reader to supplement Ranke's treatment of topics with newer works. He must be read for his strengths, not his omissions.[57]

Nearly a century after Ranke's death, many of his works are available in reprint, both in English and in his native German. This is due not solely to his status as a monument; though his information is in many places outdated, he remains, like Gibbon, a literary classic. His unerring choice of the significant which served him so well in research also gave to his finished works drama and meaning: he captures for us the great moments of the great nations in modern history.[58] Acton for a long time disapproved of him, not only for his reluctance to sit in judgment on past characters, but as a typically scholarly "dryasdust." "The dust of archives blots out ideas. No man had so few as Ranke." In contrast, Heinrich Heine also dismissed him, but as superficial, claiming his "pretty talent was fit only to carve historical figurines."[59] The reader can form his own judgment of Ranke's calm, flowing narrative, artfully building its scenes into climaxes, sparkling with insightful portraits and trenchant summations. An examination of his fragmentary notes, letters, and lectures reveals quite a different style, epigrammatic, with a quite original syntax and spelling, sharp. Ranke consciously sought to "dissolve himself" in his published works, and avoided there the value judgments and highly personal expressions with which his private papers abound. In his books everything seems on a higher, Olympian, harmonious—even too classic—plane. Friedrich Meinecke, himself no mean stylist, praised "the music of Ranke's speech, the interweaving of his sentences, and the rhythms of his narrative, delicate as Goethe's, not translatable without loss into modern speech." An American translator can only ruefully concur.[60]

When Ranke took up his pen, after the example of his model, Thucydides, history had been written for two thousand years as a form of literature. Ranke's own work, and that of his generation, were to raise its claim to status as a science, based solidly on painstaking research, and cleansed of distorting personal interpretations. And of a sort, scientific it has continued. Science is superseded; art endures. Though much of Ranke's work was solid enough to stand the test of time, subsequent researchers have enlarged his answers, and added new dimensions in such areas as economics and society, so that he is no longer a first reference to be consulted when we look for information about an event in European history. Yet he remains a classic, and not only of the German language. Ranke's art endures. Like Gibbon, he can be read as literature which also informs, an artist who paints with facts. Nor is that artistic conception necessarily invalidated by later, different, and more informed versions. As Hayden White pointed out in a seminal study of nineteenth-century historical thinkers, not only Ranke, but Burckhardt, Marx, Hegel, were men who built their philosophic or scientific versions of history on essentially artistic foundations. In each case, the thinker's approach to history and his use of it depended on his more fundamental level of consciousness, the preconditions of his approach to history, which then formed the basis for his selection of what is significant in history. To describe this process, perhaps the terms of classical poetics are more useful than those of the philosophy of science. Thus White classifies Ranke and others according to classical modes of literature: Romance, Comedy, Tragedy, Irony; and asserts that Ranke's essentially Comic approach is not invalidated by later approaches to history cast in an Ironic mode. Indeed, a return to other modes of approaching history may be required if history is to regain wider influence on modern thought than it has achieved in its present, largely Ironic approach.[61]

It is in the light of the enduring value of Ranke's art, and in the hope of presenting him, not simply as a museum piece, but as a person capable of seeing history in a different way from that of most contemporary historians, that this anthology has been compiled.

Ranke's pupil Jacob Burckhardt once defined history as what one age finds worthy of note in another. In the depressed post-Hitler Germany of 1948, Meinecke reappraised pupil and master. He noted that the critical spirit of Burckhardt, who deplored the excesses of state power and forecast the evils of demagogic mass industrial society, was more relevant to the twentieth century. Yet he hoped that a time might come when the tranquil, optimistic spirit of Ranke might again serve as an inspiration.[62]

Our own decade of the eighties does not offer much grounds for tranquillity, but Ranke's viewpoint of universal history is still useful. In the century of Lenin, Mao, Hitler, De Gaulle, the notion that ideas come to bear on human history through personification in certain leaders, that universal history has to be understood, not in separate events or personalities—though we have to start with them—but in their relation to the wider whole, can refine the perception of the historian.

"Apart from and beyond the histories of individual nations," Ranke remarked,

I assume a specific principle of universal history: it is the principle of a common life of the human race which dominates the nations without resolving itself in them. One could call it culture, preservation and expansion of civilization, not of culture alone, as it is usually understood, which would restrict the horizon to sciences and arts. Civilization comprises at the same time religion and state, the free development of all these forces looking toward the ideal. Civilization forms the foremost acquisition and possession of humanity handed on and augmented from generation to generation . . . it is inseparably bound together with politics and war and with all the events which constitute the facts of history. The idea of universal history does not appear in universally valid forms, but in a variety of forms according to the special life of the nations, and not at all in peaceful and undisturbed development but in the continuous conflict and struggle; for to quarrel is the nature of man.[63]

To Ranke, as Holborn noted, "History had become . . . instead of the critical and optical exploration of isolated subjects, the critically enlightened awareness of human civilization in its totality." This was his unique and lasting contribution, after his critical method had been assimilated, appropriated, and surpassed, his archival discoveries extended by successors, his philosophy and politics largely ignored or repudiated by following generations: his vision of the universal history of man. He stood above the rising nationalism of his century like a last monument of the cosmopolitan age of Goethe. For Ranke history was not a meaningless process. Ideas did matter; great men who embodied them did change the course of history; history was free, not determined. Yet he never lost sight of the individual and the limits imposed on him by the general course of events. If he thought in terms of critically derived facts, he also thought of dynamically related facts; the context was never far from his consideration of any particular man, idea, nation, or event. To read Ranke is not merely to experience the perception of history by the vanished school of German Idealism; it is to review the tangled pattern of events with fresh eyes, from a mountain top, as Ranke once did with King Max, a divine landscape in which all ages become immediate to Ranke and to us. With him we gaze wonderingly at "humanity as it is, explicable and inexplicable, the life of the individual, of generations, of nations; and, at times, the hand of God over them."[64]

## NOTES

1. For a discussion of the nineteenth-century historical revolution, see Georg G. Iggers, *The German Conception of History: The National Tradition of Historical Thought from Herder to the Present* (Middletown, Conn., 1968); Friedrich Meinecke, *Die Entstehung des Historismus*, ed. Carl Hinrichs, Werke III (Munich, 1959); G. P. Gooch, *History and Historians in the Nineteenth Century*, rev. ed. (Boston, 1959); Eduard Fueter, *Geschichte der neueren Historiographie*, 3rd ed. (Munich, 1936); Heinrich von Srbik, *Geist und Geschichte vom deutschen Humanismus bis zur Gegenwart*, 2 vols. (Munich, 1950, 1951). Steven Toulmin and Jane Goodfield, in *The Discovery of Time* (New York & London, 1965), discuss the impact of the past on Western thought generally. The eighteenth-century background to German historiography is examined in Herbert Butterfield, *Man on His Past* (Cambridge, 1955; repr. Boston, 1960).

2. See Wilhelm Dilthey, "Erinnerungen an deutsche Geschichtsschreiber," in *Vom Aufgang des geschichtlichen Bewusstseins: Jugendaufsätze und Erinnerungen*, ed. Erich Weniger, Gesammelte Schriften XI (Leipzig & Berlin, 1936), pp. 216ff., for the comment on his old teacher Ranke. For Acton's remarks, see "Inaugural Lecture on the Study of History," *Essays on Freedom and Power*, ed. Gertrude Himmelfarb (Boston, 1948), p. 20. Butterfield, *Man on His Past*, Appendix VII, pp. 225–32, gives Acton's July 20, 1867, review of Ranke from *The Chronicle*.

3. Acton, *The Chronicle*, July 20, 1867, in Butterfield, *Man on His Past*, p. 226. See also Gooch, *History and Historians*, pp. 72–97; and Fueter, *Geschichte der neueren Historiographie*, p. 485.

4. For biographical treatments of Ranke see especially the autobiographical dictations and letters in Volumes 53/54 of his Sämtliche Werke, 54 vols. (Leipzig, 1868–1890), hereafter cited as SW; Eugen Guglia, *Leopold von Rankes Leben und Werke* (Leipzig, 1893); Hans Helmholt, *Leopold Rankes Leben und Wirken* (Leipzig, 1921); Theodore H. von Laue, *Leopold Ranke: The Formative Years* (Princeton, N.J., 1950). The last section of the present volume gives further suggestions for readings on Ranke.

5. Ranke, dictation of October 1863, SW 53/54:25.

6. SW 53/54:27. See also Ranke to Friedrich Thiersch, April 28, 1822, in Leopold von Ranke, *Das Briefwerk*, ed. Walther Peter Fuchs (Hamburg, 1949), p. 28; hereafter cited as *Das Briefwerk*.

7. For a survey of Ranke's political views, see Wilhelm Mommsen, *Stein, Ranke, Bismarck* (Munich, 1954); von Laue, *Leopold Ranke*; O. Diether, *Leopold von Ranke als Politiker* (Leipzig, 1911); Stephan Skalweit, "Ranke und Bismarck," *Historische Zeitschrift* (hereafter cited as HZ), 176 (1953), 277–90.

8. Ranke, dictations of October 1863 and November 1885, SW 53/54:26–31, 58–59.

9. Ibid., 31, 59. Carl Hinrichs, *Ranke und die Geschichtstheologie der Goethezeit* (Göttingen, 1954), pp. 161ff.

10. Ranke, dictation of May 1869, SW 53/54:33–44; Helmholt, *Rankes*

*Leben und Wirken*, pp. 17ff. See also Hermann Oncken, *Aus Rankes Frühzeit* (Gotha, 1922).

11. SW 53/54:60–63.

12. Ibid., 61.

13. Ranke to Heinrich Ranke, February 18, 1824, *Das Briefwerk*, p. 53.

14. Ranke to Heinrich Ranke, March 1820, SW 53/54:89.

15. Ranke's direct relationship with Wilhelm von Humboldt is difficult to document, despite the striking similarity in their basic view of history. Though Ranke undoubtedly had personal contacts with him, and had the 1821 edition of Humboldt's essay "On the Task of the Historian" in his personal library (now in the Ranke Collection in The George Arents Research Library for Special Collections at Syracuse University; the volume has no marginal comments by Ranke), he never referred to Humboldt in print, as he did to other romantic thinkers such as Fichte or Goethe who influenced him. But Ranke's pupil Sybel asserted that in his 1839 Berlin lectures on historiography Ranke did mention Humboldt as an influence; see HZ, 56 (1886), 471. An English translation of Humboldt's essay edited by Georg G. Iggers is in *History and Theory*, 6 (1967), 57–71, and has been reprinted in Leopold von Ranke, *The Theory and Practice of History*, edd. Georg G. Iggers and Konrad von Moltke (Indianapolis & New York, 1973), pp. 5–23. Other discussions of the problem include: Richard Fester, "Humboldts und Rankes Ideenlehre," *Deutsche Zeitschrift für Geschichtswissenschaft*, 6, No. 2 (1891), 235–56; and Eduard Spranger, "Wilhelm von Humboldts Rede 'Über die Aufgabe des Geschichtsschreibers,' und die Schelling'sche Philosophie," HZ, 128 (1923), 415–45. See also Gerhard Masur, *Rankes Begriff der Weltgeschichte*, Beiheft 6 of HZ (Munich, 1926), p. 89.

16. "After criticism . . . ," Gunter Berg, *Leopold von Ranke als akademischer Lehrer* (Göttingen, 1968), p. 212; ". . . sympathetic comprehension . . . ," SW 53/54:569. Ranke's exact philosophic relationship to Hegel has been the subject of much controversy. See Ernst Simon, *Ranke und Hegel*, Beiheft 15 of HZ (Munich, 1928), and Friedrich Meinecke, "Leopold von Ranke: Gedächtnisrede," in *Die Entstehung des Historismus*, p. 597, for discussions of Ranke's *Ideenlehre*. Other useful treatments include Helmut Diwald, *Das historische Erkennen* (Leiden, 1955); and Joachim Wach, *Das Verstehen*, 3 vols. (Tübingen, 1926–1933). See also Helmholt, *Rankes Leben and Wirken*, p. 15.

17. Ranke, Introduction to the *History of the Latin and Teutonic Nations*, SW 33:vii. For a discussion of the meaning of Ranke's famous phrase "wie es eigentlich gewesen," see Hajo Holborn, "The Science of History," in *History and the Humanities* (Garden City, N.Y., 1972), pp. 81–97. Wilma Iggers, in *Theory and Practice of History*, edd. Iggers & Moltke, p. 137, prefers to translate it as "how, essentially, things happened."

18. Ernst Schulin, "Ranke's erstes Buch," HZ, 203 (1966), 581–609. See also Masur, *Rankes Begriff der Weltgeschichte*.

19. See Oncken, *Aus Rankes Frühzeit*, pp. 20ff.; Ranke, dictation of November 1885, SW 53/54:63; Helmholt, *Rankes Leben und Wirken*, pp. 28–36. See also E. Rothacker, "Savigny, Grimm, Ranke," HZ, 128 (1923), 415–45.

20. Ranke, Introduction to the *History of the Reformation in Germany*, SW I:x. See also Helmholt, *Rankes Leben und Wirken*, p. 33.

21. Ranke, dictations of December 1875 and November 1885, SW 53/54: 48–49, 66–67; Helmholt, *Rankes Leben und Wirken*, pp. 37–40. For Niebuhr's comment, see Gooch, *History and Historians*, p. 77.

22. Ranke, dictation of November 1885, SW 53/54:67, 71. Helmholt, *Rankes Leben und Wirken*, pp. 41–44 for Italy. "No one should regret . . . ," Introduction to the *History of the Reformation*, SW I:vii. See also Leopold von Ranke, *Neue Briefe*, edd. Bernard Hoeft and Hans Herzfeld (Hamburg, 1949), hereafter cited as *Neue Briefe*, as well as *Das Briefwerk* and SW 53/54 for numerous letters dealing with his Italian travels.

23. Ranke describes his involvement with the *Historisch-Politische Zeitschrift* in the dictations of December 1875 and November 1885, SW 53/54: 50, 68, 70–75. See also J. Varrentrapp, "Rankes Historisch-Politische Zeitschrift und das Berliner Wochenblatt," HZ, 97 (1907), 35–119.

24. An original copy of Ranke's inaugural lecture, "De historiae et politicae cognatione atque discrimine" (Berlin, 1836) is in the Ranke Collection of The George Arents Research Library for Special Collections at Syracuse University. It was reprinted with a German translation by Ranke's brother Ferdinand in SW 24:280–93.

25. The "Politisches Gespräch," which first appeared in *Historisch-Politische Zeitschrift*, 2 (1836), 775–807, is reprinted in SW 49/50:314–39. An excellent translation by Hildegard Hunt von Laue is available in von Laue, *Leopold Ranke*, pp. 152–80. See also the selection in chap. 6 below.

26. Ranke's "Die grossen Mächte," from the *Historisch-Politische Zeitschrift*, 2, No. 1 (1883), 1–51, is reprinted in revised form in SW 24:1–40. See the translation in this present volume. The best introduction is in the edition of *Die grossen Mächte* by Friedrich Meinecke (Leipzig, 1916).

27. ". . . victory falls . . . ," SW 53/54:570.

28. Hajo Holborn, "Der deutsche Idealismus in sozialgeschichtlicher Bedeutung," HZ, 174 (1952), 359–84; Iggers, *German Conception of History*, pp. 82ff., 89.

29. Pieter Geyl, "Ranke in the Light of the Catastrophe," *Debates with Historians* (Cleveland & New York, 1958), pp. 9–29. See also Ranke to Edwin von Manteuffel, October 4, 1869, *Neue Briefe*, p. 528; Mommsen, *Stein, Ranke, Bismarck*, p. 173, and Werner Stark's introduction to Friedrich Meinecke, *Machiavellianism* (New Haven, Conn., 1957), p. xvi.

30. On Ranke's teaching, see Berg, *Ranke als akademischer Lehrer*; Heinrich von Sybel, "Gedächtnisrede auf Leopold von Ranke," Preussische Akademie der Wissenschaften, *Abhandlungen* I (1886) (Berlin, 1887); and Alfred Dove's comments in *Allgemeine Deutsche Biographie*, XXVII 258–59. Also useful is Edward G. Bourne, "Ranke and the Beginning of the Seminary Method," *Essays in Historical Criticism* (New York, 1901), pp. 265–74. A valuable new publication includes fragments of many of Ranke's own lectures: Leopold von Ranke, *Aus Werk und Nachlass. IV. Vorlesungseinleitungen* (Munich, 1975), with an introduction by Walther Peter Fuchs.

31. Iggers, *German Conception of History*, p. 269.

32. Georg G. Iggers, "The Decline of the Classical National Tradition of German Historiography," *History and Theory*, 6 (1967), 382–412; idem, *New Directions in European Historiography* (Middletown, Conn., 1975), pp. 25–27, 80ff.

33. Ranke, *Die römischen Päpste, ihre Kirche und ihr Staat im sechszehnten und siebzehnten Jahrhundert*, 3 vols. (Berlin, 1834–1836); revised edition in SW 37–39. See Thomas Babington Macaulay's classic essay on Ranke in *The Miscellaneous Works of Lord Macaulay* (London, 1870), pp. 45–89; and Acton's comments of July 20, 1867, in Butterfield, *Man on His Past*, p. 225.

34. Ranke, dictation of December 1875, SW 53/54:52. Sybel, as cited in G. P. Gooch, *Studies in German History* (London, 1958), p. 234. See also Sybel's comments in HZ, 56 (1886), 463, 481. Ranke, *Deutsche Geschichte im Zeitalter der Reformation*, 6 vols. (Berlin, 1839–1847), reprinted as SW 1–6. The best edition is the Academy one edited by Paul Joachimsen (Munich, 1925–1926) with an excellent introduction.

35. Ranke, *Neun Bücher preussischer Geschichte* (Berlin, 1847–1848), reprinted in revised form as *Zwölf Bücher preussicher Geschichte* in SW 25–29. The Academy edition (Munich, 1930) edited by G. Küntzel is preferable. On Treitschke, see Gooch, *Studies in German History*, p. 253.

36. Hans Herzfeld, "Politik und Geschichte bei Leopold von Ranke im Zeitraum von 1848–1871," *Festschrift für Gerhard Ritter zu seinem 60. Geburtstag* (Tübingen, 1950), pp. 322–41. There is an interesting manuscript letter by George Bancroft, dated November 9, 1867, in the Bancroft Papers at The New York Public Library, describing an encounter which Bancroft had with Ranke, strolling in the Tiergarten, and their discussion of the merits of Macaulay as an historian.

37. For Ranke's family, see Helmholt, *Rankes Leben und Wirken*, passim; and Giesbert Bäcker-Ranke's dissertation "Leopold von Ranke und seine Familie," University of Bonn, 1955. Bäcker-Ranke has also published an interesting sketch: *Rankes Ehefrau Clarissa geb. Graves-Perceval* (Göttingen, 1967). Ranke's numerous affectionate letters to his wife, in English, French, Italian, and German, appear in the several collections mentioned above.

38. Herzfeld, "Politik und Geschichte bei Leopold von Ranke," 325.

39. Ranke taught his last class in the fall semester of 1870. His planned lectures for the spring of 1871 were canceled for lack of students, at about the same time as his wife died. Henceforth, he lived alone, assisted by one or two secretaries and busily engaged in scholarship. See the reminiscences of his assistant, Dr. Theodor Wiedemann, in the *Deutsche Revue*, during 1891–1893.

40. Herbert Baxter Adams, "Leopold von Ranke," *American Historical Association Papers* III (New York, 1888), pp. 101–20. For Ranke's influence in America, see also Jurgen Herbst, *The German Historical School in American Scholarship* (Ithaca, N.Y., 1965); and Helmholt, *Rankes Leben und Wirken*, p. 131.

41. Ranke, *Weltgeschichte*, 9 vols. (Leipzig, 1881–1888); Helmholt, *Rankes Leben und Wirken*, pp. 142–57; Wiedemann, in *Deutsche Revue*

(February 1892), 215ff.; Acton, "Lecture on the Study of History," p. 20.

42. SW 53/54:239. See Diwald, *Das historische Erkennen*, pp. 77–106, for a discussion of concepts which Ranke used. For American misinterpretation, see Charles A. Beard, "That Noble Dream," *American Historical Review*, 41 (1935), 78–87, and Georg G. Iggers, "The Image of Ranke in American and German Historical Thought," *History and Theory*, 2 (1962), 17–40.

43. Diwald, *Das historische Erkennen*, pp. 81–89. See also Friedrich Meinecke's discussion of a *Stufenbau*, a series of levels, of historical individualities, in "Kausalitäten und Werte in der Geschichte," HZ, 137 (1928), 17ff.

44. Simon, *Ranke und Hegel*, p. 43.

45. Ranke, *Weltgeschichte* IX, Part I, p. 270.

46. Ibid., Part II, p. 7.

47. Meinecke, "Leopold von Ranke," p. 592.

48. Ibid., p. 586.

49. Ranke, *Weltgeschichte* IX, Part II, pp. xiv, 77ff.

50. For Acton's criticism, see Butterfield, *Man on His Past*, p. 92.

51. SW 31/32:viii.

52. ". . . every epoch is immediate to God," *Weltgeschichte* IX, Part II, p. 2.

53. Ranke to his son Otto, May 25, 1873, *Das Briefwerk*, p. 519. "History will always be rewritten," SW 53/54:569; 1845 lecture quoted in Berg, *Ranke als akademischer Lehrer*, p. 212; "impulse of the present," SW 53/54:569.

54. Diwald, *Das historische Erkennen*, pp. 72–76; Iggers, *German Conception of History*, pp. 109–13.

55. From Ranke's *History of England*, SW 21/22:113.

56. Ranke to Heinrich Ritter, October 4, 1830, SW 53/54:242. Karl Marx, in *Marx–Engels Gesamtausgabe* (Frankfurt, 1927–1935), III 228, derides Ranke as one of the "born palace servants of history." For a contemporary Marxist critique, see Gerhard Schilfert, "Leopold von Ranke," in *Die deutsche Geschichtswissenschaft vom Beginn des 19. Jahrhunderts bis zum Reichseinigung von oben*, ed. Joachim Streisand (East Berlin, 1963), pp. 241–70.

57. Karl Kupisch, *Die Heiroglyph Gottes: Grosse Historiker der bürgerlichen Epoche von Ranke bis Meinecke* (Munich, 1967), p. 31.

58. Antoine Guilland, *Modern Germany and Her Historians* (London, 1915), p. 116.

59. Acton's comment as cited in Butterfield, *Man on His Past*, p. 91; see also pp. 92–94. Heinrich Heine, *Sämtliche Werke*, 20 vols. (Leipzig, 1910–1915), VI 89.

60. Meinecke, "Leopold von Ranke," p. 586.

61. Hayden White, *Metahistory: The Historical Imagination in Nineteenth-Century Europe* (Baltimore & London, 1973). See also the comments on Ranke as an artist in Peter Gay, *Style in History* (New York, 1974).

62. Friedrich Meinecke, "Ranke und Burckhardt," Deutsche Akademie der Wissenschaften zu Berlin, *Vorträge und Schriften*, Heft 27 (Berlin, 1948); trans. Karl W. Deutsch in *German History: Some New German Views*, ed. Hans Kohn (Boston, 1954), pp. 142–56.

63. Quoted in Holborn, "Science of History," pp. 95–96.

64. Ibid., p. 96. Hinrichs, *Ranke und die Geschichtstheologie der Goethe-zeit*, p. 130. *See* also Masur, *Rankes Begriff der Weltgeschichte*, and Ernst Schulin, *Die weltgeschichtliche Erfassung des Orients bei Hegel und Ranke* (Göttingen, 1958). "Humanity as it is . . . ," from the Introduction to the *History of the Latin and Teutonic Nations*, SW 34:viii.

# I

# Autobiographical Dictation
### (November 1885)

Although Ranke never composed a formal autobiography, in his old age he did dictate to his secretaries several short fragments, of which the dictation of November 1885 is the most complete. The passages not only reveal little-known events, especially of his earlier years, but also indicate those parts of his career which he considered particularly significant. The following dictation by the 90-year-old scholar is really a reflection on the main events of his lifetime, and allows Ranke to introduce his own life and work. The following selection is taken from SW 53/54:56–76.

I WAS BORN IN THE YEAR OF THE PEACE OF BASEL, that first attempt at an agreement between a revolutionary, transformed France and the Prussian state, which embodied the conservative principles of the European world. It was more of an attempt at an understanding than a peace, in which the two contradictory elements of the century stood in opposition to one another. You must pardon me for relating to my own trivial existence the great events of the world, but it can never be otherwise than that everyone lives under the influence of the stars which dominate the world. The first decade of my life was passed in tranquillity, for the Electorate of Saxony, to which my birthplace belonged, enjoyed both internal and external peace as a close ally of Prussia. It was a quiet life of a singular sort, which was occasionally affected by ties to that literary movement which then formed a classical age for Germany. I remember how one day one of the family, whose visits I enjoyed, showed me a portrait which hung under the mirror and told me that the man portrayed—it was Schiller—had just died. He described him as the greatest man in all Germany.

I experienced the year 1806 with full awareness. I remember very well how at first a Prussian cavalry regiment rode by our little town; they avoided crossing directly through the place. The hussars stationed there also armed themselves to go into the field. All were in expectation of a great decision. On October 14 we had an intimation of the battle of Auerstadt. We boys ran to the Hoheruth, a neighboring hill, and a few dug into the earth and asserted that they detected the sounds of cannon fire; I must confess that I didn't hear anything. But very shortly we learned of the outcome. The first sign was a long column of wagons, filled chiefly with ladies, who led the retreat. Then came refugees, whom my father took into our home, and fed at our round table. Shortly thereafter the first of the French appeared. Just as we boys had previously admired the deaths-head attire of the Prussian cavalry, so now we were struck by the French chasseurs. One began to distinguish between Prussia and Saxony, and to speak of the defeat as a purely Prussian one. No one had any real idea what had happened to us: a decision between the two great elemental forces of the world had occurred, but Saxony was at first only slightly affected by it.

For me, the time had now come when my studies were extended beyond the horizon of a rector and cantor at Wiehe. I attended in succession the two monastery schools of Donndorf and Pforte, which were still maintained completely in the old style of education, but which opened to me a new way, in which I breathed and lived. World events also found a certain echo here. While we busied ourselves at Donndorf with the deeds of the legends of the Homeric world, we were still impressed greatly with the Napoleonic proclamations which we got to read, and which we sometimes imitated or copied on our slates. What was begun there continued on a higher level at Pforte. I cannot describe how much I owe to the school at Pforte: not simply the instruction itself, but the spirit which pervaded the institution and deepened the study of the classics. There I read through the greatest part of the poets of antiquity, and, under the guidance of a young instructor, the tragedies as well, touching even on Pindar. Several of us could recite whole books of Vergil. Among the historians the most famous of all was among the first with whom we made our acquaintance. Then followed the great fall of Napoleon's star in the year 1812. I was studying the *Agricola* of Tacitus when the popular disturbances occasioned by the fall of the French became known. I was struck by the identity of the viewpoints which Tacitus ascribed to Queen Boudicca. The inner connection of the most remote things with the present and the similarity between the exercise of power and the rebellion against it appeared before my eyes. The already-mentioned friend and teacher agreed with me, remarking on the sameness of events. We elevated our viewpoint to a universal historical outlook, above the motivations which had previously dominated the day. Before our eyes, in our very neighborhood, was fought the great fight which would decide the world. We saw Napoleon in the midst of his generals and marshals draw past the cloister door. Shortly afterward the battle of Lützen was fought; once again the revolutionary and imperial principle triumphed.

But with what eagerness did we await the news of the arming of the allies! We greeted the first Cossacks we glimpsed on the road as the messengers of an approaching salvation from the pressure which all of us now felt. How long it seemed until the delayed decision occurred, at the battle of Leipzig! We received our first news of the outcome from the mouth of General Thielmann, who told the young people who gathered about the school door about the incomparable battle, with the count of the wounded and dead which astonished us and which awoke our sympathies all the more since Thielmann himself had gone over to the allies. A few days later we saw the French army, which previously had always marched to the east, fleeing westward. They covered the heights again, as before. By the pass of Kösen there occurred a clash of artillery from both sides. With what astonishment did old Professor Schmidt, the school's mathematician, who had seen in Napoleon a man with a divine mission, now behold the retreat of the army, though he himself did not give up hope!

Thus was the fate of the world now decided. The power of the ancien régime, as it had been formed through the centuries, returned to view, and everyone now perceived that the future of the world would depend upon how far the reaction advanced, on where it would find its borders. The Treaty of Paris resulted in the suppression of the revolutionary attack, but ensured that constitutional reform, which still contained within itself some revolutionary elements, would remain.

At this time I entered the University of Leipzig. The scholarly lectures, which I took in relationship to one another, made an impression on me. First philosophic and then historical studies followed in their turn. It is true, as often has been noted, that I entered the university somewhat earlier than most, to gain more time and room for my own proper studies.

Even the lectures of Gottfried Hermann were not fully satisfactory to me, since he placed a value upon versification [*Metrik*] which I was never able really to comprehend. But his lectures on Pindar were unforgettable, and first taught me to understand him properly. So were those on Hesiod, and those on Greek mythology, but perhaps, most of all, the lectures about Greek grammar, which breathed a complete understanding of the language as a whole, and contained a logical foundation for the grammatical rules which satisfied the mind.

Krug's lectures were useful to me for their dialectical precision, but I thirsted to proceed from the Kantians to Kant himself, skipping over his well-known followers. I procured Kant's *Critique of Pure Reason* and studied a great deal by my lamp. Fichte made the greatest impression on me, actually the popular works most of all, which were connected with religion and politics. The *Addresses to the German Nation* gained my unlimited admiration. But I still remained somewhat foreign to history. In the handbooks I saw only an immense number of facts, whose arid incomprehensibility scared me. Niebuhr's *Roman History* was the first influence upon my historical studies. The copying and the repetitions from Livy and Dionysius, and Niebuhr's own narrative, which breathed a classic spirit in many places, gave me the conviction that history could also exist in the modern age. In that period the name of Goethe stood out above all others. He introduced a modern classicism into life and studies, and contributed infinitely to the formation of the national consciousness in this connection; and at that time he stood at the zenith of his reputation. Among my companions I was his greatest admirer, but I lacked the courage at that time to imitate him, or the right inclination; he was really too modern for me. Even then I sought for an older style of language, more rooted in the depths of the nation. I seized upon Luther, at first only to learn his German and to master the fundamentals of the modern German written language. But at the same time I was deeply stirred by the greatness of his content and his historical role. In the year 1817 I actually made an attempt to narrate Luther's history in his own language. You can understand that I was also engaged deep in my soul with theological problems for I had never abandoned theological studies. Tzschirner's lectures on church history were among those for which I was most grateful. And when I continued to translate Greek authors, I added to these German translations made from Hebrew texts as well.

I was torn from these incoherent but zealous studies in every discipline by an appointment to the *Gymnasium* at Frankfurt on Oder. This I owed to a very excellent philologist who had studied with me in the seminar of Christian Daniel Beck and who had risen very young to the directorship of the Frankfurt *Gymnasium*. In this respect there was no difference between Prussia and Saxony, but in every other way moving from the social life of Leipzig to a dignified Prussian city was the greatest change which I have ever experienced, in spite of the fact that Thuringia and my fatherland had become united with Prussia. Public life was completely different. In Frankfurt memories of the last war were still prevalent and dominated even the table conversations. It was a different spiritual atmosphere, which could not fail to attract and capture me. I refer here to my distinction between the differing tendencies of the European spirit. Prussia belonged to the conservative and monarchichal tendency, which, however, had infused itself in a moderate way with heterogeneous elements, by means of the great innovations which had prepared the way for victory. Everyone knows how actively the contradictory waves broke upon one another in the years 1819, 1820, and 1821. My younger brother, who soon followed me to Frankfurt, attached himself to Jahn and those ideas which were part of the Turnverein movement. I came close to them, but never joined.

Meanwhile, my studies had taken a positive direction. I had now become completely an historian, which was occasioned by my teaching office. But from the very beginning I combined historical studies with original research and made them my own. At that time I first read through the Greek and Roman historians, and worked them into my lectures, which made the latter unusually colorful, and won me a certain amount of applause.

But I did not remain with antiquity. The public situation induced me to progress toward more recent times. No one could conceive how much I was captured and seized by the age when the Roman period changed into the German. With a sort of delight I pored over the reports which Gropius had collected about the period called the Barbarian Invasions, and those which followed. I had the good fortune of being permitted the use of the large library, which the librarians of the former University at Frankfurt had collected and which was then no longer in use. I could thus gradually employ the authentic monuments of all the centuries, so that I was less subjected than others to the controversies of the contemporary moment. And yet I ought not to neglect to mention one other impulse. In the 1820s the conviction gained momentum that only a deeper study of the foundations of states and kingdoms would satisfy the future. The romantic–historical works of Sir Walter Scott, which found a reception in all languages and nations, contributed principally toward awakening a participation in the deeds and achievements of the past.

They were also attraction enough for me, and I read these works with lively interest; but I also took objection to them. Among other things, I was offended by the way in which Charles the Bold and Louis XI were treated, which seemed, even in particular details, to be completely contradictory to the historical evidence. I studied Commynes, and the contemporary reports which were appended to the modern editions of this author, and became convinced that a Charles the Bold or a Louis XI as they were pictured by Scott had never existed. That worthy and learned author himself was aware of this; and I could not forgive him for accepting in his narrative biased tendencies which were totally unhistorical, and presenting them as if he believed them. The comparison convinced me that the historical sources themselves were more beautiful and in any case more interesting than romantic fiction. I turned away completely from such fiction and resolved to avoid any invention and imagination in my work and to keep strictly to the facts.

Now that I had addressed myself to modern authors, an analogous

difficulty became apparent. When I next turned to the two most repu-
table writers dealing with the beginnings of modern history, Guicciardini and Jovius, I found in comparing them so many unresolved
discrepancies that I did not know on which I could chiefly depend.
Jovius is by far the more objective, and reveals a variety of good information about details. In contrast, Guicciardini is far more informed
and informative about the politics of the period. But it was no more
possible to choose between them than to reconcile them, if truth itself
were to be my first consideration. Many other authors of this era could
be named, who were supposed to have had their own original information, and it was necessary to draw upon them for comparison to
gain a solid ground and foundation.

It then appeared that Guicciardini, by far the most talented of
them all, had disagreements with them on some points, and, on the
other hand, had copied from them in other places. Thus a critique of
the historians of this period became an inescapable necessity. It was
even necessary to extend a similar effort toward a few German authors
of the period. One result was that the famous report by Sleidanus
about the imperial election of Charles V proved to have been taken
from a biased, largely fictional, account, and that this author was not
even acquainted with the authentic documents which would allow
him to gain a solid knowledge of events. My work was not based upon
Niebuhr, who was really more engaged in giving significance to a
tradition, nor completely on Gottfried Hermann, who had criticized
particular details of authors, although I had hopes of gaining applause
from men such as these. My procedure was derived in its own manner, without any pretensions, out of a sort of necessity; and for the
period which I next treated it sufficed properly. The letters of Louis
XII, which had been known for a long time, offered a secure basis for
judging the most important political decisions. At the point when
these letters ceased, I also had to break off my work.

My first book, the *History of the Latin and Teutonic Nations*, appeared in the year 1824. Its unique style aroused a good deal of criticism. I must confess that the mode of expression of French and German
chroniclers found repetition in my work, while the difficult construc-
tions which I had borrowed from classical studies often dominated
the word order. Still, the method of research and the content of the

narrative won such recognition that I owed my appointment to the University of Berlin in 1825 to the book. I will not discuss my first attempts at the lectern, from which one might have concluded only too quickly that I was not familiar enough with the area which I was supposed to cover, but they went off not at all badly. I gained enough friends from them, and a decent number of students. There remained for me only further progress in my studies.

Since I was already committed to continuing the work which I had begun, which could make no further progress without manuscript sources, I felt it necessary to search through a large collection of manuscript remains from the sixteenth and seventeenth centuries which I found in the library at Berlin. Actually, I was not able to achieve a continuation of my project, but there opened to me a new world. I had never expected such a rich source of information about the states and princes of the sixteenth century as was now presented. I found it advisable to work on a few chapters of the history of the sixteenth century on the basis of this information. Thus in 1827 the book *Princes and Peoples of Southern Europe* [the *History of the Ottoman and Spanish Monarchies*] appeared.

I must confess that the company of men and, I should not omit, women of universal education exercised a strong formative influence on me. The atmosphere of the capital affected me in this regard even more than my residence in a provincial town. So it happened that I was able to avoid much in my second book which was done heavily in the first. It found the best reception in the highest circles in Germany and even the praise of the most widely read French authors.

But I could not remain standing still. I readily determined that the Berlin collection, voluminous as it was, could only be very insignificant in comparison with the material which Italian archives and libraries could offer, and I secured the necessary support to allow me to excavate this treasure. I turned next toward Vienna because a good part of the records of Venice had been brought to that city during the occupation, and were to be found in its archives. These days one has no idea how difficult it was then to gain entry to the archives. Prince Metternich did me an eternal service when he gave me permission, on the advice of the gifted Gentz, to use the archives. I did not fail to ransack them thoroughly. I found a rich treasure of Venetian relations concerning Turkey and Germany. My industry was at once aroused, and I researched them thoroughly, from day to day encountering something new, unexpected, and instructive. But along with this, my visit to Vienna, which lasted from October 1827 to October 1828, was fruitful in every other way. Oral information was added to the written. In Vuk Stephanovitch, the most learned of all living Serbs, I found a friend, who gave me his collection of Serbian history. I was touched in the depth of my heart and spirit by this living witness to an event of universal historical and political significance. In the summer of 1828 I composed out of these materials a history of the revolution in Serbia. Unforgettable in connection with this was the assistance rendered to me by Kopitar, who then served as the middleman between German and Slavic scholarship.

Understandably, I did not lose sight of my chief goal. In October 1828, I journeyed to Venice. My first Venetian visit lasted until February 1829. I then went to Florence. On March 22 I beheld the first green shrubs of the Roman Campagna. I remained in Rome, making one excursion to Naples, until April 1830. Once again my studies led me to Florence, where I got to read the newspapers describing the last disturbances which preceded the July Revolution. I did not let myself be deterred from my project, which had just reached a very important stage, for I had now obtained permission to use the Venetian archives themselves in Venice. Here I first got the full series of Venetian relations, which had lain there unnoticed, brought to light, and could use them to my heart's desire. Never did I learn or think more, or gather more, than in the second half of the year 1830 and the first of the year 1831. But I will now not go any further into my Italian stay, in hopes that I may give in the future a more detailed account. Here I wish to speak only of my connection with the great division which now filled the world.

I need not go into great detail about my stay at Frankfurt on Oder in this respect. Those were the days in which the results of the previous century, the victory of the allies and the principle of legitimacy over independent powers, found the greatest resistance; and a *Gymnasium* teacher could not remain untouched by them. The institutions to which I belonged were drawn into the controversy. I was never a member of the *Burschenschaften*. But through my brother, who had studied at

Jena, the idea of independence and the Germanic tendencies held by young people were brought extremely close to me. Society at that time was stirred by a vigorous debate over the revolutions which broke out in Italy and Spain. But what could have filled our spirits or been more disturbing than the revolt of the Greeks against the yoke of the Turks? I will not deny that my studies of the Ottoman Empire, which were presented in my first volume of *Princes and Peoples*, were stimulated by this source. They are chiefly obvious in a few notes about the survival of the Greek world under the Turkish yoke. Then in Berlin I proceeded to the study of revolution in general; I was decisively pushed in this direction by the society of those who were close to me, and who eagerly studied the communist newspaper *Globe* and all the memoirs which had any connection with the revolution. As a result in the year 1827 I undertook my own study of the most illustrious and authentic memoirs of that period. But that was not enough; I immersed myself in the *Moniteur*, so that I at once became personally acquainted with the original inspirers of the revolutionary movement. I learned not only the motives which they proclaimed, but the tendencies which bore them along, coming to know them better than if I had first consulted secondary authorities. I reached my own decision as to whether the revolution possessed a universal soul and spirit, and an interest which necessarily determined participation in it, or whether it was an event like any other, whose original roots lay in events and which arose out of their interaction, and which also could have turned out otherwise.

I recognized fully what an infinite importance lay in the revolution for the world and for every individual, yet reconciled it with the opposing efforts of that part of the European world not included in its turbulence. My papers still contain attempts at criticism of the most important biographical monuments of this era. Enough; I attained after the most energetic study a position which had an understanding of both sides, and which provided me a certain inner peace which could not be shaken by daily events.

I now belonged, by virtue of my own personal position, to the system which was in possession of power. But I could not hide from myself the fact that it had been shaken. On my first and, unfortunately, last visit to Prague I heard protests by the national movement against the Vienna Hofburg. I even heard the question raised, whether it would be better for Bohemia to attach itself to Prussia. But my greatest experience came at the Hofburg itself, or at least in its direct vicinity. Court Councilor Gentz still directed, as they then used to say, the politics of Austria and Europe from a stable stall. Gentz did the great kindness of bestowing his confidence on me. He was well known as a man who did not hide in the dark; he conversed without reservation, and well, in such a way as to suit himself. I gradually became one of the best-informed men in Vienna, as far as current events were concerned. But the impression which this information from Gentz made on me was much deeper. Not only was he one of the vehement opponents of the English and French policy of supporting Greece—when Lord Canning died, they felt in Vienna as if an Alp had been lifted away—but he feared nothing so much as a daily increasing misunderstanding with Russia. Gentz repeated to me the impressions which the English, and principally the Russian, diplomatic dispatches made upon him. At that time he told me directly: from Russia we receive decrees no worse than Napoleon might have sent. I never put any of this to paper, though perhaps I should have; by so doing I might have introduced a false element into my studies.

Only once in the midst of these studies did I take notice of the above, in an essay in which I stressed the impossibility of avoiding a new revolution, which would necessarily be based on the same political principles as the first, though not repeating the intensity of the former. When I then came to Italy, I noticed in Venice movements similar to those which I had seen in Prague, but they were not yet so strong. In general, the Venetians felt themselves to be well off under a just government. But who would have revealed such dissenting opinions to a *prussiano* who was very close to the *tedeschi*?

People expressed themselves much less timidly in the rest of Italy, and particularly in Rome, where the strongest opposition was voiced against the contemporary governments of Leo XII and Pius VIII, and, above all, against the domination by the clergy and the cardinals. I was in direct contact with public opinion as expressed in the salons. It was the most brilliant period for our Bunsen, who was engaged in important negotiations with the Holy See on behalf of Prussia's interests. Men of the most varied nations and parties gathered about him, so that a free exchange of fears and hopes took place. The subject of public attention was the movement in France, which became continually more serious and threatening. At that time it was said that the Bourbons were finished in France, that Charles X would not be able to preserve his throne. Chateaubriand himself, who was then French ambassador in Rome, was in disagreement with his court. But few believed that the changes in the French government which he envisaged would occur. The example of England was advanced; people predicted that Charles X would fall and would be succeeded by the Duke of Orléans, just as William III had replaced James II.

This was all quite lively to me, when the revolution in France actually began. I received word of it through a newspaper, on the heights of the Apennines. By the time I arrived in Venice, it was all over: Charles X was in flight, the Duke of Orléans now really on the throne.

But in the Venetian archives, which I now frequented, there was no sharing in the general rejoicing which accompanied these great events. The archivists felt too much gratitude toward Emperor Francis, who had first united and then established the archives in an impressive new building—under the Republic there had been none. They were afraid of a universal upheaval, and discussed the question of whether the allied powers should again invade France and restore the Bourbon government. I knew better—that, on the one hand, a universal revolution was not to be feared, and that, on the other, it was not to be expected that the powers would agree with one another to repeat their struggle against the revolution in this manner.

King Friedrich Wilhelm III was the most decisive opponent of such an attempt. He had no desire to see the fate of the world rest again on the point of a sword. Count Nostiz, whom he then sent to the Rhineland, to the side of Prince Wilhelm, made it his duty to prevent the outbreak of war. But it happened that the revolutionary forces were not at all stagnated, and when brought to full awareness of their power by the events in France, broke out everywhere, while the conservative principles hastened strongly to oppose them.

It was during this conflict, on March 22, 1831, that I arrived back in Berlin. Men's minds there were caught up in a most lively antagonism. One might well think that I would have had nothing to do but to evaluate and communicate the treasures which I had collected on my travels. That did take place, at once, with my publication of an essay on the conspiracy against Venice in 1618, but this essay involved only a few, nearly forgotten incidents, which could be easily mastered. The larger project required of me a greater concentration of effort, which, under the influence of the Berlin society which I had re-entered, I could not manage to achieve. Sympathies with the events in France were so strong and overpowering that I became impassioned and threw myself into the discussion.

In Berlin there raged both sympathy for and antagonism toward the Revolution of 1830, but there were also many who opposed the extreme consequences of both the revolutionary and the counter-revolutionary ideas. These included to a large extent my best friends, men of intact reputation and unclouded intelligence. I found support from them, without being directly influenced by one or the other. So I became a political journalist, but on the basis of ideas which were formed by my study of history and my experience in life. But a position of this sort cannot be understood. I maintained a certain distance from the ideas which appeared in the political weeklies and which were considered by many to be orthodox. Those on the opposing side perceived increasingly my opposition to the universal validity of revolutionary ideas. The one regarded me as an Ultra; the others wanted to see me painted with a Jacobin hue. My intention was merely to fight for the position midway between the two systems which was already occupied by the Prussian state. It was obvious that my leanings were more toward the positive and existing than to the wild impulses of revolutionary tendencies; and it soon became clear to me that nothing decisive could be accomplished in this manner, and I again took up the work which I had previously laid aside.

The last decade of the reign of Friedrich Wilhelm III was of boundless importance for the movement of ideas. At the University of Berlin both tendencies encountered each other, without either's having any hope of a decisive victory. From my studies in the documents which I had brought back with me, there arose works which suited my spirit. First was the *History of the Popes*, which no one could say was written more for or against the papacy. It was intended neither to favor nor to expose, but was solely the result of thorough and impartial study. And thus it was received. But it seemed, even to me, that the Protestant movement had not received complete justice in the *Popes*. After completing the first work, I was walking once with Savigny in the garden. He inquired with hearty interest what I would undertake next. I told him about a task which I had long wanted to attempt, an intention which had been strengthened by my visit to Frankfurt on Main, where I saw the collections of documents there dealing with the Imperial Diet. I aimed to dedicate my efforts to the development of the German Empire at the time of the beginning of Protestantism, and this project won his complete approval. Now I had to add to my studies from the Italian archives still others from the German, which represented this side in a more lively way. The collections of Diet reports which Frankfurt offered were of only secondary or tertiary value for my researches, since they reflected only the city's interests. Far more important were the reports and remains which I collected at the princely courts, especially the Saxon ones, which were to be found for the earlier period in Weimar, and for the later at Dresden. For me a visit to those cities offered the double advantage of studying the past and getting a closer acquaintance with the present in a few important respects. The visit in Weimar led me to the grand ducal court, which was then governed by a woman who simultaneously belonged to the European world and closely affected Germany. I found no sympathy for Luther at Weimar; he was still blamed strongly for the loss of their Electoral dignity to the Albertine line of the Saxon family. But the collections were infinitely important, and those dealing with the Diets under Maximilian I were priceless. My studies of ancient times were tied together with the modern age. My involvement with the Reformation led me still farther. In the year 1839 I discovered that, in addition to the princely collections, there was also a reliable source for the center of events, the imperial court. I cannot describe the delight with which, in Brussels, I picked up the well-ordered volumes containing the relics of the House of Austria in the Netherlands, especially those of Charles V. My astonishment and, at the same time, my satisfaction grew even greater when the still unorganized papers of the ruler's last years came to light and were made available to me. This was exactly what I needed to complete my work.

These were later published as the correspondence of Charles V, but only after I had used them. The new discoveries gave the work a particular charm, even when I had to leave them behind, so that my progress could continue. There was now plenty of work to be done, since even the theological disputes retained a contemporary interest. Even friends later felt that the work on the age of the Reformation was inferior to that on the history of the popes. I felt that myself: it seemed to me impossible to compose a readable book out of Diet records and theological confessions; but the material produced its own form, and the purpose was completely different. I intended to write a basic book about the fundamental events of modern history. I thought, not of the readers of the wider world, but in terms of satisfying German scholarship and German religious convictions. May the work continue to enjoy in the future the acceptance which it then worthily received!

But while I had been occupied with it, things in Prussia and in Germany had all been completely altered by the death of Friedrich Wilhelm III. Thus was buried the last remaining prince who had led the wars of the Restoration era. Friedrich Wilhelm III had, as was mentioned, been chiefly responsible for preventing a new war against the July Revolution, which was able to establish its stability because it neither faced resistance nor was feared. For the present, the July Monarchy was based on a compromise of the two principles [monarchy and revolution]. This was only a personal balance, but it produced a quasi-legitimacy. However, it rested upon a revival of the revolutionary idea and on its victory, which gave such ideas an infinite predominance in Europe. Through the press, such ideas also found entry into Germany. The main point of controversy was over the demand for a constitution which would limit princely power by popular assemblies. This movement was followed in Berlin with the closest attention. It was discussed in all social conversations, since the government of Prussia, by its earlier promises, seemed to be bound to take a similar step. But Friedrich Wilhelm III was afraid to undertake such a great change, and the personal authority which he possessed hindered any demonstrations for this cause. But it was expected that the new monarch would act energetically and decisively. Friedrich Wilhelm IV, who always embodied the idea of the Restoration wars, had a horror of anything which smacked of revolution; even the word "constitution," which appeared at that time in a thoroughly revolutionary context, met his opposition. But he was equally opposed to the routine rule of an absolute bureaucracy. His idea was to establish a constitution based on the Estates, on the old foundations of historical development, but, at the same time, one which unified the country under the king himself.

I had made, if I might call it that, the acquaintance of Friedrich Wilhelm IV in Venice in 1828. I saw him twice at St. Mark's library, and more than once at the Hotel Danieli. He received me as an old acquaintance, with a comment so flattering about my *Princes and Peoples* that I dare not repeat it. From that time he was my gracious lord and patron. Standing at his father's side, he adopted a position suitable to his spirit. At that time, I saw him occasionally, without belonging to his intimate circle, which was well known to me through Radowitz, Voss, and Gerlach. The first was a man of brilliant spirit and comprehensive knowledge. The second, an offspring of an old Brandenburg family of government officials, was doctrinaire, well informed about the country, thoroughly upright, and completely filled with the ideas of his class. Gerlach was his friend; they had met at the University of Heidelberg, and shared tendencies which inclined to the right. Both were thoroughly orthodox in religious and political conviction. Gerlach had absorbed the teachings of Haller. At the time, Gerlach and Radowitz were not at court. Friedrich Wilhelm IV carried on his administration relying on the advice of his adjutant general, Thiele. To my astonishment, Thiele then put the question to me, whether I would like to serve the king by advising him on his effort to establish Estates. It was one of the most important moments of my life; and I could reply, with all decisiveness, only in the negative. I certainly did not know the internal conditions of the Prussian provinces well enough to give advice on the formation of an Estates-type constitution which could be followed without difficulty. I was still occupied with the last portion of the *History of the Reformation in Germany*, and I lived so completely in the sixteenth century that it would have been hard for me to consider it.

And when I had completed this work, I was again directed into other studies which suggested themselves. For one thing, I felt a gap in my general historical education, which consisted in my lack of close personal acquaintance with the great nations whose culture and power had played the greatest role on the world stage. Only by remedying this could I realize my long planned hope of an overall comprehension [of modern history]. On the other hand, in the course of that comprehension, I felt it a hindrance that I had not been able to evaluate properly the position of Prussia itself. Its most important moment lay in the rise of the rather limited Electorate of Brandenburg into a European power of the first order. This was well known in general—I wanted to develop it with suitable thoroughness, and strove to attain that end. The first step which I took toward this goal came with my first long visit to Paris, in the year 1843.

My book on the popes had paved the way for me, and to it I owe my acquaintance with Thiers. Shortly before, he had done me the honor of calling upon me at the Luisenstrasse in Berlin, and expressed the most lively admiration for my work. I then saw him again in Paris, and he accorded me a friendly relationship of a most intimate sort, insofar as such a relationship could develop between a man who had grown up in the revolutionary tradition, and who, according to a certain point of view, had contributed most to its development, and a German scholar who belonged more to the opposing side and who saw in the revolutionary element only an aspect of the world which could no longer be suppressed. Thiers had vigorously and eagerly suppressed the communist tendencies during the few years in which he wielded power. He fell from power with his monarch, who resisted democratic movements. He lived in the midst of conditions which led to the establishment of a stable government on the foundation of a revolution. But he was, in addition, a man of spirit; he understood when I declared that all this was impossible. He expected everything from the workings of a constitution; I told him that no one would ever be able to find a born prince who would subject himself completely to the conditions which a constitution imposed.

When I first arrived in Paris, my intention was to make the Revolution itself, on which I had done some preliminary work, the object of my research. Though I also discovered in the national archives many items which were unknown, these would not have been sufficient for a thorough treatment of the subject. When I was about to give up the topic, I came across a relation of the greatest value, which dealt with Prussia itself.

These were the letters of the French ambassador to Frederick the Great, Valori, many details of which were known, but the richness of their contents was scarcely guessed. The director of the Archives of Foreign Affairs, Mignet, who was very friendly toward me, raised no objection, and allowed me unlimited use of the papers. For many a day I made excerpts from them from 10 until 3 P.M., until my hand tired, since the strict regulations of the archives at the time forbade the use of a stranger to assist me. I returned to Berlin with a treasure of original information about Prussia. It would have perhaps been good if I had published them as they were, but they would not have been basically instructive. If I wished to accomplish anything, it was unavoidable that I search the Prussian archives for enlightenment and information. Up to then they had been strictly closed, but they were opened willingly to me. The only requirement was that here too I copy with my own hand. One has no idea how much time such a thorough search through individual documents can take! But the things which I sought were there; they were the chief joy of my curiosity, and were otherwise close to my heart. Herr von Thiele told me that I had the opportunity to lead the forces, whose origins in the sixteenth century I had described, into battle. I was inspired by another interest, already mentioned: to learn to understand how the Electorate of Brandenburg attained the rank of a European power. To do that, I first had to portray the man who organized its military forces and organized its state. I turned to the study of Friedrich Wilhelm I. The first volume of my nine books of the *History of Prussia* was dedicated to this creative administrator and organizer of the state. He had a bad reputation in Prussian history; it caused a great sensation when I showed that he possessed a worthy and admirable side. From there I went to Friedrich II, and, understandably, to his struggle with Austria. His own historical works do not picture this struggle with the evidence which the documents provide. That I had previously studied and assimilated the correspondence of Valori proved a great advantage to me.

My work received a great deal of applause from some, but considerable opposition from others. At the time when it came to the king's notice, he himself was being assaulted by a storm which no one would have expected. The turmoils of the year 1848 went even deeper than the Revolution of 1830; they were also of a social sort. They were at first directed against the system established by the July Monarchy, but since all Europe was involved in similar instability, the overthrow of the July Monarchy was unhealthy for the rest. A moment arrived in which universal upheaval seemed to stand at the door. Friedrich Wilhelm IV had already brought his constitutional plans into existence by convening a united Diet, but against this universal upheaval he could not maintain his own ideas for an instant. He was forced to proceed to a second constitution, which allowed the revolutionary element free play. In the meantime, I had been indirectly drawn on for advice in those rather doubtful moments. Edwin von Manteuffel, at that time aide-de-camp and later field marshal, offered himself as an intermediary, and I learned that the king at least listened to his words and was emboldened to a stronger position by them. He acquired confidence in me because one or another of the predictions which I had made—for example, the presidential victory of the young Napoleon—came true.

Since then I saw the king more often than I had previously, and I rejoiced in and was edified by his talented nature, and depth of his character, and the unclouded outlook with which he regarded the world. But it became impossible for me to continue work on the history of Prussia. The disturbances which I viewed induced me to return to the study of the ancient world, from which sprang my lectures on ancient history in general, and on that of Rome in particular. With regard to my literary activity, I now for the first time returned to the collections which I had made in Italy.

My history of France arose out of the conflict between the documentary evidence and accepted opinions. I was still able to read it to the king. He loved the French in general, and also understood them. His comments were so pertinent that I sometimes wished that I had presented one section or another to him earlier. For I must say this: he was a man from whom one always departed better than when one came. One day I discussed with him in detail a few ideas about English history, particularly the great catastrophe which we call the Revolution of 1688. Never had I found him to be so attentive as when I told him that these events would form the basis of my next work. He called to me in a joyful, appreciative manner, "Do it; perhaps you will master it!"

Two decades earlier, I had delivered a few lectures, not really very many, to Crown Prince Maximilian of Bavaria, who was studying at the University of Berlin, and they gained for me his appreciation and favor for life. When he succeeded to the throne amid the storms of the Revolution of 1848, which also seized Bavaria, had strengthened his control somewhat, and felt himself secure, he had the kindness to remember me and to offer me a very honorable position. One could not compare Maximilian II with Friedrich Wilhelm IV in terms of talent of character or extent of education, but he was calm, considering things quietly, and then was very firm. All his efforts were directed toward raising the cultural level of Bavaria. He loved scholarship for itself and in relation to his country. I owe him my gratitude for inviting me to join him in his trip through the mountains from Berchtesgaden, which began in the fall of 1854. He revealed to me a side of German nature and the German nation with which I had not previously been acquainted. His conversations were always directed toward universal things. On our walks from Berchtesgaden, the plan was conceived for the academic society which has since performed great literary and historical service as the Historical Commission of the Bavarian Academy of Sciences. If only Maximilian had lived longer! Politics were not raised, and they played no large part in our discussions. He was thoroughly well-intentioned; there was nothing false in him. Bavaria was the most powerful of the middle states between Prussia and Austria. The king was in no way agreeable to the politics of the coalition of middle states which was then being negotiated, but his unexpected death certainly was the moment which first completely destroyed this system. The king of Bavaria would never have decided to join the Austrian side when war broke out, yet it occurred in the confusion which ensued after his death. He had many plans, well thought out— if only he had lived!—including an all-German academy for language and literature. But the war which followed brought an end to the situation of that period, and to any plans which were based upon it.

Then followed the two great wars, the Austrian–Prussian and the Franco-Prussian, which changed the fate of the world, and whose chief effect was to develop political relationships on a uniformly equal level. The general outlook for Germany and the world then prompted me to dedicate my last efforts to a work on universal history, with which I am still engaged.

# II

# The Historian's Craft:

## Four Working Statements

# INTRODUCTION TO THE
## *HISTORY OF THE LATIN*
## *AND TEUTONIC NATIONS*

One of the most quoted of Ranke's pieces is the first he ever published. In 1824 the unknown *Gymnasium* teacher from Frankfurt on Oder appeared before the German public as the author of the *History of the Latin and Teutonic Nations, 1494–1535*. It was a small work, offering a survey of Europe at the turning point between medieval and Renaissance times. Though not a best seller, the book attracted scholarly notice and some criticism. Above all, it won the attention of officials in the Prussian ministry of education, and led to Ranke's appointment as extraordinary professor of history at the University of Berlin in the spring semester of 1825. His career was launched.

The *History* covers the chief European nations from 1494 only to 1514; a planned second volume intended to carry the story to 1535 was never completed. The narrative is colorful, but the research was not profound; Ranke depended chiefly on printed sources and contemporary histories by Machiavelli, Guicciardini, and others. In a critical appendix he compared these earlier writers and their sources. Painstakingly he uncovered a host of errors: misinformation, distortion of the facts, and plagiarisms. Ranke may have exaggerated in some respects—Guicciardini's reputation has been somewhat restored by later historians—but the result of his work was to demonstrate clearly the impossibility of writing accurate history from contemporary historians and memoirists.

The same critical talent which gained him appointment to the university faculty at Berlin was too dissatisfied with completing the work based on the same printed sources, and the second volume was dropped after Ranke's attention had been brought to an extensive manuscript collection of relations by ambassadors of the former Republic of Venice, housed in the Berlin library. These opened his eyes to the possibility of an historical reconstruction done from eyewitness accounts and official documents. This led to his more ambitious expedition in 1827 to explore the archives of Austria and Italy, and his whole future work.

Fifty years later, in 1874, the aging Ranke debated whether to include his imperfect youthful book in his edition of his Collected Works. After some consideration, he concluded that he should, at least to present to his reading public the series of colorful vignettes of historical figures which it contained. Its originality, unlike that of the later works, lies more in its critical use of facts than in new discoveries, and in its different interpretation of European history.

The Introduction set Ranke apart from most contemporary Romantic historians. History was to be scientific, impartial, liberated from dependence on contemporary politics or philosophical systems; he rejected the paths of Hegel and of Michelet. History could only show "what actually happened [*wie es eigentlich gewesen*]."

Secondly, the book was quite original in its conception of Europe as the result of the interaction of two groups of peoples, the Latin and the Teutonic. The Slavs were excluded from consideration as peripheral. The description of Europe as a dynamic entity is typically Rankean, and was refined further; a more mature version can be seen in his essay on "The Great Powers." Thirdly, the critical appendix set new standards for the use of the printed sources of the Renaissance, and is useful even today. Its virtue was chiefly negative; it showed the difficulty of using such printed material and pointed the way toward recourse to archival research—a development in which Ranke followed the mandates of his own early work, and led the profession along the lines which he proposed.

The Introduction has been translated from Ranke's SW 33:v–viii.


THE PRESENT BOOK, I must confess, appeared more perfect to me before its printing than after. Nevertheless, I rely upon kindly readers who will pay attention less to its deficiencies than to its possible values. So as not to entrust it solely to its own powers, let me begin with a short explanation of its purpose, its material, and its form.

The purpose of an historian depends upon his point of view. About my viewpoint in this volume, two things must be said. First, I regard the Latin and Germanic peoples as a unit. This notion differs from three analogous concepts: the concept of a universal Christendom (which would include even the Armenians); the concept of Europe (for the Turks there are Asiatics, and the Russian empire embraces the whole of northern Asia and cannot be understood without investigating and penetrating a complete range of Asiatic affairs); and, the most analogous concept, the concept of Latin Christianity (for Slavic, Lithuanian, and Magyar races belonging to the latter have their own special and peculiar nature which I shall not include here).

By touching upon what is foreign to this unity only where necessary and only as a passing and subordinate matter, the author will remain close to the racially kindred nations of either purely Germanic or Latin-Germanic origin whose history forms the heart of all modern history.

In the following Introduction I shall try to show—by tracing the threads of international affairs—how these peoples have developed in unison and along similar lines. This is one aspect of the present book. The other is manifest from the contents: that it includes only a small portion of the history of those same nations, which we could call the beginning of the modern age. It contains only histories, not History. It comprises, on the one hand, the founding of the Spanish monarchy and the collapse of Italian freedom; and, on the other, the formation of a double opposition: political opposition by the French and religious opposition by the Reformation—in short, that division of our nations into hostile camps upon which all modern history is based. It begins at the moment in which Italy was still enjoying at least external freedom, and, if the position of the papacy is taken into consideration, perhaps even a predominance. The narrative then describes the division of Italy, the invasion by the French and Spanish, the destruction of freedom in some states and of self-determination in others, and, finally, the victory of the Spanish and the beginning of their domination. Starting with the political insignificance of the Spanish kingdoms, it proceeds to their unification and to the crusade of the united kingdoms against the infidels and for the inner renewal of Christianity. The book seeks to make clear how this crusade led to the discovery of America and the conquest of its great empires, and how, above all, it led to the Spanish domination of Italy, Germany, and the Netherlands. Thirdly, the work proceeds from the moment when Charles VIII went forth as a defender of Christendom against the Turks, through all the fortunes and misfortunes of the French, to the time 41 years later when Francis I called upon those same Turks for aid against the emperor. Finally, by following the beginnings of a political opposition in Germany against the emperor and of a religious opposition in Europe against the pope, it attempts to open the way toward a complete view of the history of the great schism caused by the Reformation. The first phase of that schism itself will be considered. The book seeks to comprehend all these and other related events in the history of the Latin and Germanic nations as a unity. History has had assigned to it the office of judging the past and of instructing the present for the benefit of the future ages. To such high offices the present work does not presume: it seeks only to show what actually happened [*wie es eigentlich gewesen*].

But from what sources can such a new investigation be made? The basis of the present work, the sources of its material, are memoirs, diaries, letters, ambassadors' reports, and original accounts of eyewitnesses. Other writings were used only if they were immediately derived from such as these, or seemed to be equal to them in some original information. These sources will be noted on every page; the method of investigation and the critical conclusions will be presented in a second volume, to be published concurrently.

Aim and subject shape the form of a book. We cannot expect from the writing of history the same free development as is, at least in theory, to be expected in works of literature; I am not certain that it was right to ascribe this quality to the work of the Greek and Roman masters. A strict presentation of the facts, contingent and unattractive though they may be, is the highest law. A second, for me, is the development of the unity and the progress of the events. Therefore, instead of starting, as might be expected, with a general account of the political situation of Europe, which would have confused if not distracted our attention, I have preferred to discuss in detail each people, each power, and each individual only at the time when each played an importantly active or leading role. I have not been disturbed by the fact that here and there they have had to be mentioned earlier where their existence could not be ignored. But thereby we are better able to grasp the general line of their development, the paths which they followed, and the ideas by which they were motivated.

Finally, what will be said of my treatment of particulars, the essential part of the writing of history? Will it not often seem harsh, disconnected, colorless, and tiring? There exist noble models for this work, ancient and—we should not forget—modern as well. I have not tried to emulate them; theirs was another world. There is an exalted ideal toward which we can reach: the event itself in its human intelligibility, its unity, its diversity. I know how far from it I have remained. One tries, one strives, but in the end it is not attained. Let none be impatient with this! The important thing, as Jacobi says, is always how we deal with humanity as it is, explicable or inexplicable; the life of the individual, of generations, of nations; and, at times, with the hand of God above them.

# TWO INTRODUCTIONS: THE
# *HISTORY OF THE POPES* AND THE
# *HISTORY OF THE REFORMATION*

Quite aside from the works which they precede, Ranke's introductions are interesting both for the light which they cast on his research methods and for his own personal ideas about history. In them we see unfolding the nineteenth-century revolution in history, the progress in transforming history from a story based on memoirs to a story based on archival research. We see Ranke earning Lord Acton's accolade as "the real originator of the heroic study of records." Ranke used these short pieces not only to introduce his own works but to lay down a standard for others to emulate; if he only partially achieved his goal in his earlier works, from the *History of the Popes* on he produced a series of masterworks of enduring value. There are some short excerpts from other introductions in the last section of the present volume.

The selection from the *History of the Popes* is based on the translation by Elizabeth Foster (London, 1847; pp. xi–xix); that from the *History of the Reformation in Germany*, on the translation by Sarah Austin in 1845 (repr. New York, 1905; pp. vii–xi).

# Introduction to the
# *History of the Popes*

THE POWER OF ROME IN ANTIQUITY AND THE MIDDLE AGES is universally known: in modern times, she has exercised renewed influence over the world. After the decline of her importance, in the first half of the sixteenth century, she raised herself to be once more the center of faith and opinion for the Romantic nations of southern Europe, and made bold, and often successful, attempts to recover her dominion over those of the North.

It is my purpose to describe, at least in outline, this period of the revived temporal power of the Church—its renovation and internal development, its progress and decline. This is an undertaking which, however imperfectly it may be performed, could never have been attempted, had I not had the opportunity to avail myself of certain materials hitherto unknown. My first duty is to give a general indication of these materials and their sources.

In an earlier work [the Preface to the *Ottoman and Spanish Monarchies in the Sixteenth and Seventeenth Centuries*], I indicated the contents of the manuscripts in Berlin; but Vienna is incomparably richer than Berlin in treasures of this kind.

Besides its essentially German character, Vienna possesses an element more extensively European: the most diversified manners and languages meet in all classes, from the highest to the lowest, and the Italian in particular is fully and vividly represented. Even the collections in this city present a comprehensiveness of character, attributable to the policy of the state and its geographical position; its ancient connection with Spain, Belgium, and Lombardy; and its proximity to and ecclesiastical relations with Rome. The Viennese have from the earliest times displayed a taste for collecting, possessing, and preserving; whence it arises that even the original and purely national collections of the imperial library are of great value: to these, various foreign collections have since been added. A number of volumes similar to the Berlin *Informazioni* were purchased at Modena, from the House of Rangone. From Venice were acquired the invaluable manuscripts of the Doge Marco Foscarini, including his materials for a continuation of his literary undertaking, the "Italian Chronicles," of which no trace is elsewhere to be found. And the bequest of Prince Eugene added a rich collection of historical and political manuscripts, which had been formed, with comprehensive judgment, by that distinguished statesman. The reader is animated by feelings of pleasure and hope, on examining the catalogues, and perceiving the many unexplored sources of knowledge which will enable him to supply the deficiencies manifest in almost all printed works of modern history. A whole futurity of study! And at the distance of only a few steps, Vienna presents literary subsidies still more important. The imperial archives contain, as might be expected, the most authentic and valuable records for the elucidation of German, and general, but particularly Italian, history. It is true that the greater part of the Venetian archives has been restored, after many wanderings, to Venice; but there remains in Vienna a mass of Venetian manuscripts far from unimportant: despatches, original or copied, and abstracts thereof made for the use of the state, and called "Rubricaries"; reports which, in many instances, are the only copies extant; official registers of public functionaries; chronicles and diaries. The notices to be found in the present volumes relating to Gregory XIII and Sixtus V are for the most part derived from the archives of Vienna. I cannot sufficiently acknowledge the unconditional liberality with which I was permitted to have access to these treasures.

And perhaps I ought here to particularize the many and various aids afforded me in furtherance of my attempt, both at home and abroad, but I feel restrained by a scruple (whether well founded or not, I am unable to decide) that I should have to mention so many names, some of them of great eminence, as would give my gratitude the appearance of vainglory; and a work, which has every reason to present itself modestly, might assume an air of ostentation ill suited to its pretensions.

Next to Vienna, my attention was principally directed to Venice and Rome.

It was formerly the almost invariable practice of the great houses in Venice to form a cabinet of manuscripts, as an adjunct to the library. It was in the nature of things that these would relate principally to the affairs of the republic. They served to show the part taken by the respective families in public affairs, and were preserved as records and memorials of the house, for the instruction of its younger members. Some of these private collections still exist, and I had access to several; but much the larger number were destroyed in the general ruin of 1797, or since. If more have been preserved than might have been expected, the gratitude of the world is due chiefly to the librarians of St. Mark, who labored to save, from the universal wreck, whatever the utmost resources of their institution would permit them to secure. Accordingly, this library possesses a considerable store of manuscripts, which are indispensable to the history of the city and state, and which are even valuable aids to that of Europe. But the inquirer must not expect too much from it: it is a somewhat recent acquisition; gathered, almost at hazard, from private collections; incomplete and without unity of plan. It is not to be compared with the riches of the state archives, especially as these are now arranged. I have already given a sketch of the Venetian archives, in my inquiry into the conspiracy of 1618, and shall not repeat what I said there. For my Roman investigations, the reports of the ambassadors returning from Rome were above all desirable; but I had great reason to wish for assistance from other collections, because none is free of lacunae, and these archives must necessarily have sustained losses in their many wanderings. In different places, I gathered together 48 reports relating to Rome: the oldest date from the year 1500; 19 are of the sixteenth century, and 21 of the seventeenth. These formed an almost complete series, with only a few breaks here and there. Of the eighteenth century, there were only eight, it is true, but these, too, were very instructive and welcome. In the majority of cases I saw and used the originals. They contain a great number of interesting notices, the results of personal observation, which had passed out of memory with the generation. It was from these that I first derived the idea of a continuous narrative, and the courage to attempt it.

It will be obvious that only Rome herself could supply the means for verifying and extending these materials.

But was it to be expected that a foreigner, and one professing a different faith, would be permitted to have free access to the public collections, there for the purpose of revealing the secrets of the papacy? This would not have been perhaps so ill-advised as it might appear, since no search can bring to light anything worse than what is already assumed by unfounded conjecture, and received by the world as established truth. But I cannot boast of having had any such permission. I was enabled to take cognizance of the treasures contained in the Vatican, and to use a number of volumes suited to my purpose; but the freedom of access which I could have wished was by no means accorded. Fortunately, however, other collections were thrown open to me, from which I could acquire information, which, if not complete, was very extensive and authentic. In the flourishing times of aristocracy, more particularly in the seventeenth century, it was customary throughout Europe for the great families, who had administered the affairs of state, to retain possession of some of the public documents. This practice prevailed in Rome, to a greater extent, perhaps, than in any other state. The reigning kinsmen of the pontiff, who in all ages exercised considerable power, usually bequeathed as an heirloom to the princely houses which they founded a large part of the state papers accumulated during their administration. These constituted a part of the family endowments. In the palaces which they erected, a few rooms, usually in the upper part of the building, were always reserved for books and manuscripts, which each succeeding generation contributed to enrich. Thus, to a certain extent the private collections of Rome may be regarded as the public ones, since the archives of state were dispersed among the descendants of reigning houses, without any objection's being made to the practice; much in the same manner as the superfluity of public wealth was suffered to flow into the coffers of the papal kindred, and certain private galleries, such as the Borghese or the Doria, became greatly superior to the Vatican, both in extent and historical importance (though the latter is distinguished by its selection of masterpieces). The manuscripts which are preserved in the Barberini, Chigi, Altieri, Albani, and Corsini palaces are, accordingly, of inestimable value, for the aid which they give toward a history of the popes, their state, and the Church. The Vatican public records office, which has recently been established, is particularly important for its collection of registers illustrative of the Middle Ages; for that period, it will still repay the inquirer, but, so far as my knowledge extends, I do not believe that much is to be gained from it for later centuries. Its value sinks into insignificance, unless I have been purposely deceived, when compared with the wealth and magnificence of private collections. Each of these comprises, as may readily be supposed, that epoch in which the pope of the family reigned. But since the kindred of each pontiff usually retained an eminent station, since men are in general desirous of extending and completing a collection once begun, and since opportunities were frequent in Rome because of the literary traffic in manuscripts established there, the whole of these private collections possesses many valuable documents illustrating other periods, both proximate and remote. The richest of all (in consequence of important bequests) is the Barberini; that of the Corsini Palace has been remarkable from its commencement for the care and judgment with which it has been formed. Fortunately, I was permitted to use all these collections, as well as others of less importance—and in some instances with unrestricted freedom. An unhoped-for harvest of authentic and suitable materials thus lay before me: for example, correspondences of the nuncios [*nunciaturae*], with the instructions given them, and the reports which were brought back; circumstantial biographies of different popes, written with greater freedom, because they were not intended for the public; lives of distinguished cardinals; official and private journals; investigations of particular circumstances and transactions; special opinions and deliberations; reports on the administration of provinces, their trade, and manufactures; statistical tables; and accounts of receipts and disbursements. These documents, for the most part entirely unknown, were prepared by men practically acquainted with their subject, and of a credibility which, though it does not supersede the necessity for a searching and critical examination, is equal to that usually accorded the testimony of well-informed contemporaries. The oldest of these manuscripts of which I made use related to the conspiracy of the Porcari against Nicholas V. Of the fifteenth century I met with only a few; but at the beginning of the sixteenth, they became more numerous and more comprehensive at every step. Through the entire course of the seventeenth century, during which so little is known with certainty respecting Rome, they afford information, the more valuable because of its previous dearth. For the period after the beginning of the eighteenth century, they decrease in number and intrinsic value; but at that time the Roman court and state had already lost much of their influence and importance. I shall go through those Roman manuscripts, as well as the Venetian, in detail, at the end of the work, and shall note there whatever I may find which is deserving of attention and which I could not well introduce in the course of the narrative. The large mass of materials, both manuscript and printed, which is lying before me, renders a stringent condensation indispensable.

An Italian or Roman, a Catholic, would enter into the subject in a spirit very different from mine. By indulging in expressions of personal veneration, or perhaps, in the present state of opinion, of personal hatred, he would give to his work a peculiar, and, no doubt, more brilliant coloring; on many points he would be more elaborate, more ecclesiastical, more local. In these respects, a Protestant, a North German, cannot be expected to compete with him. He regards the papal power with feelings of more indifference, and must, from the first, renounce that warmth of expression which arises from partiality or hostility and which might, perhaps, produce a certain impression in Europe. For mere matters of ecclesiastical or canonical detail, we can have no true sympathy; on the other hand, our position affords us different, and, if I am not mistaken, purer and less partial views of history. For what is there in the present day which can make the history of the papal power of importance to us? Not its particular relation to us; for it no longer exercises any essential influence, or creates in us solicitude of any kind; the times are past in which we have anything to fear; we now feel ourselves perfectly secure. Popery can now inspire us with no interest other than what results from the development of its history and its former influence.

The papal power was, however, not so unchangeable as is commonly supposed. If we consider the question apart from those principles upon which its existence depends, and which it cannot abandon without consigning itself to destruction, we shall find it affected, quite as deeply as any other government, and to the very essence of its being, by the various destinies to which the nations of Europe have been subjected. As the history of the world has varied, as one nation or another has gained the ascendancy, as the fabric of social life has been disturbed, so also has the papal power been affected: its maxims, its objects, and its pretensions have undergone essential changes, and its influence, above all, has been subjected to the greatest variations. If we cast a glance at the long catalogue of names so frequently repeated through successive ages, from Pius I in the second century, to our contemporaries, Pius VII and Pius VIII in the nineteenth, we receive an impression of uninterrupted stability; but we must not permit ourselves to be misled by the semblance of constancy. The popes of different periods are, in fact, distinguished by differences as strongly marked as those existing between the various dynasties of a kingdom. To us, who are lookers-on at a distance, it is precisely these mutations which present the most interesting subject of contemplation. We see in them a portion of the history of the world, and of the general progress of mankind; and this is true, not only of the periods when Rome held undisputed sovereignty, but also, and perhaps even more remarkably, of those shaken by the conflicting forces of action and counteraction, such as the times which the present work is intended to comprise: the six-teenth and seventeenth centuries—times when the papacy was menaced and endangered, yet maintained and fortified itself; nay, even re-extended its influence; striding onward for a period, but at last receding again, and tottering to its fall; times when the mind of the Western nations was pre-eminently occupied by ecclesiastical questions; and when that power, which, abandoned and assailed by one party, was upheld and defended with fresh zeal by the other, necessarily assumed a station of high and universal importance. It is from this point of view that our natural position invites us to consider it, and this I shall now attempt.

# Introduction to the
## *History of the Reformation*
## *in Germany*

FROM THE FIRST TEN YEARS OF THE FIFTEENTH CENTURY to the beginning of the Thirty Years' War, the constitution and political condition of Germany were determined by the periodical Diets and the measures there resolved on.

The time was long past in which the public affairs of the country were determined by one supreme will; but its political life had not yet (as at a later period) retreated within the several boundaries of the constituent members of the empire. The imperial assemblies exercised rights and powers which, though not accurately defined, were yet the comprehensive and absolute powers of sovereignty. They made war and peace, levied taxes, exercised a supreme supervision, and were even invested with executive power. Together with the deputies from the cities, and the representatives of the counts and lords, the emperor and the sovereign princes appeared in person. It is true that they discussed the most important affairs of their respective countries in their several colleges, or in committees chosen from the whole body, and the questions were decided by a majority of voices. The unity of the nation was represented by these assemblies. Within the wide borders of the empire nothing of importance could occur which did not come under deliberation here; nothing new arise, which must not await its final decision and execution here.

In spite of all these considerations, the history of the Diets of the empire has not yet received the attention which it deserves. The Recesses [documents summing up all the decisions of the emperor and Diet published at the conclusion of the session] of the Diets are sufficiently well known; but who would judge a deliberative assembly by the final results of its deliberations? Projects of a systematic collection of its transactions have occasionally been entertained, and the work been taken in hand; but all that has hitherto been done has remained in a fragmentary and incomplete state.

Since it is the natural ambition of every man to leave behind him some useful record of his existence, I have long cherished the project of devoting my industry and my powers to this most important work. Not that I flattered myself that I was competent to supply so large a deficiency, to exhaust the mass of materials in its manifold juridical bearings; my idea was to trace with accuracy only the rise and development of the constitution of the empire, through a series (if possible unbroken) of the Acts of the Diets.

Fortune was so propitious to my wishes that, in the autumn of 1836, I found in the archives of the city of Frankfurt a collection of the very kind I wanted, and was allowed access to these precious documents with all the facility I could desire.

The collection consists of 96 folio volumes, which contain the Acts of the imperial Diets from 1414 to 1613. In the earlier part it is very imperfect, but step by step, in proportion as the constitution of the empire acquires form and development, the documents rise in interest. At the beginning of the sixteenth century, from which time the practice of reducing public proceedings to writing was introduced, it becomes so rich in new and important materials that it lays the strongest hold on the attention. There are not only the Acts, but the reports of the deputies from the cities—the *Rathsfreunde*—which generally charm by their frankness and simplicity, and often surprise by their sagacity. I profited by the opportunity to make myself master of the contents of the first 64 of these volumes, extending down to the year 1551. A collection of imperial Rescripts occasionally afforded me valuable contributions.

But I could not stop here. A single town was not in a position to know all that passed. It was evident that the labors of the Electoral and princely colleges were not to be sought for in the records of a city.

In the beginning of the year 1837, I received permission to explore the Royal Archives of the Kingdom of Prussia at Berlin, and, in the April of the same year, the State Archives of the Kingdom of Saxony at Dresden, for the affairs of the empire during the times of Maximilian I and Charles V. They were of great value to me: the former as containing the records of an electorate; the latter, down to the end of that epoch, those of a sovereign principality. It is true that I came upon many documents which I had already seen at Frankfurt; but, at the same time, I found a great number of new ones, which gave me an insight into parts of the subject hitherto obscure. None of these collections is, indeed, complete, and many a question which suggests itself remains unanswered; yet they are in a high degree instructive. They throw a completely new light on the character and conduct of such influential princes as Joachim II of Brandenburg and, still more, Maurice of Saxony.

Let no one pity a man who devotes himself to studies apparently so dry, and neglects for them the delights of many a joyous day. It is true that the companions of his solitary hours are but lifeless paper, but they are the remnants of the life of past ages, which gradually assume form and substance to the eye occupied in the study of them. For me (in an introduction an author is bound to speak of himself—a subject he elsewhere glady avoids) they had a peculiar interest.

When I wrote the first part of my *History of the Popes*, I designedly treated the origin and progress of the Reformation with as much brevity as the subject permitted. I cherished the hope of dedicating more extensive and profound research to this most important event of the history of my country.

This hope was now abundantly satisfied. Of the new matter which I found, the greater part related, directly or indirectly, to the epoch of the Reformation. At every step I acquired new information about the circumstances which prepared the politico-religious movement of that time, the phases of our national life by which it was accelerated, and the origin and working of the resistance which it encountered.

It is impossible to approach a matter originating in such intense mental energy, and exercising so vast an influence on the destinies of the world, without being profoundly interested and absorbed by it. I was fully aware that if I executed the work which I proposed to myself, the Reformation would be the center on which all other incidents and circumstances would turn.

But to accomplish this, more accurate information was necessary as to the progress of opinion in the evangelical party (especially in a political point of view), antecedent to the crisis of the Reformation, than any which could be gathered from printed sources. The archives common to the entire Ernestine line of Saxony, deposited at Weimar, which I visited in August 1837, afforded me what I desired. Nor can any spot be more full of information on the marked epochs at which this house played so important a part than the vault in which its archives are preserved. The walls and all the interior space are covered with the rolls of documents relating to the deeds and events of that period. Every note, every draft of an answer, are preserved here. The correspondence between the Elector John Frederick and the Landgrave Philip of Hesse alone would fill a long series of printed volumes. I endeavored, above all, to make myself master of the two registers, which include the affairs of the empire and of the League of Schmalkald. As to the former, I found, as was to be expected from the nature of the subject, many valuable details; as to the latter, I hence first drew information which is, I hope, in some degree calculated to satisfy the curiosity of the public.

I feel bound here publicly to express my thanks to the authorities to whom the guardianship of these various archives is entrusted for the liberal aid—often not unattended with personal trouble—which I received from them all.

At length I conceived the project of undertaking a more extensive research into the archives of Germany. I repaired to the Communal Archives of the House of Anhalt at Dessau, which at the epoch in question shared the opinions and followed the example of that of Saxony; but I soon saw that here I should be in danger of encumbering myself with too much matter of a purely local character. I remembered how many other documents relating to this period had been explored and employed by the industry of German inquirers. The work of Bucholtz on Ferdinand I contains a most copious treasure of important matter from those of Austria, of which too little use is made in that state. The instructive writings of Stumpf and Winter are founded on those of Bavaria. The archives of Württemberg were formerly explored by Sattler; those of Hesse, recently, by Rommel and Neudecker. For the more exclusively ecclesiastical view of the period, the public is in possession of a rich mass of authentic documents in the collection of Walch, and in the recent edition of Luther's letters by De Wette; and still more those of Melanchthon by Bretschneider. The letters of the deputies from Strasburg and Nuremberg, which have been published, throw light on the history of particular Diets. It is hardly necessary for me to mention how much has lately been brought together by Foerstemann respecting the Diet of Augsburg of 1530, so long the subject of earnest research and labor.

Recent publications, especially in Italy and England, lead us to hope for the possibility of a thorough and satisfactory explanation of the foreign relations of the empire.

I see the time approaching when we shall base modern history no longer on the reports even of contemporary historians, except insofar as they were in possession of personal and immediate knowledge of facts; and still less, on works yet more remote from the source; but rather on the narratives of eyewitnesses, and on genuine and original documents. For the epoch treated in the following work, the prospect is no distant one. I myself have made use of a number of records which I found when in the pursuit of another subject, in the archives of Vienna, Venice, Rome, and especially Florence. Had I gone into further detail, I should have run the risk of losing sight of the subject as a whole; or in the necessary lapse of time, of breaking the unity of the conception which had arisen before my mind in the course of my past researches.

And thus I proceeded boldly to the completion of the work, persuaded that when an inquirer has made researches of some extent in authentic records, with an earnest spirit and a genuine ardor for truth, though later discoveries may throw clearer and more certain light on details, they can only strengthen his fundamental conceptions of the subject—for truth can be but one.

# CRITIQUE OF GUICCIARDINI

Ranke's programatic statements on the need for critical research and a careful use of the sources are stated briefly in the Introductions to his major works, and are glimpsed occasionally in the narrative of his major histories. However, it is in a number of his smaller, more technical essays and fragments that we see the critical faculties of the historian actually at work. His most famous piece of extended criticism, indeed a book-length work, is to be found in the second part of his first published work, on the history of the Latin and Teutonic peoples. Following closely on the publication of the narrative came a long critical appendix, *Zur Kritik neuerer Geschichtsschreiber*, in which Ranke systematically evaluated the major historians upon whose work study of the Renaissance era had previously depended, and upon whose work much of his own first book was based. More than the narrative, it was the critical appendix which won the young scholar a reputation among colleagues, and his appointment to the professorial position at Berlin. It represented the most detailed and sharply evaluated survey of the historiography of the early-sixteenth century which had yet appeared.

Ranke's most famous piece of criticism was directed against Francesco Guicciardini, whose *History of Italy* was regarded both as the best Renaissance historical work, and as a reliable source for much of the complicated politics of that era.

The following selection, slightly abridged for reasons of space, gives Ranke's account of Guicciardini. It is critical to the point of being hostile, and some Guicciardini scholars have protested that he distorted his subject.

Yet this essay represents more than a young historian's seeking to make his reputation at the expense of a predecessor. It shows us Ranke at the very outset of his career, when he first turned his attention to a careful use of printed sources and memoirs, before he developed his skills and opportunities in the unpublished archives of Europe. It is the judgment of one great historical mind upon another, and reveals something about both.

The following excerpt from the second part of his first book, unlike the narrative, has never before been translated. It was included in Ranke's Sämtliche Werke under the title "Zur Kritik neuerer Geschichtsschreiber." SW 33/34 includes the 1874 revision of Ranke's original text of 1824; the later version is used in this selection.

Guicciardini's *Storia d'Italia* was first published in Florence, in

1561, with numerous later editions, some enlarged. Abridged modern English translations include *The History of Italy by Francesco Guicciardini*, ed. and trans. Sidney Alexander (New York & London, 1969); *History of Italy and History of Florence*, trans. Cecil Grayson (New York, 1964). For critical comment on Guicciardini, see Roberto Ridolfi, *The Life of Francesco Guicciardini* (New York, 1968) and Wallace K. Ferguson, *The Renaissance in Historical Thought* (Cambridge, 1948). For Ranke's *Kritik*, see Eduard Fueter, "Guicciardini als Historiker," *Historische Zeitschrift*, 100 (1908), 486–540, and Ernst Schulin, "Ranke's erstes Buch," *Historische Zeitschrift*, 203 (1966), 581–609.

# Introduction

## (To the First Edition, 1824)

I INTEND THE PRESENT BOOK to have three purposes: first, to justify the manner and method in which the sources were used in my attempt at Latin and Teutonic history; second, to indicate to those who wish to educate themselves in depth about the beginnings of modern history the books upon which they can and cannot rely; and third, to contribute to a thorough evaluation of the nature and worth of the available documentary writings, the collection of which forms the unfalsified basis of modern history; this is the most important and purely scholarly intent.

When entering a great collection of antiquities gathered from many countries and from many ages, and placed next to one another in disorder, one could be overwhelmed by the genuine objects and the forgeries, the beautiful and the repulsive, the most brilliant things and the most dull. One could feel the same way looking at once at the manifold monuments of modern history; they speak to us with a thousand voices, display the most varied natures, and are clad in all colors. A few arrive with ceremony.

They pretend to represent the ways of the ancients. Others seek to draw from the past lessons for the future. Many wish to defend or accuse. Not a few strive to develop the events out of deeper motives of emotion or passion. Then there are a few whose only purpose is to transmit what happened; alongside these are the reports of eyewitnesses. Actions are turned into words; crowds of documents become available, both supposed and real.

Most important, the person accustomed to original knowledge of so many items has to ask himself, "From which of these can I really learn?" The principal purpose of this essay is to throw some light on the contemporary, or nearly contemporary, written connections with the beginnings of modern history. Our purpose aims merely at making some contribution; it cannot and will not exhaust the subject. It takes the following course.

We begin with those historians who appear to be at once the most comprehensive and the most famous. Guicciardini is the basis of all the later works about the beginnings of modern history and easily has precedence.

Beaucaire, whose authority Sismondi cites some 27 times in Chapter 104 and not less than 27 times in Chapter 105 of his *Italian History*, follows next. Of all the Spanish historians, Mariana has the greatest fame and the greatest readership on this side of the Pyrenees, and he is the third. After this follow Fugger, Sleidanus, and Jovius, so that in the first section we speak of two Italians, two Germans, one Frenchman, and one Spaniard.

Italy, Germany, France, and Spain—these were the nations which played the most active role in the events of the period, and to them as well belong the other writers whom I handle in their turn. In four following sections I treat in sequence the Italian, Spanish, German, and French writers. One cannot make equally significant remarks about all of them, and sometimes the unimportant must occasionally be supported by the more important. Of some, I found so little to say that I should have preferred not to have mentioned them at all. About others, especially three English writers, I myself remain in the dark, since I was lacking a comparison with contemporary chronicles, and it would be asking too much for any reader to expect a section dealing with them.

Machiavelli is not really an historian of our period, but he transmits to us such essential information about it, gives us such a picture, so deeply based on the times, and provides such a profound insight into the age, that we may omit him least of all. He is treated in a separate appendix.

Truly this book represents just one fragment of another fragment. One can indeed find ideas in it, such as the progress of historiography, the distinctions between the nations, the commonly agreed upon principles which united the individual historians. But the role of guiding ideas [*leitende Ideen*] in such a limited work is as dangerous as it is attractive. When one errs once, one does it doubly and triply. Truth itself, under the guise of error, becomes falsehood.

Thus no one should expect to find here something complete. Nonetheless, much is said, which previously has not been said; and the author awaits with close attention the contradiction or agreement of men of insight.

Written at Frankfurt on Oder, in October 1824.

# Guicciardini's
## *Storia d'Italia*

1. *Life of the Author*

The youth of Francesco Guicciardini, who was born in Florence in 1482, occurred at the time of the greatest disturbances which his native city had ever experienced. These were closely connected with all the events which were happening in Italy and throughout the world. We must remember that his father, Piero Guicciardini, was the representative of the older branch of the House of the Medici in Milan at the time it broke with Ludovico Sforza. Piero de' Medici was reminded by his ambassador just how dangerous this estrangement might be. We can gather from the *Florentine History* which Francesco wrote in his youth that the appearance of Girolamo Savonarola as an opponent of Medici rule also made a strong impression on him. Guicciardini dedicated this youthful work to the aim of a thorough and impartial account.

The father, Piero, had a large family, and, as a result, his third son, Francesco, had to make his own career. He chose to study law, which led him to Pavia, which was then the greatest legal school in the world. There he dedicated himself to the study of Roman law, a subject which even the Germans came to study there, since it was new for them also. Francesco Guicciardini also read law at Florence, where a school had been established a few years earlier. After this school was discontinued, he was fortunately able to jump into the membership of the bar in his native city, and landed himself a solid position.

But this did not satisfy his ambitions.

At first there was talk that one of his relatives might transfer to him one of his ecclesiastical benefices, and Francesco was very interested in accepting it, in the hopes of rising in this manner to the cardinalate in the Roman Church. But the plan failed: his father, who had no love for the clergy at all, opposed it. Nor was the father really happy with the marriage his son then contracted. Francesco sought his bride from one of the great families of Florence, the Salviati, whom he discerned to be the most respected of all at that time. His father, however, was afraid of that family's opposition to the then Gonfaloniere Piero Soderini. He did not wish to alienate him, although the Guicciardini were also members of the aristocracy of the city. The son, for whom piety toward his father and forefathers formed an important point of his character, nearly regretted his willful conduct in this matter. But his connection with the most distinguished families, which he had now joined, together with the respect earned by his studies and profession, led to his appointment at a very young age as the republic's ambassador to Spain. His father was most agreeable to this, especially since he did not have to contribute any of his own money toward it. Francesco was thus raised far above the level of a Florentine lawyer.

His mission to Ferdinand the Catholic broadened him and gave him a worldly point of view. He observed at first hand the relationships between England, France, and Spain. At the same time he was made aware of the great transformation which had occurred in the trade with the Indies and the riches which Spain acquired from its West Indian discoveries. He was on good personal terms with Ferdinand the Catholic, which benefited his republic, and at the time of his departure, in 1513, the king assured him that Florence was as dear to his heart as any of his own cities.

The situation of Florence itself was basically altered when the Gonfaloniere Soderini was overthrown by the great families and the House of the Medici, and a member of that family was elected to the papal throne. This led to the closest entanglement of the affairs of Florence with those of the Papal States and the Church. Francesco was not in the closest agreement with the government of Florence, led by the younger Lorenzo. He complained about being neglected, and when amends were made, he thought the action derived more from a necessary respect for his person than from favor and grace.

The measures which Lorenzo undertook were not at all in accord with the claims and ambitions of the Florentine aristocracy. But Guicciardini did not sever his connections with the House of the Medici over these matters. At precisely the moment when Pope Leo X concluded peace at Bologna with Francis I, he entered the papal service, though he never lost sight of his native city.

One of his memoranda survives written after the death of Lorenzo, in which he advises the pope to favor the leading families, and to have the closest alliance with them, so that they would join the party of the Medici . . . and establish that House on a sound basis. However, his own activity was dedicated to the service of the pope. He achieved a high administrative position in the Romagna, not without difficulty, since the papal authority in that territory was recent and the world was disturbed.

In 1521, when a breach of faith again occurred between Leo X and Francis I, it was Guicciardini's task to halt the first attack of the French on Reggio, where they had pushed the refugees from Milan. We will treat later his own account of these events. The elements of this situation were most significant and of world importance. The war between Francis I and Charles V was to decide the predominance of one or the other over Europe. The power of the Medici—which now encompassed Rome and the old States of the Church, the newly won cities, particularly the Romagna, and Florence and Tuscany—seemed suited to lay the foundations of the independence of Italy, working in between the two contending powers. A situation presented itself in which one could hope to see the Spanish driven out of Milan and Naples.

Francesco Guicciardini also supported this. He played no small part in forming the alliance which Pope Clement VII—also a Medici—made with King Francis against the emperor. But everyone knew how unfortunately that war proceeded after its start; the pope was held prisoner for a long time, and he was able to recover his power over Florence only with the aid of the emperor. Instead of being struck down, the domination of the Spanish was established for centuries.

There remained for Guicciardini's ambition only to accommodate itself to the events which had taken place. We find him in papal service as governor of Romagna, entrusted with the difficult task of suppressing the perpetual clash of rival factions. He applied the laws with severity to everyone, no matter who, and though he insisted that it was essential to do so and took no personal pleasure in the cruel sentences which he imposed, he made himself thoroughly hated. At the same time, he did all he could to strengthen the authority of the Medici in Florence. He and his friends above all deserve the credit for the installation of the new duke, Alexander, which they accomplished while respecting the rights of the chief dignitaries. With the duke at his side, Francesco and the oligarchical faction guided the government of the city. But this government was so hard and violent that it awoke decisive opposition, especially after the death of Pope Clement, and was able to maintain itself only with the help of the emperor, whose daughter was engaged to the young duke. Guicciardini's high and imposing manner and his stern appearance kept everyone in fear and at a distance. But while the people truly might describe him by the name used for the old servant of tyrants, "The Corrector," he maintained an unweakened respect among the upper classes.

He seemed to be a man who thoroughly understood world affairs, and was excellent in deliberation. He combined the authority of high office with a reputation for steadiness, competence, and spirit. His highest aim continued to be the maintenance of the newly established duchy. When Jacopo Nardi was so bold as to complain about Alexander to the emperor, Guicciardini undertook to defend the duke's atrocities.

His entire life now centered in the alliance, which he had once opposed, of the House of the Medici, the leading families, and the emperor. When Charles V entered Florence, Guicciardini himself was seen at his side; he even accompanied the emperor on his campaign against France. But Alexander was murdered. There was now no longer a Medici from Lorenzo's old line. But the constitution which had been introduced required a duke.

Another young man of the same age from the second branch of the Medici family, which had often in the past been opponents of the older line, was supported by the great families for the dukedom. But they also wished to restrict him; Guicciardini's thoughts had already been moving in this direction for some time. Many years earlier, in his *Discorsi*, in which he opposed Machiavelli's *Discorsi*, we can find the idea expressed that a combination of the forms of monarchy, aristocracy, and democracy would be the most desirable. Making finer distinctions, he proposed the principle that neither the prince nor the people should decide the most important questions. The people's freedom of speech and advice in their assemblies should be restricted. Only those persons should speak who were empowered by the magistrates to do so. He rested the weight of power in a senate which would decide all the essential questions of war, peace, and political negotiations. This was the type of government which he sought to establish.

The Council of Eight, which was formed to assist the new duke, consisted of Guicciardini's friends and relations, and he was its leader. It appeared almost inevitable that he would continue to exercise the predominant authority. To the duke, he wrote "as good as your son"; to the king of France, "to my cousin." He even dared to hope that he would become father-in-law to Duke Cosimo of Tuscany.

But the duke preferred a direct alliance with the Spanish, who were the only ones who could defend him against his enemies, to a one-sided alliance with the great families of the city. The duke kept his distance from those who wished to dominate him with their advice, Guicciardini among them. In this state of discouragement, Guicciardini died on May 23, 1540.

His life can in no way be described as happy—for the two greatest goals which he had in sight, the independence of Italy and the aristocratic rule of his native city, were not attained. But it was rich in great events, in untiring and honorable activity in important places, and in the highest society. Guicciardini not only had a practical nature; he also loved theory, political abstractions, and history. The most varied activities in which he participated never deterred him from writing continuously. During his lifetime he never appeared in print as an author, but among his literary remains a great number of works were discovered. These included the *Avvertimenti*, the *Discorsi*, memoranda, autobiographical statements, and the already-mentioned *Florentine History*, which was written in 1508, but remained unknown down to our own period. But by far his most important legacy was the complete *History of Italy* from the invasion of Charles VIII. It was written, as far as we know, in the not entirely voluntary retirement which marked the last days of his life at his country home, Monticci. Twenty years after his death his nephew published it, and from that moment on it has attracted the greatest interest. It serves even today as the foundation for any study of that period. It has dominated the perception of subsequent ages. The goal of the following essay is to inquire whether it is deserving of its reputation, and whether other works can maintain their value in relation to this one.

## 2. *The Form of the Work*

In its frequent interruptions and resumptions, Guicciardini's history is comparable to the poem of Ariosto. But an historian's work requires a stricter rule. Let us search for it.

In Book IV, Guicciardini retells the campaign of Cesare Borgia against Imola and Forlì, the state of the countess Caterina Sforza. Imola was conquered in December 1499; Forlì, in January 1500. The undertaking itself was carried on without interruption. Nonetheless, after Guicciardini speaks of Imola, he breaks off. The end of the year reminds him of an event which he then recounts: the attack of the Turks on Friuli, which had taken place in July, and might perhaps have had something to do with the war of Ludovico, but had not the least to do with Cesare's campaign. After he discusses this, he also recalls that 1500 had been a Jubilee Year—he then returns to the subject of Forlì.

He is even more rigid in observing the form of a yearbook. Alexander and Cesare Borgia made a joint attack against the Orsini. The son succeeded on December 31, 1502; the father, on January 3, 1503. This was sufficient motivation for Guicciardini to interject the story about a clash at Mirandola, which he himself admits has little significance, into the middle of his narrative.

We can see that he intended strictly to write a yearbook. If we look further, at the conquest of Navarre, for example, which was closely related to the events in Italy in the summer of 1512, we find that he does not discuss these together, but pushes the conquest off to the end of the year. Similarly, he treats the war between Henry VII and Louis XII in the summer of 1513, which was directly connected with Cardona's attack that fall against Venice, only at the end of the year. Thus it appears that his intent was to write an annual chronicle of Italy, although he does not always strictly adhere to this aim.

But are the accidental distinctions made by each annual calendar so important that an historian should conform to them in all essentials, and allow them to hinder the progress of his narrative? If this were carried to extreme lengths, the narrative would then be bound to the events month by month and day by day. The notion of a yearbook is not essentially different from the notion of a diary.

I do not believe that anyone can read this history without taking offense at the great scrambling of events. In nine pages of Book 17—pp. 433–461 of the 1604 (Treviso) edition—we can find these points described divided from one another, in the following order:

1. the liberation of Florence
2. the strengthening of the imperial army at Rome
3. the alliance of France with England and Venice
4. plague in the army at Rome and the army of the League
5. the treaty of the Florentines
6. Lautrec's march from France
7. Venice's attack against Marignano and Medici's against Mus
8. the advice of the emperor
9. Wolsey's mission to France and the alliance itself
10. the situation of the army at Rome
11. the situation of the pope
12. the situation of the army of the League
13. the disturbances at Siena
14. once again the situation of the army at Rome, and the opposing League army
15. Lautrec's arrival in Bosco
16. Doria's undertaking at Genoa.

Here Guicciardini handles the army at Rome four times, the army of the League three times, speaks of the alliance between France and England twice, and the same number of times of Florence, Venice, and Lautrec. They are only connected together or introduced with such phrases as "in those times," "in this manner," "at such a time," "before such." In most cases, at least a more exact definition of the dates is required. Suffice it to say that the parts seem to have been put together more by accident than by intent. . . .

In this manner the history is constructed. It is scarcely different from Ariosto's poem. Moreover, its form is essentially distorted by discourses about "why" and "if" and "why not." There are speeches and digressions; at the least one could say that the latter do not always fit. Thus, in spite of the fact that he asserts that Henry VII's war of 1524 was influenced not at all by the old claims of England against France, but rather by the ambition of the king and the cardinal, Guicciardini then goes on to detail in length these same old claims.

### 3. *Whether Guicciardini Is to be Regarded at all as a Source*

The first question to be asked regarding those documentary histories, which we generally regard as sources, is whether they are written by participants or eyewitnesses or merely by contemporaries. In the year 1492, where Guicciardini begins, he was only ten years old. One could easily think that for the next two decades while he was studying and completing his legal training his observations must be incomplete. He himself, even after he was sent as ambassador to Spain, could have had only an inadequate knowledge of Italian affairs. But thereafter, when he was President of the Romagna, commander in Reggio and Parma, and Lieutenant of the Pope with the allied army, he participated in affairs himself and witnessed many remarkable events with his own eyes.

As a result, his history falls into two parts: one which contains the events in which he played a role, and the other in which this was not the case. It is obvious that for the latter, as extensive as they were, he must have based his work on documents and research. Therefore before we make any use of his book, we must ask if his information was original, or if borrowed, in what manner it was borrowed and what kind of research was employed to compile it.

It would be reasonable to assume that the second part of the *History*, that dealing with the period in which the historian often held high offices and had the best opportunity to ascertain the facts correctly, would be the most original, most instructive, and best researched account. But it is precisely here that his work shows itself to be unoriginal and dependent upon the work of another.

There is a book by Galeazzo Capra, called Capella, the private secretary of the Milan minister Morone, *Commentarii de rebus gestis pro restitutione Francesci ducis Mediolanensis*. Currently, this book has been forgotten, but in the first eleven years after its publication it enjoyed eleven editions in Latin, two in German, one in Spanish, and one in Italian. It was the source of many later works.

I must begin by remarking that Guicciardini follows this Galeazzo sentence for sentence, even for the most important events, for which he must have had numerous original reports available. . . .

What battle was more important than the battle of Pavia? Nonetheless Guicciardini practically dismisses all sources, and copies a strange account—and one which is even incorrect! He went still further. One could convincingly argue that he composed his Book XV, pp. 277–299, essentially from Book IV of Galeazzo, more or less literally, though with occasional additions and subtractions, without giving credit. We read in Guicciardini, p. 279: "the entire imperial army departed . . . by the Porta Romana toward the Via del Lodi at the very same time as the enemy began to enter through the Porta Ticinese and Vercellina; and if those at Milan had pursued the imperial army, which was exhausted by the long march, they would have destroyed a great number of soldiers and cavalry. Certainly this would have scattered the forces in great disorder . . . and placed them in doubt. But the king . . ." Compare this with the words of Galeazzo, p. 194: "Just as Davalus was leaving through the Porta Romana . . . the French army was arriving through the gates of Ticine and Vercellina, and no one doubts that had they overtaken the imperials, the latter would have been overcome; certainly if the enemy had made such an effort, a greater part of the army and cavalry would have been destroyed, since they were weakened by the long march; certainly they would have been scattered shamefully. But the king etc."

We can recognize that Guicciardini had not a note about these matters other than what he obtained from Galeazzo. So it is with the conquest of the Castel Sant' Angelo, . . . so with the victory of Meino over the advancing French, the enterprise of Giovanni Jacopo Medici against Mus, the defeat of Pallavicini—all these are transcribed from Galeazzo with only very few alterations. It appears that Guicciardini not only used Galeazzo's book merely for single incidents, but also used entire sections of it.

It would be interesting to know where he got some of the pieces here and there in the rest of his account. In the portion referred to above, there are certainly a few errors. When he relates that the emperor was overcome by a fever because of the retreat from Marseilles, this is definitely in error. The withdrawal occurred on September 29, 1524; Peter Martyr assures us in his Letter 800 that Charles had already had his fever at the beginning of August. Further, when Guicciardini mentions that the chief leaders of the French, especially Tremouville, advised the king to seek a fortified place, this is more than suspicious. Jean Bouchet, who wrote about the actions of Tremouville as early as 1527 and who was most accurately informed about the deeds of his hero, recalled that instead he had urged his king to seek a battle; it was the others who advised that he "remain." This is false, but I do not know from which source Guicciardini took it.

Perhaps one other piece in this section will reveal the source. Guicciardini gives special attention to the negotiations between the emperor and the pope. Guicciardini has the pope declare in a proud style "a pope has other duties than a cardinal. He disapproved of the campaign against Provence; he hindered the enterprise of Stuart against Naples, and he sought to assist the imperial forces in their great need with a treaty." Guicciardini then has the emperor reply "Clement himself arranged his alliance first with Leo, from which all the wars originated, then with Adrian. The emperor's people were not at all in any great need, and the conditions which Clement had suggested to his viceroy were very poor." It is possible that this negotiation is taken from original documents, which Guicciardini in his position as ambassador had the opportunity to see. But a book was published in 1527 *Pro divo Carolo apologetici libri duo, nuper ex Hispania allati, Haganoae per Secerium*, which contains among other documents, a letter of the pope's from June 23, 1526, and an answer of the emperor's of September 16, 1526. . . .

[Ranke quotes the texts paralleling
the passage from Guicciardini]

. . . What can we say about such a great correspondence and agreement? But Guicciardini speaks of the year 1524; the later correspondence dates from 1526. Would these words have been spoken two years earlier and then repeated without any indication that they were repetitions? For the later period, at least, the imperial correspondence with the various ambassadors has been preserved.

It is certain that in this account of an important period, when Guicciardini was a very important man with some of the most significant connections, most of his material is taken from well-known books of his era; some of it is false, and some of it doubtful. I would prefer to praise this historian heartily and gladly. But would it not be unjust to deprive Galeazzo of this praise? He deserves it for originally presenting these important events; can we ascribe it to another who has not earned it nearly as much? We must keep in mind above all that Galeazzo's book, from its beginning in 1521, is used by Guicciardini, or translated, or serves as the chief source, always without credit. This extends from Guicciardini's Book XIV to the end. . . .

As a result of these remarks, it would be difficult for Guicciardini's historical work to retain the fame for its documentary basis and exact research which it has heretofore enjoyed. We would have to research thoroughly all the reports and accounts upon which it is based; still it would be unjust to place Guicciardini with those writers who merely reproduce others' material.

It is quite remarkable that he should have used a foreign source for the events which occurred in Florence and were so vastly important for that city: namely, the arrival of Charles VIII in Tuscany. The account appears in Rucellai's book *De bello italico*. Rucellai begins with a discussion of the routes which Charles could take, through either Tuscany or the Romagna. So does Guicciardini. Though they vary somewhat in their descriptions, note their account of Pontrémoli, where Charles arrived. Guicciardini (1 5) speaks of "Pontrémoli, a land belonging to the Duchy of Milan, lies at the foot of the Apennines, at the river Magra; this river divides the country of Genoa, called in antiquity Liguria, from Tuscany. . . ." This is apparently a translation of Rucellai's Latin text "Pontrémoli, . . . a town located on the borders of Milan, surrounded by the Apennine mountains, where the river Macra flows, which divides Tuscany from Liguria. . . ."

Then a few original or otherwise derived sentences of Guicciardini follow; but the next, about the importance of Sarzana and the infertility of that district, is from Commynes.

A description of the situation in Florence follows next. Rucellai distinguished three main parties. The first thoroughly disapproved of any resistance against the French, the second complained about the stupidity of the government, and the third thought of innovations. Guicciardini makes a similar distinction. But it is far more complete and instructive. As I mentioned, he had composed a history of Florence in his youth in which he had written about these events and from which he now extracted the most important ones. In his new version, nonetheless, much appeared which was from Rucellai's book, especially about the catastrophe of the Medici. . . .

Guicciardini followed the tradition, which he had already employed in his *Florentine History*. I will add a word about this later. Between the accounts of Guicciardini and Rucellai there is no doubt a certain family resemblance. They both begin with the invasion of Italy by Charles VIII, which they regard as the beginning of a great era. Both blame chiefly the advice of the princes. . . . Both perceive the invasion as a warning to and a lesson for the future. In the exposition of the situation of Italy both agree almost word for word with one another, and both lay great weight upon the balance of power in the Italian states which Lorenzo de' Medici and King Ferdinand of Naples were able to maintain. . . .

This is far from saying that Guicciardini simply copied Rucellai. There is no doubt that the older author had an influence on his young friend and determined the composition of his work. . . . Nonetheless, we also find many divergences: much of what Rucellai provides, Guicciardini openly rejects, and in general maintains his own original spirit.

The most original parts in Guicciardini's work are his discourses. There is nothing more instructive than to compare the way Rucellai treats Charles' calling of Piero de' Medici and the advice which Venice gave about it, with the account by Guicciardini. We recognize how the latter not only presents more factual material, but also makes so many incise observations about Piero's morale, the custom of asking for advice, and the dangers of following such advice.

### 4. *About Guicciardini's Speeches*

Five years after Guicciardini's work first appeared, Jean Bodin in his *Method for the Study of History* remarked, "It is admirable how the search for truth is carried on in this study. Letters, decrees, and treaties are produced, drawn clearly and distinctly from the sources. We frequently find in his work the expressions 'it was spoken in these words' or 'it was spoken in these sentences.' . . ."

We can see what Bodin meant: the speeches of Guicciardini are genuine, and are distinguished even between those in which Guicciardini presented the actual words of the orator and those in which he presented only the speaker's thoughts. This interpretation has persisted, though not without some criticism, down to the present day [written 1824]. We need not think of Sismondi; only five years ago

Pierre Daru incorporated many of Guicciardini's speeches in his Venetian history and explained that he found still others which were authentic (III 25).

This assumption would be justified only if one could show at least for a few of the speeches from definite evidence derived from another source that they had been delivered in such a form as Guicciardini presents. But as far as I know, no one has done this. What shall we say if it appears that some of the Florentine speeches of which Guicciardini must have had personal knowledge appear in his work in an altered condition?

In his *Commentaries* (p. 100) Philippo Nerli recalls a speech which Soderini delivered to the Great Council of Florence. It was elegant and suited to the occasion; he himself heard it. In his speech Soderini recounted all the actions of his ten years of administration, and offered the thought that his entire work was intended to preserve a free constitution. Carmignola says that "the war was waged only against him, the Gonfaloniere; he was now prepared to resign, but only if the people, who had put him in his place, agreed. He would place himself completely in their hands." One can see that Soderini's speech was wholly personal and about himself. The motive was his danger and the political situation.

Guicciardini here employs not this, but another, speech. In this account Soderini says nothing about his ten years of activity. After a very short introduction he speaks in a very subdued way about himself, and then presents his real topic: "the Medici will come back with nothing, the way they departed." Sismondi also excerpts this theme from him, as if Soderini were not such a complete populist, or as if he wanted to cause trouble for the Medici. . . . It is clear that these two speeches differ greatly from one another in meaning and in words. Guicciardini was not pursuing the truth; he merely wanted to set the stage for the subsequent reply of the Medici. Thus he omits the advice of the Gonfaloniere and Soderini's noble gesture.

Now, when Nerli says that this speech was written "molto elegantemente" by Francesco Guicciardini, we should recognize that he does not state "truthfully." He who had heard the speech and indirectly refers to it here spares himself the trouble of revealing Guicciardini's departure from the truth. But we should also recognize that at that time no one in Italy would have expected more from an historical speech than elegance. Thus the speeches which concern the popular and aristocratic governments after the time of the exile of Piero cannot depend for confirmation upon Nerli, who describes them as elegant. . . .

Among these fabricated speeches we can distinguish three types: those which were actually delivered, and are reported here with some alterations; those which were never delivered; and those in which the facts were rearranged, in order to make possible a fabricated speech.

The third type is without a doubt very unworthy of the historian.

I cannot fail to remark that just as the speech of Soderini was changed, and that of the emperor was invented, there is a third speech in which Guicciardini appears to have been untrue to history by allowing the speech to have taken place at all. This is the talk of Hieronimo Morone in the same section of Book XV in which the historian, as we have earlier shown, based himself chiefly on Galeazzo. As the latter describes (IV 792), Morone was with Francesco Sforza at Pizzighettone; both had wanted to proceed to Milan but were frustrated by the closeness of the enemy and had gone to Pavia. Guicciardini reports the same story, but only about Sforza. . . . Instead Guicciardini has Sforza return, but tells us that Morone arrived in Milan where he gave a speech.

If Galeazzo is to be trusted anywhere, it has to be at this place, and at this time, for, as he himself tells us, he was Morone's secretary and no doubt accompanied him on this trip; the action which Guicciardini ascribed to Morone was honorable enough, and was crowned with a favorable outcome, and there was no reason to conceal it. . . .

Did Guicciardini only wish to give an Italian credit for the decision to leave Milan, as he had for so many other shrewd suggestions? Perhaps he only wished to present the remarkable situation, in which prince and people were true to one another, but were unable, as much as they wished, to support each other. . . .

We recognize that of these speeches of Guicciardini it is likely that a few were never delivered, that a few others were given in a manner different from the way in which he reports them, and that only a few of them can be shown to be completely genuine. . . . They serve only as a point of departure, a consideration of the present circumstances from every point of view and every possible course; they have almost nothing to do with historical evidence. But it was not only Guicciardini who was seduced in this matter by the example of the ancient writers. All the scholars of his age were deeply immersed in the ancient manner, and the same attitude as Livy assumed in introducing composed speeches into his *Histories* was also taken for granted by historical writers of the period.

### 5. *About Guicciardini's False Stories*

Nowadays, we have a different concept of history: we want the naked truth, without any decoration, and with thorough research into the particulars, and let God take care of the rest! But no poetry, not even in the smallest matters, and no fantasy. We might consider that Guicciardini's method, in and of itself, did not eschew the commission of many errors. The fact is that we find the work crowded with them. Let me rest my case upon only a few of them, those in which the changes in events are falsely presented.

### THE CONQUEST OF MILAN IN 1499

Guicciardini presents Galeazzo Sanseverino as the very epitome of the cowardly traitor: "he could certainly have protected Alessandria, and even the land on that side of the Po. He had 3,000 infantry and 2,400 cavalry, but he said not a word, except to Luzio Malvezzo, and secretly departed." Alessandria determined the outcome of the entire war. Here, above all, we require some research and certainty.

Now, we have Ludovico Sforza's own report, in which we can read that "Galeazzo had 2,000 cavalry and 400 infantry"—which is in agreement with the old arrangement of Italian armies—"but because of the overwhelming number of the French cavalry, he was unable to hold the field; and because of the French artillery, to hold the city."

Guicciardini says that Bornia was retreating and that Galeazzo should have attacked. But how could he have done that without inflicting greater damage on himself than on his enemy? Furthermore, the French held the best fortified positions on either side. . . .

One can see that the city could not be held, and that Galeazzo was trying to rescue his troops, which were the principal forces which his lord possessed. In fact, the greater portion of them reached Monserrat, but here they were plundered anyway, as Ludovico relates. This is no doubt the truth. Where did Guicciardini receive his false impression?

It is drawn, I believe, from Corio's *Storia di Milano*, p. 972. Throughout this passage Guicciardini follows in the footsteps of Corio, though not without adding a few embellishments of his own. Coria says, for example, that Ludovico held a council with the Primates of Milan, and states exactly who was present. Guicciardini expands on this; he has the populace summoned and addressed in heated words—despite his aristocratic leanings, Guicciardini loves demagoguery. Corio further states that Francesco Sanseverino, Count of Galeazzo, made a secret agreement with the victors. Guicciardini knows why: "Corio was jealous because Galeazzo was favored over himself." This citation of such a suspicious source becomes even more suspect since Guicciardini himself was once such an enemy of the count's that the latter wanted to murder him. . . .

## MIRACLES

It is remarkable that such a shrewd man as Guicciardini occasionally retells the stories of miraculous events in the credulous words of a believer.

In the year 1512, as the Spanish laid siege to Bologna, their hopes depended on a mine laid by Pedro Navarra. Guicciardini tells us (p. 573) that the mine was tunneled under a chapel named Baracano. He continues: "the chapel was blasted into the air, went up like a curtain in a theater, but came back down again in place and stood undamaged. . . ." This is also related by Jovius, Muratori, and Fabroni; Rosmini tells us that the citizens of Bologna still celebrate the event. I shall not say that something of the sort is simply impossible, but the two good and authentic accounts which were written at the time and based on a secure knowledge of the siege mention the mine (one of them, Le Veau, comments that the mine caused the greatest surprise— it had extended deep under the city and as it went off people thought that the town itself was collapsing) and the battle which followed, but they say not one word about the miracle. These accounts are by Coccinius, who was in Modena in the close entourage of the emperor, in his book *De bellis italicis*; and by Jean Le Veau, who came to Bologna from France. According to Le Veau, the ruins were almost impassable, and the French very brave—there were Germans among them —but the attack failed.

How could the French reports have failed to mention such a clear sign of God's favor toward them? Here silence is the most significant evidence. Even Bishop Karl Sigonius, who otherwise delights in talking about the miracles of the Virgin Mary, . . . says nothing about the actual miracle. . . . It seems certain to me that there is no basis for this tale, except perhaps an unsuccessful attack in the neighborhood of the chapel. The story may well have been expanded, and accepted by Guicciardini later while he was governing Bologna for the pope. One can never disagree with the people. What story could have expressed better the great peril, and the aid of God which preserved the city from the fate of Brescia, keeping it in memory? Guicciardini casually remarks, "we attribute this affair to a miracle," and ignores the Virgin Mary. He also tells the story of someone who had one eye torn out and replaced so well by a doctor that no harm ensued. . . .

## TREATIES

. . . One of the most important treaties in his entire *History* and the one which first opened the way for the Spanish into Northern Italy was the League between Pope Julius, Ferdinand, and Venice in October 1511. Guicciardini says that Julius promised to augment the Spanish forces with 400 lancers, 500 light cavalry, and 6,000 infantry. But we note in the letters of Louis XII, and in the text of the treaty itself, "Item: our Holy Lord shall send 600 heavily armed knights," and nothing further. We have the public proclamation of the pope which was read in Santa Maria del Popolo in Rome, stating His Holiness' obligation to the League to send 600 men. Now, we may ask, what is so significant about these numbers? This is their meaning: the essential fact about the treaty was that the pope was renting the Spanish with his money, just as on other occasions he had rented the Swiss, the Bresignels, and the Romagna troops. For that reason, the pope could not have promised to provide a new army of his own. The entire situation is confused in Guicciardini's account. There is one other pos-

sible excuse: these numbers referred to men whom the pope was con-
tributing out of good will, over and above the agreement. But when
this event is described (p. 568), Guicciardini's history gives us a completely different count of the numbers.

From this we conclude that Guicciardini is quite far from describing
the treaties accurately, and that he often essentially changed their
contents.

Enough. Pindar says "I have still many other arrows in my quiver."
But believe that I must regretfully complain about this matter for the
sake of truth.

## 6. *About Guicciardini's Account of His own Role*

It is said that in 1527 Guicciardini intended to write Commentaries
about his own life and deeds, but that Jacopo Nardi pointed out to
him how much envy this could direct against him, and he thus determined to write the history of Italy. But in spite of this, he could
hardly fail to describe fully the role which he played in the latter, and
since his knowledge was both original and sufficient, this was certainly
all to the good.

There are four events in particular in which he took part and which
he regarded with satisfaction: the defense of Reggio, of Parma, and
of Modena, and his personal mediation of the first Florentine disturbances of 1527. If we look to see the action on which he laid the
most stress, it would be his decisiveness at the critical moment when he
first discovered the plans of Lescun at Reggio and prepared to frustrate
them. Secondly, there is the incident where Lescun entered the outer
fortified works for a parley and, after a fateful shot was fired, was taken
into the fortress as a prisoner, only to be released afterward by Guicciardini. Here Guicciardini simultaneously defends himself without
doing harm to his opponent (XIV 184), with whom he subsequently
was able to enter into negotiations at Parma, drawing them out until the
moment when it was reported that the Spanish were ready to attack . . .
(XIV 217).

. . . His greatest achievement, he considered, occurred when the
Palazzo Pubblico at Florence had been seized by the young insurgents,
while the army of the League stood ready to storm it. When Fedrigo
da Bozzulo came out of the Palazzo, doubting the possibility of any

agreement, Guicciardini took him aside and said "an agreement is as possible as it is necessary." When these words were passed on by Bozzulo, a pact was soon concluded (XVIII 442). Guicciardini played an exceptional role in these events.

But in the case of Reggio, Bellay (Mem. 38 B) ascribes the most credit to Count Guido Rangone. Concerning Parma, Carpesan (*Commentarii*, p. 1333) does concede Guicciardini's courage and presence of mind, but maintains that the citizens themselves were already greatly desirous of supporting the papacy. Galeazzo (p. 1218) assures us about Modena that Bartolomeo Gattinara accomplished the essential matters, and it is striking that Guicciardini, who often faithfully follows Galeazzo as a source, here pays no attention to him.

Even Guicciardini's Florentine action seems to have attracted scarcely any notice among other historians. Nardi, who was one of those inside the Palazzo, and who accurately described the events, says nothing about it. Varchi, who composed a most complete work about a few years of Florentine history which seems to omit nothing, makes no mention of it. We may attribute less significance to Nerli's silence, in that he had read Guicciardini's work, and was of the same party. But even Jovius, who is generally favorable to Guicciardini, also fails to mention this event. These historians ascribe a large role to him, but not quite the one which he himself describes. . . .

Among his enterprises there were still others which did not succeed. He was Lieutenant-General of the Pope in the military campaigns of the League which were undertaken against Milan to free Francesco Sforza, and against Rome to liberate Pope Clement. Both were directed against the Spanish–German army and both failed completely.

Here Guicciardini blames Francesco Maria, Duke of Urbino, the general of the Venetians—he never dared to attack. Giovanbattista Leoni in the *Considerationes*, which I mentioned earlier, and in the life of Francesco Maria, thoroughly refutes this accusation. I shall not repeat Leoni; his works may as easily be read by anyone as by me. . . .

To understand Guicciardini's displeasure, we have to understand the necessity of this war, as it appeared to him. In Machiavelli's personal correspondence, we can find a few letters which Guicciardini wrote to him immediately after the death of Pescara, at the beginning of Sforza's imprisonment by the imperial forces, in December 1525. "Everyone will perceive the evil of this peace," Guicciardini remarks, "when the opportunity to make war is gone." It is more than likely that he was influential in the pope's decision to enter the conflict. And now look at the result! His lord was ruined, as was all of Italy. Guicciardini sought the cause of all this misfortune in the personal interests of the Duke of Urbino.

Nor was the latter silent. "The avarice of the Lieutenant was the sole cause of the disaster." He suspected that Guicciardini slandered him in Venice. It would not have taken much to make him do violence, but the duke restrained himself; if we can believe Leoni, he recalled Gajazzo, who was determined to murder Guicciardini.

## 7. The Success and Utility of this Historical Work

The results of this present investigation reveal that this *History* often loses our interest because of its completely disordered chronology; that it is to a large extent put together from other works, without any particular research; that a great part of it, the speeches, is in no way an historical monument, but an exercise in the art of oratory; that important facts are completely omitted, treaties changed, and miracles described, which never happened; that the narrative which the author writes about his own activities rests at the very least on a doubtful basis. With these conclusions, it would hardly seem likely that this same history, despite its voluminous size, should have appeared in its first fifty years in ten Italian editions, three Latin, three French, and three Spanish, with additional translations as well into German, English, and Dutch. It became a book which has enjoyed a comparable reputation to the classics, and one which has retained its fame to the present day. On what can the great success of such a work be based?

The shrewdness with which a Catholic writer described the pope and the ways of the Church, with which he uncovered the most secret decisions of the princes, without a trace of flattery, may well have earned the work some of its applause. But the main reason lies in something else. There has never been an age like the last half of the sixteenth century for such lively participation in public life, in even the least important events. There was widespread independence of states, and yet such a great interdependence and interconnection through the two parties, that no history of any state can be written which is not also bound together with the general events. Then there are the discourses of Guicciardini, his considerations regarding every event, at the right moment. . . .

One feels, at the same time, that this is the most important aspect of Guicciardini's work. As Montaigne says, the parts which "seemed to be the most valuable were his digressions and his discourses."

We must concede that these discourses in Guicciardini have something original in them, full of spirit and critical sense. They are not modeled on those of Machiavelli, whose discourses are aimed at a future which is still to be attained, or proceed from some general concept, or attempt to return to one. Guicciardini, in contrast, presents a pure consideration of an object which lies before us. He wants to show what can be expected, what can be done, what the real basis of such a transaction might be. His explanations of the extent to which every human affair derives from passion, ambition, greed show him to be a true virtuoso and master. These discourses do not proceed solely from Guicciardini's spirit alone, but are also, in a double sense, based on the situation of his native city, Florence.

First of all, Florence was never an independent power; and as the course of public affairs swung from one extreme to the other, its attention was of necessity directed toward the possible things which might succeed. To get some idea of this, one could read Francesco Vettori's letter to Machiavelli describing the intentions of the powers in 1513. He constantly prefaces remarks with "if" or "if not" or "if, however." The ambassadors were schooled in such thinking. The representatives of the smaller powers were rarely informed about the intentions of the great states, and completely uninformed about their negotiations. They had to reach what conclusions they could, as we can see in the legations of Machiavelli, from whatever they knew. This is the first point.

But even in internal politics the same style and manner were followed. We can read in Varchi and Nardi how even the election of a Gonfaloniere produced so many schemes, negotiations, suspicions, and judgments. There were in this smaller circle the same relationships, alliances, and counter-alliances as in European affairs, and all to gain a few more votes. If we can understand how many factors there were to consider, how the rules, the insights, the advice to follow developed, we can see the origin of such a work as Guicciardini's. Its soul is primarily or exclusively concerned with literature and ambition. These two contend with each other in sagacity. They compete in the presentation of past events, or in the estimation of the future; they proceed from one close event to the next, and in presenting these relationships, they are unusually powerful.

And so it can be said of Guicciardini, "he was one of the shrewdest minds in Italy; and he knew very well how to discuss human affairs." In his discourses we find the usefulness of his work, and thanks to them his original nature has earned eternal fame.

For the purpose of presenting these ideas, it would not have been right for him to relate the major events without interruption by lesser ones. Each was as important as the other; their connection during the period was one of the most essential things. Above all, the situation of these independent states and their interactions with one another are brought to our consideration. This is the reason why Guicciardini chose the strictly chronological form which we observe. The contemporary interrelationships were as important to him as the successive cause and effect. This was why he could write such a complete work, without being afraid to include the strange and the obvious event. For him it was more a question of causes and events than of the facts. But we find only rarely in him a joy in affairs and in life.

III

# The Relationship
# of
# History, Politics, and Philosophy

# HISTORY AND PHILOSOPHY

In 1877 the aging Ranke attended a lecture at the University of Berlin in which Wilhelm Scherer maintained that Ranke's work was an outgrowth of Romantic philosophy and that Ranke himself was essentially close to the position of Hegel. The old historian rebuked the speaker: "I am indeed much more original than you think!" and stalked away.

Yet we know that behind the careful student of the sources lurked a mind of deep philosophical and religious interests; Ranke expected to derive some insight into the plan of the universe, a philosophy of history, but one derived only from careful historical research. The fine distinctions of method and position between Ranke and his contemporaries have been explored by modern scholars such as Wilhelm Mommsen, *Stein, Ranke, Bismarck* (1954); Helmut Diwald, *Das historische Erkennen* (1955); and Carl Hinrichs, *Ranke und die Geschichtstheologie der Goethezeit* (1954). Another good survey of the problem can be found in Georg G. Iggers, *The German Conception of History: The National Tradition of Historical Thought from Herder to the Present* (1968).

Since Ranke rarely discussed philosophy in his histories, most such research has been based on his notes and private papers. A clear statement of his views early in his career can be found in the following fragment, which was written in the 1830s and offers a good counterpart to the lecture on history and politics. In reviewing his career, Ranke declared that "It is laughable to hear that I am lacking in philosophical and religious interests; it was just these, and these alone, which drove me to history." Yet he maintained that he was far from an Hegelian in method. "From the particular we can indeed thoughtfully and boldly ascend to the universal; but from the universal, there is no way to the particular." What Ranke rejected was, not philosophy as such, but the notion that philosophical systems could be used to explain history; yet there certainly was room for contact between the two.

The selection was chosen from Ranke's papers, and posthumously published by Alfred Dove in *Weltgeschichte* IX, Part II, pp. vii–xi.


IT HAS OFTEN BEEN NOTED that there is a certain contradiction between immature philosophy and history. Some thinkers have decided on *a priori* grounds what must be. Without observing that others,

more doubting, will disagree with their ideas, they set forth to redis-
cover them in the history of the world. Out of the infinite array of
facts, they select those which they wish to believe. This has been called
the philosophy of history! One of the ideas which is continually repeated in the philosophies of history is the irrefutable proposition that
mankind is involved in an uninterrupted progress, a steady development of its own perfection. Fichte, one of the first philosophers of
this type, assumed that there are five epochs of what he called a world
plan: the rule of reason through instinct, the rule of reason through
law, the liberation from the authority of reason, the science of reason,
and the art of reason. Or, put otherwise: innocence, original sinfulness,
complete sinfulness, initial justification, and completed justification.
These stages can also appear in the life of an individual. If this or
similar schemes were somehow true, then universal history would have
to follow a progression, and the human race would travel in its appointed course from one age to another. History would be completely
concerned with the development of such concepts, with their manifestations and representations in the world. But this is largely not so.
For one thing, philosophers themselves are extraordinarily at odds
about the type and selection of these dominating ideas. Moreover, they
consider only a few of the peoples in the world's history, regarding
the activity of the rest as nothing, merely superfluous. Nor can they disguise the fact that from the beginning of the world to the present
day the peoples of the world have experienced the most varied circumstances.

There are two ways to become acquainted with human affairs:
through the knowledge of the particular, and through the knowledge
of the abstract. There is no other method. Even revelation consists of
the two: abstract principles and history. But these two sources of
knowledge must be distinguished. Those historians who disregard this
err, as do those who see history as only a vast aggregation of facts
which must be arranged according to a utilitarian principle to make
them comprehensible. Thus they append one particular fact to another, connected only by a general moral. I believe, instead, that the
science of history is called upon to find its perfection within itself, and
that it is capable of doing so. By proceeding from the research and
consideration of the individual facts in themselves to a general view of

events, history is able to raise itself to a knowledge of the objectively present relationships.

To make a true historian, I think that two qualities are needed, the first of which is a participation and joy in the particular in and for itself. If a person has a real fondness for this race of so many, so varied, creatures to which we ourselves belong, and for its essential nature, always ancient and somehow always new, so good and so evil, so noble and so brutish, so refined and so crude, directed toward eternity and living for the moment, satisfied with little yet desirous of everything; if he has a love of the vital manifestation of humanity at all, then he must rejoice in it without any reference to the progress of things. To his observation of humanity's virtues he will add an attention to its accompanying vices, to its happiness and misfortunes, to the development of human nature under so many varied conditions, to its institutions and customs. In summary, he must seek to follow the kings who have ruled over the races, the succession of events, and the development of the chief undertakings. All this he should do for no purpose other than his joy in the life of the particular individual, just as we enjoy flowers without considering to which genus of Linnaeus and Oken they belong. Enough: he must do this without thinking how the whole appears in the individuals.

But this is not enough. It is essential that the historian also have an eye for the universal. He ought not to conceive of it *a priori* as the philosopher does. Rather, his consideration of particular individuals will show him the course which the development of the world as a whole has taken. This development is related, not to the universal ideas which have ruled in one or another period, but to something completely different. No people in the world has remained out of contact with the others. This relationship, inherent in a people's own nature, is the one by which it enters into universal history, and must be emphasized in universal history.

There are some peoples who have armed themselves more powerfully than their neighbors on the planet, and these above all have exercised an influence upon the rest. They were the chief cause of the changes, for good or ill, which the world has experienced. Our attention ought to be directed, not to the ideas which some see as the directing force, but to the peoples themselves who appear as actors in history, to their struggles with one another, to their own development which took place in the midst of these peaceful or warlike relationships. It would be infinitely wrong to see only the effects of brute force in the struggles of historical powers or to conceive of the past in that way. There appears a spiritual essence in power itself, an original genius which has its own proper life, fulfills more or less its own requirements, and forms its own sphere of action. The business of history is to perceive the existence of this life, which cannot be described by a thought or a word. The spirit which appears in the world is not of such a conceivable nature. It fills all the boundaries of its being with its presence; nothing about it is accidental; its manifestation is founded in everything.

# ON THE RELATION OF
# AND DISTINCTION BETWEEN
# HISTORY AND POLITICS

Ranke's address "On the Relation of and Distinction Between History and Politics" ("De historiae et politicae cognatione atque discrimine") was delivered in 1836 as his formal inaugural lecture as professor at the University of Berlin. Actually, the promotion had been awarded earlier, in 1834, in reward for his services as editor of the *Historisch-Politische Zeitschrift*. As the foreign minister, Ancillon, remarked to the minister of education, Altenstein, Ranke's promotion was desirable "more in the general interest of the state than in that of the university," and initially he was paid out of the general treasury rather than from the university budget. The philosophical faculty was never asked to vote on the appointment, and was informed only afterward that it had taken place. Ranke's great series of works, beginning with the *History of the Popes*, which earned him an international reputation, were published after he had gained his professorial rank. Though his editorship of the journal ceased in 1836, Ranke remained a conservative supporter of the Prussian government in university controversies relating to academic freedom.

In 1841, after his appointment as Prussian Royal Historiographer, he began to research and publish his first version of the *History of Prussia* in nine books. During the Revolution of 1848 he addressed several memoranda to King Friedrich Wilhelm IV urging him to resist liberal demands, and joined some 60 professorial colleagues in petitioning for a dismissal of the Frankfurt assembly. Ranke's conservatism was sincere (when Bismarck ruthlessly overrode principles in order to make Prussia supreme in Germany, Ranke thoroughly disapproved); but it was also opportune, though closely related to his whole way of viewing politics as part of the historical process.

This lecture should be considered, in conjunction with his 1836 "Political Dialogue" and 1833 essay on "The Great Powers," as one of the basic statements of his thoughts on history.

In it Ranke describes some of the common misapprehensions about the usefulness of history in politics, decisively rejects the Enlightenment approach of seeking universal laws of society and politics, and argues that each state can be governed correctly only by those who, through the study of history, can understand the past experience and development of their state, and govern in accordance with the principles which underlie its particular and unique nature. He differed from many conservatives in allowing for gradual change and historical development of these underlying principles, but was repelled by what he regarded as the doctrinaire approach of liberals. Here he has attained a much more mature view of the relation between history and politics than was manifest in his earlier disclaimer of their connection, in order to study only "what actually happened." But he warns that the value of history to politics is indirect, not a matter of simple imitation.

The style is rather formal, with a certain stiffness of expression, which betrays in part its Latin origin, in part a personal aversion to the ceremonial occasion. In April 1834 he had written to his friend Heinrich Ritter, "Unfortunately, a Latin dissertation and similar lecture are still required, which I have little desire to do, so that I am not yet famous among the faculty." In 1836, which saw the close of his political-journalistic activities, as well as this inaugural lecture, Ranke took leave of politics to retire to his study and lecture room, to fulfill the program of national histories which enlarged the insights laid down in "The Great Powers." The political experience, even this summation of it, was not without value for that larger task. In 1872, when revising his Prussian History for his Collected Works, Ranke pointed to the significance of this lecture for his career: "It included a few sentences which almost serve as a motto for the enlarged Prussian history which will follow."

This selection has been translated from the German version written by Ranke's brother Ferdinand, in SW 24:280–93, and compared with the original pamphlet from Ranke's library, now in The George Arents Research Library for Special Collections at Syracuse University.

As you are well aware, my honored audience and dear colleagues, nothing occupies people in our times more than the desire and inclination to improve government or to cast it into new forms. I believe that this urge originates from two causes: partly from boredom with the institutions of our ancestors, which they say have changed and deviated from the original intentions of their creators; and partly from a certain preconceived notion about the best forms of government, which has, somehow, been absorbed into every soul like a physical necessity and to whose standard the state must conform itself for its own good, either at once or gradually. Nor can we say that only ignorant or evil persons, seized with an inordinate desire for novelty, have chosen this path. We know rather that there are honorable men, patriots, who have adopted the same viewpoint, or at least have not condemned it.

But it is marvelous that this general tendency of thought and spirit has not brought forth its expected fruit! How many states are there which have not been troubled and shaken by this pressure? And have we not seen men driven to complete blindness and criminal acts in the carrying out of such plans, which they dreamed would lead them to wisdom and virtue? Indeed, we have observed that the praiseworthy zeal to improve a bad and perverted form of government has been transformed into a rejection of good laws, into public disorders, and, finally, into a frenzy of madness. Thus great storms break out, preventing the pilot from controlling the rudder of government or steering the ship by a fixed course. The people are deprived of their ability to consider or to recognize what would be useful or harmful; one would be fortunate indeed to rescue oneself safe and sound from the dark clouds and stormy winds which sweep the sea.

The freedom for which men have aspired has often been turned into a slavery detested by honorable men through the domination of a foolish and terrible mob. And when we inquire about the form of government which has resulted from this change, we can discover nothing based on solid foundations which could promise or ensure that security which is necessary for the real development and cultivation of the human spirit. Indeed, the more a state is shaken and torn by these storms of opinion and party, the more it seems to drive itself into still more violent disturbances. In the words of Vergil, it flows with burning sorrow here and there. The most extreme tendencies are always preferred to whatever is good and healthy. Thus whenever a division of minds occurs today, it suddenly seizes upon and poisons an otherwise peaceful people. At times we fear that the entire series of previously overcome misfortunes is about to occur once again.

I have no doubt, dear listeners, that most of you have thoroughly studied the reasons why such justified hopes and expectations have so seldom met with success. The causes, we all understand, are of many kinds and differ in different countries. They can be explained only with great thoroughness and completeness, as our own age has certainly learned. But there is one reason, and a very universal one, which is often advanced, and it is a discussion of this reason which I should like to bring to your attention.

History, they say, not only is no longer listened to by the younger generation, but is even intentionally set aside. If youth paid more attention to its precepts and to its continuing series of events, and considered their necessity, then matters might have gone more according to our liking. Though this argument has the appearance of complete truth, it is actually somewhat dubious. For many deny decisively that history can or must be drawn upon to bring order to government. What does history, which gives us a supply of knowledge of previous ages, have to do with the improvement of contemporary states? The establishment or improvement of their political constitutions requires a completely different science. History sometimes excuses deep-rooted evils by explaining their origins, but their remedy can be obtained only by the new science of politics, first developed in our time. There is a steady progress of the human race, and we can raise no longer those questions which occurred in other ages, only those which concern us today. When one is afraid to trust one's own strength and looks to untrodden paths to find newer or better things, the human situation appears to resemble more the sorry picture of a stagnant pond or dirty swamp than the joyful and happy image of a running stream.

And, in fact, to concede the undeniable: drawing history into the governing of a state involves the greatest difficulties, and not only for the reason cited above. History itself does not offer such certain prescriptions that no one could doubt their worth. Writers appear daily who neither seek nor find anything in history which does not agree with their political doctrines. Do not the same differences in opinion which divide states into parties also appear no less passionately in the researching and retelling of the events? There are disputes over the nature and character of the Middle Ages, over the original customs and mores of the German peoples, over the virtue of men honored in antiquity, and, finally, over the origin and beginnings of the human race. So far is history from improving politics that it itself is more usually corrupted by it.

But how are we to judge all this, my dear listeners? Is it really true, as a few maintain, that there is nothing at all which is really certain and true in the study of the humanities? Do we, or do we not, know the events of ancient periods, and their history? Is it possible to understand their inner nature, or shall we remain ignorant of it for all eternity? Can we not draw up ways in which a well-governed state can be distinguished from a corrupt one, the constitution of Tarento distinguished from that of Rome, of the ways in which virtue differs from vice? God forbid! Humanity would then descend to the level of beasts; everything would then be given over to a game of blind chance. No, no one can deny that nature and Divine Providence have afforded us a deep insight into the causes of misfortune and happiness, and the ability to determine how good laws differ from evil customs. No one will maintain that we suffer such great blindness or lack of understanding that we are unable to distinguish anything about the nature and ways of previous ages.

What is your verdict, my esteemed audience? Do you believe that some knowledge of past events contains nothing useful which is applicable to the present or future? Will you agree that there is no close connection and kinship between history and politics? I cannot think that you would agree to such a view. But there is a question as to what relationship exists between the two. This question can hardly be raised in our days without the danger of error. Nonetheless, its utility and necessity are so great that I do not shrink from raising it, especially amid a gathering whose good intentions are beyond doubt. I shall thus discuss the relationship between history and politics, attempting to show what the borders of these disciplines are, where one touches upon the other, where they part ways, and what distinctions exist between them.

Starting with history, as the better known of the pair, let us mention that its aim is not so much to gather facts and to arrange them as to understand them. History rests not solely on memory, as some believe, but above all on critical understanding. Nor can we deny that it is difficult to distinguish truth from falsehood, and to select from many accounts the one which is factually the best. Those who know only by hearsay the role of criticism are aware of its use in historical circles. And yet this is only part of the task of historical studies.

Another still more glorious and difficult part consists in observing the causes and premisses of events, as well as their results and effects, and in distinguishing exactly the intentions of men, the mistakes which cause some to fail while others succeed. We recognize why one arises and another declines, and how states are strengthened or dissolved: in short, we comprehend equally the hidden causes of events as well as their visible appearance. Whoever wishes to accomplish this turns profitably to history. Just as natural science not only attempts to draw a careful picture of nature, but also strives to investigate the higher goal of the eternal laws governing the world itself in its parts and members; just as science endeavors to press on to the inner sources of nature from which all things spring, so it is with history. Although it pursues the succession of events as sharply and accurately as possible, and attempts to give each of them its proper color and form, and ascribes to these efforts the highest value, still history goes beyond this labor and moves on to an investigation of origins, seeking to break through to the deepest and most secret motives of historical life.

Some presume to fly to such heights but deceive themselves, embracing a cloud instead of Juno. Their efforts secure them only formulas and empty wind in place of truth. A few of them are aware of an obscure sense of dissatisfaction with their ideas, take refuge in philosophical or theological doctrines, and transform their historical studies. But we should not conclude from these errors that the goal which they have set for themselves does not exist. Though they cannot attain their object, the goal is there. The victor's palm which they fail to win will one day be awarded; and like the victor's prize at Elis, in Horace's phrase, be accompanied homeward in the awareness of divine happiness.

But we must proceed, if I am not mistaken, in a completely different way to make progress.

History by its nature must reject poesy and empty shadows, and can accept only the completely certain and sure. It requires prudence as well as boldness of spirit. On the one hand, it must research individual events with the greatest care, and avoid errors; on the other, it must not allow itself to be dissipated in the multiplicity of events, but must press on with steady gaze toward its final goal, despite the fact that this procedure denies the human yearning to comprehend everything on the first attempt. History leads us to unspeakable sweetness and refreshment at every place. For what could be more pleasant and more welcome to human understanding than to become aware of the inner core of events, of their deepest mysteries; or to observe in one nation or another how men's enterprises begin, increase in power, rise, and decline? Or gradually to attain a knowledge, either directly through a justified intuition or indirectly through a sharp-eyed, thorough recognition, of those things in which each human age excelled, or sought or strove to attain and achieved? For this is likewise a part of divine knowledge. This is what we seek with the help of history to attain; history is motivated wholly by this effort. Who will ask whether this be useful or not? It suffices to recognize that such knowledge is as useful as any other, that it belongs to the perfection of the human spirit.

We now approach politics. The question as to whether it is an art or a science requires us to begin with a few remarks about government. If I am not mistaken, there ought to appear in the life of states the same continuity of life we ascribe to the human race. Men die; one age follows another or supplants it. But states, which far outlast the longevity of the individual, enjoy a very long and always regular life. We can take Venice as an example. From the time when the city was founded in a lagoon of the Adriatic Sea, we see how it proceeded in the same manner for a thousand years: its marriage with the sea; its conquest of neighboring lands: often by craft and often by force; its creation of a secret state power; its favoring of the populace and suppression of the aristocracy; its growth, development and flowering, and its eventual decline and fall. These can be perceived by anyone who follows the history of Venice. The same theme appears in all its marvelous persistence and succession through different centuries like the life of a single person. Similarly [the Roman historian] Florus artfully distinguished certain ages in the character of the Roman state. In the course of time, collapse comes even to states themselves, and not only to those which must endure a conqueror's law and authority, but also, astonishingly, to those who have been victors and have imposed their yoke on others. The Roman state was unable to preserve or even to retain its old city laws when it began to dominate and rule the world. For it is in the nature of human affairs that the stronger part, whether it leave the battleground as victor or as vanquished, gradually gains the upper hand and destroys the individuality of the weaker part. But, as it happens, the latter's life is not wholly destroyed; nothing is ever completely abolished. Though something appears to collapse, it is only merged into a more perfect society. Thus a new life is born, and another course of events established, which are closely related to the former existence, and connected with it in retrospect.

And if we now ask, "What is it which enables a state to live?" then it is the same as with the individual, whose life incorporates both body and spirit. So too with the state. Everything depends on spirit, which is the pre-eminent of the two. Although we are not granted the privilege of bringing the hidden to view, revealing the soul and its activity, the very source and current of life, by indicating it precisely with definite proper names, still we are able to observe what lies before our eyes, and to reach conclusions about the remote causes of events by reflecting on its mysteries. For the spirit cannot be touched with the hand or the eye; it is known by its successes and its effects. Who would be foolish enough to think that he could see God with his eyes? And yet no one would hesitate to maintain that He exists and that everything has its origin in Him.

I come now to the point which I have undertaken to prove. We perceive states and peoples, whether contained in larger or smaller boundaries, living and flourishing according to their own customs, which they share with no other people, and according to their own laws and particular institutions. It is obvious that each state has a completely definite character and a life of its own, which distinguishes it from all others, and that everything which it has and does derives from this character. Since this is so, it is not hard to indicate the task and duty of those who govern the state. Esteemed listeners, how would you judge those who, caught up in some attractive prejudice, seek to achieve their own ends, regarding everything older as outmoded and useless; men who set aside everything without considering whether its forms and laws have been blessed by usage, and who undertake to transform abruptly a state which they do not really know? It seems to me that they hardly fulfill their duty, but instead tear down rather than build. Let us listen to a man who has some experience in governing. "Every people," Cicero tells us, "every social institution, which is a creation of the people, every state, which belongs to the people, must be ruled according to a certain plan if it is to endure." It is self-evident how much this viewpoint agrees with our own. For by nature every living thing flees death and seeks its self-preservation. It is ap-

parent that the chief point of civic wisdom is that those who are entrusted with the honor and authority of ruling the state should take
care to maintain and preserve it, leading it daily toward ever greater
perfection. Cicero describes for us in the same passage how this should
take place: "this plan is always to be derived from the foundations
on which the state was established." In those foundations are contained the source and origin of the inner life of which we speak. Thus
the helmsman of a ship must know the difference between a warship
and a merchantman. No one should control the rudder of a ship of
state who does not completely know not only the nature of the sea in
which he sails, but also the nature of his vessel. He who lacks this
thorough knowledge would do better to take his hands off the wheel.
For he would necessarily destroy the very institutions which he is
supposed to preserve, scattering and extinguishing their life. I believe
that only those who have achieved the closest relationship and identity
with the nature of the state which they represent can distinguish themselves in politics.

Up to now, dear listeners, we have considered separately the offices
and limits of history and politics. It should not be hard to derive from
this the connection which exists between the two, and to determine in
what their relationship and distinction consist.

First, it is clear that the basis of both is one and the same. Just as
there can be no politics which does not rest on a complete and exact
knowledge of the state which is to be ruled—and that knowledge is
inconceivable without knowing the events of past ages—and just as
history incorporates this very knowledge, or attempts to comprehend
it, so it is clear that in this matter both are most closely connected. I
do not say that politics is impossible without a perfect historical understanding. For there is a critical use of human reason which likewise
with divine inspiration can penetrate into the nature of things. Nor do
I recommend a special type of education for those who would be suited
for government. Rather, I shall try to probe the nature of the problem,
unconcerned whether a carefully achieved education or a kind of prophetic intuition is better suited to reach those heights of which we
spoke. It is, after all, the task of history to extract from past events the
nature of the state and to bring us to an understanding of it; the task
of politics, to carry on and develop it after recognition and understand-

ing are successfully achieved. The knowledge of the past is incomplete without an acquaintance with the present; an understanding of the present is impossible without a knowledge of the past. They clasp one another's hands. One cannot exist, or be complete, without the other.

Nevertheless, I am not one of those who believe that nothing new should be allowed to take place. We know from experience how human nature is prone to error, how human affairs can easily take a turn for the worse. We see in order for life itself to continue to flow and progress that new enterprises are daily necessary, and that even storms can be essential. Political wisdom consists, I think, not so much in preservation as in progress and in growth. The human race lacks much of what it needs to grow toward its highest perfection. History itself would already have reached its limits, and achieved its eternal goals, if we did not wish to continue striving to reach these heights and summits.

This is, honored listeners, the relationship between history and politics as I conceive them. Both comprise at once a science and an art. As sciences they are most closely connected, though one is more concerned with the past, the other with the present and the future. As art they are much farther apart. History is based wholly on literature. Its task consists in renewing our vision of the way in which events have occurred, and human nature behaved, and in preserving the memory of them for all time. But politics belongs to practical affairs. It strives to hold men together through the bond of the state, to preserve their peace through the wisdom of law, to bind them in free consent to join together, so that they will behave properly in their private and public lives. History and politics differ from one another, just as do theoretical and practical philosophy. One is proper to the school and to retiring persons; the other is concerned with the market place, to disputes and public strife; one is practiced more in shadow and the other in the light of day; one suffices simply to preserve, the other passes beyond preservation to the creation of something new.

I believe, esteemed listeners, that I have taken account of those who will object that there are aspects of politics which have nothing in common with history, yet are of the greatest importance. These consist in the natural laws affecting the state, not only the proper administration of field and forest, but also the way in which income is to be obtained and spent, how cities should be governed, courts held, laws given and enforced. In fact, I would not want to disparage a science which is also so rich in discernment, truth, and utility. Rather, I would see it as no less necessary for the state than medicine is for the human body. Human society forms its own body; political economy shows how the members of a state are closely bound to one another, and displays for us their arteries and veins, the location of their breathing and blood, and teaches in what the healthy functioning of the body politic consists, so that sickness can be healed or avoided. It is of such great importance that ignoring its prescriptions leads, not to the damage of one part, but to the destruction of all parts. Nonetheless, this statement does not weaken in the least our earlier argument. First of all, the historian no less than the politician requires an exact and ready familiarity with these things; the events which he studies are often the result of the health of the state. Secondly, the science of politics does not have such sufficient weight and regard that every political transaction must depend upon it. Just as a strong and healthy person will pay some heed to medical advice, but will hardly be so obedient to it that he will allow it to direct his whole life to the same extent as a sick person would, so it is with the healthy and wisely ordered state. It bases itself on the maxims of political economy and quietly observes them, but hardly remains so timidly tied to them that it does exactly only what their rules allow. It never renders them a slave-like obedience. The state keeps in sight other laws of higher significance, more comprehensive viewpoints which proceed from the drives of its own inner life, drawn from its spirit and heart, which allow mankind to play a part in divine freedom.

At this point in our discussion, we come to another distinction between the two closely related disciplines. History is by its nature universal. True, some do concentrate their efforts completely on their fatherland, narrowly conceived, on their own state, on one small dark corner of the earth. But this is more out of a certain prejudice or piety or a praiseworthy tendency toward careful work than from any intellectual forces deriving from the nature proper to the discipline. The latter consists in the conviction that nothing human can be alien to history, which aims to comprehend all centuries and all monarchies. It is quite different with the nature of politics, which always exists in relation to a given state, is exercised for the state's benefit, and, as such, is always restricted within certain limits. For who would attempt to govern by himself universally over every country? He would be fortunate indeed to understand how to administer one. Many are called to steer the ship of state; not a few are forced to abandon the rudder. This art of politics requires, if any does, keen understanding and the force of genius accompanying it to uncover and establish things. It requires courage and, if I am right, is the most difficult art of all.

And now let us return to our starting point.

The error of the philosophers of the last century was that they formulated a universal doctrine according to which every state must be ruled. They avoided the painstaking work of scholarship by which particulars could be discovered. They were so seized with disgust at the undeniable corruption which had established itself in public affairs that they convinced themselves that everything must be reformed according to the design for the best form of government. The different peoples were to receive one and the same law, and a common form of government was suggested. And so they attempted to do everything possible. They saw their role first as the weakening, dismantling, and destruction of their ancient institutions. From this, they proposed, were to follow general happiness and the return of a golden age. But soon they themselves came to realize that one cannot without penalty dislodge and bring into dispute the basic elements and origins on which human society is founded. They were taught that states possess a character of their own, which can be suppressed by force and violence, but which is not easily completely destroyed, and which can be resurrected. To their own personal regret, they opened the way for the greed and ambition of the worst men, who cleared the air at immeasurable expense to the human race, and even today, as in Spain, continue to bring calamity upon the government.

And now I turn to you, dear colleagues. History, whose professorship I have occupied for the last few years, and which I assume formally by today's celebration, has immeasurable good to offer to a healthy politics. It clears away errors and misunderstandings, which in our age affect the eyes of even the best men. A few remind us constantly that our own age can learn no lessons from history, still less derive our laws from it. They perceive things as too different, not only because of the extraordinary skills of craftsmen and factory owners and the spread of education to the lowest classes, but also because the general awareness and humanity of all classes surpass those of all previous ages. They appear great to themselves, so that they might ignore their fathers and forefathers. Others, in contrast, assure us that our age is the worst which has ever existed. They maintain that it lacks piety, religion, courage, and justice. They complain that it is so full of errors that it can hardly be improved. The one will accept only what is new and unheard of, since this alone will be suited to the changed character of the contemporary period. The other favors only what has been approved by the usage of antiquity and treads as closely as possible in the footsteps of his ancestors.

But history teaches us that every age has its own weakness for error and its own potential for virtue. We ought to proceed neither from doubt nor from pride and arrogance. We also learn that each age has its own given tasks, as does our own, and that we must attempt to perform them with effort and concern. Finally, we recognize not only that human affairs are neither guided by a blind, inevitable fate, nor steered by false visions, but that their successful conduct depends on virtue, understanding, and wisdom. I invite you, dear colleagues, to take this science to your hearts. May we follow the paths which it suggests, guided too by the fatherland, the examples of ancient and modern times, and, finally, the nature and necessity of things themselves.

IV

# Universal Tendencies
# in History

# THE GREAT POWERS

This brief essay, published in 1833 in the first issue of Volume II of the *Historisch-Politische Zeitschrift*, is probably Ranke's most famous short work. In its outlook and emphases, it has much in common with the "Political Dialogue" and the lecture "On the Relation of and Distinction Between History and Politics," both of 1836. Here the general political insights of the latter are given concrete historical form. The essay is really a history, not of any one of the great powers, but of their interaction. In that creative relationship between the European states, Ranke sees the development of power, ideas, and the future of Europe. Never far from his mind is the tension between spiritual values and armed force which shaped so much of modern history.

The discussion of the establishment of the balance of power in Europe is not novel. Many eighteenth-century writers commented upon it. It is interesting to compare the striking similarities of the 1833 essay on "The Great Powers" with the introduction of August Ludwig Heeren's *Handbuch der Geschichte des europäischen Staatensystems und seiner Colonien* (1811) which Ranke had in his personal library. The noted Göttingen historian sums up the insights of an entire century in his careful portrayal of the main events which created the European state system. Yet his cool, rational handling of the material differs from Ranke's. In the latter we can see living energies behind the merely political occurrences. For Ranke, not only are there guiding principles which explain the behavior of the dynastic monarchies such as Russia or Austria, but also deeper, fast-rushing currents which occur when the French Revolution awakens the slumbering national will of the people. Ranke also separates himself from the position of Johann Gottfried Herder, who saw history as composed primarily of cultural nations, each with its own tradition, language, and value, with universal history as an interaction of cultural values. Ranke returns to the essential center, stressing the primacy of politics. (His pupil Dilthey went so far as to attribute to Ranke the "primacy of foreign policy.") Great ideas not only inspire the states which make up the political system; they also are controlled by the outcome of that system, as the institutions in which they are embodied decline or prosper.

It is the very delicate balance on the relationship between power and values which Ranke strikes, as well as his penetrating view of the relations of the great powers which make the essay so fascinating, even to the expert on modern history.

This selection was translated from the original article in the *Historisch-Politische Zeitschrift*, 2, No. 1 (1833), 1–51. The text in brackets was later eliminated by Ranke himself when he included the essay in his SW 24:1–40.

IT IS NO DIFFERENT WITH STUDIES AND READING from what it is with the observations we make of a journey or from life itself. No matter how much we are attracted by the particular, and profit by its enjoyment, in time it retreats into the background, becomes obscured, and disappears. Only the larger impressions which we receive in one place or another, the total perception which we gain unconsciously, or through careful particular observations remains to increase the sum of our knowledge. The most important and enjoyed moments of our existence fuse in our memory and make up its living content.

Certainly we should, after reading an important work, review its important passages and list its most important conclusions. It is advisable at times to summarize a more comprehensive study. However, I shall go further and invite the reader to visualize in their sequence the events of a long historical period, which can be understood only by a variety of approaches—the period of the last century and a half.

No doubt the contemplation of the individual moment in its truth and particular development has for its own sake an inestimable value in history. The particular bears the universal within itself, but we cannot avoid the urge to survey the whole from a detached point of view. Everyone strives toward this in one way or another. Out of the variety of individual observations the vision of their unity unconsciously arises.

But it is difficult to present such a vision in a few pages with proper argumentation and a reasonable hope of securing approval. Nonetheless, I shall try to do so.

For how could I better introduce a new volume of this journal [the *Historisch-Politische Zeitschrift*] than by trying to dispel several of the nearly universally believed errors about the formation of the modern world, and bringing into clearer and more certain perspective the present moment in world history?

If I dare to attempt this effort, let me not reach too far back into the past, lest I have to write a world history. I shall restrict myself also, by relating only the great events, the progress of the external relation-ships of the different states. This approach will largely include the explanation of the internal affairs with which the external stand in such varied relation and interaction.

## THE AGE OF LOUIS XIV

Let us start with the fact that in the eighteenth century the freedom of Europe was perceived to consist in the opposition and balance between Spain and France. A state overpowered by one could find refuge with the other. When France became weakened and disorganized, it was viewed as a general misfortune. Thus Henry IV was eagerly welcomed not only because he brought an end to anarchy in France, but chiefly because he thereby restored a stable European order.

However, it happened that France, in the process both of dealing dangerous blows to her rivals in the Netherlands, in Italy, and in the Iberian Peninsula, and of defeating Spain's allies in Germany, thereby acquired a greater preponderance than Spain had possessed even at the height of her power.

Let us imagine the condition of Europe in the year 1680. France, so suited and so long accustomed to keeping Europe in ferment, was under a king who fully understood how to rule her. His nobles, whose long resistance had finally been overcome, served him with the same zeal at court and in the army, while his clergy joined with him even against the pope. France was more unified and more powerful than ever before.

In reviewing the relationship of the powers, we must remember that at the same time as the emperor was recruiting his first two standing regiments of infantry and cuirassiers, Louis XIV already had, in peace-time, 100,000 men in his garrisons and 14,000 in his guard; that, while the English navy declined in the last years of Charles II (it had 83 ships in 1678), the French in 1681 had 96 ships of the line of first and second rank, 42 frigates, 36 feluccas, and as many fire ships. The troops of Louis XIV were the best drilled and most battle-experienced known, and his ships were very well constructed. No other prince possessed fortified borders so well suited for attack or defense. But it was through not only military power that the French managed to overpower the Spanish, but also political tactics and alliances. They transformed the situation in which they found themselves into a kind of supremacy.

Let us consider first the North and East. In the year 1674, Sweden undertook a dangerous war, without preparation, without money, without real cause, solely on the advice of France and in expectation of French subsidies. The elevation of John Sobieski to the Polish throne was announced in an official paper as a triumph for Louis XIV. The king and queen of Poland acted for a long time in the interests of France. From Poland, when it was no longer possible to do so from Vienna, France supported the Hungarian malcontents. The French assisted the latter in their negotiations with the Turks, for France continued her old accustomed influence on the Porte. It all formed a system. A principal concern of French diplomacy was to maintain peace between Poland and Turkey; for this purpose, they used even the Tartar khan. Another concern was to keep Sweden from being invaded by Russia. The Venetian envoy Contarini noted in 1681 that when Moscow showed an inclination to attack Sweden, France's ally, the Turks threatened to send their armies against the land of the czar. Suffice it to say that war and peace in these distant parts depended on France.

We know directly how this same sytem affected Germany, chiefly through Sweden. But even without this interference, our fatherland was divided and weakened. Bavaria and the Palatinate were bound to the French court by marriage alliances, and all the other princes received subsidies at one time or the other. The Elector of Cologne, through a formal treaty which he concealed behind various feigned agreements, delivered his fortress Neuss over to French occupation.

It was not much different in central and southern Europe. The Swiss at times had more than 20,000 men serving in the French armies. Under such strong public and still stronger secret influence, their assemblies could hardly boast too much about their independence. Richelieu had seized Pinerolo in order to keep the passage to Italy open. Even more important was Casale, through which Milan and Genoa were directly threatened. Everyone knew what a peril it would be to allow this fortress to come into French hands; yet no one dared to protest against it, during the prolonged negotiations which Louis

XIV conducted on the subject with the Duke of Mantua, and finally a French garrison occupied the place. Like the Duke of Mantua, most of the other Italian princes were in the service of France. The Duchess of Savoy, and, on the other side of the Pyrenees, the Queen of Portugal were Frenchwomen. Cardinal d'Estrées exercised over both of them such undoubted influence that it was said that he ruled over them despotically and, through them, over their countries.

But who would have believed that France would even have been able to gain a decisive influence over her rival, the House of Austria, from which she had just won her predominant position? She understood how to divide the Spanish and German lines of the Habsburg family. The young king of Spain was married to a French princess, and the actions of the French ambassadors soon made themselves apparent in the internal affairs of Spain. The most important man in the country at that time, Don Juan of Austria, was, as I have discovered, brought into bad repute by the French and died in that state. In Vienna too, even in the midst of wartime, France knew how to gain a foothold, if only secretly. Only by such an assumption can we explain the fluctuations in policy of the Vienna cabinet. Montecuculi complained that the decisions of the imperial war council were known sooner in Versailles than in his own headquarters. Under these circumstances, England should more than any European state have felt the call to oppose France, and only she had the power really to do so. But we know through what a strange combination of various motives Charles II was bound to Louis XIV: politics and love, luxury and religion, interest and intrigue. For the king of France, even these ties were not strong enough. At the same time he made efforts to win over the most important members of parliament. No matter how independent or republican their ideas, he had only to employ the proper method. "The arguments which I presented did not convince him," the French ambassador Barillon reported of one such member, "but the money I gave him made him secure." By such means, Louis XIV brought England under his control. Had the English king opposed him, he would have found resistance in his parliament; if the parliament expressed the national antipathy toward the French, the king would object. Louis XIV's policy, which Barillon expressly describes as close to his heart, was to keep the English divided and to prevent a reconciliation between king and parliament. He succeeded only too well, and thereby neutralized England's power.

And so Europe was, in the face of the French, "without heart," as one Venetian reported, "and without gall." European politics were in such a condition that Louis XIV could set up at the suggestion of one of his legal councilors Chambers of Reunion at Metz which summoned powerful princes before them to render decisions concerning land and populations protected by state treaties as if they were matters of private law! What a condition the German Empire was in that he could so forcefully and unnaturally tear Strasburg away from it! Allow me to quote what a foreigner wrote long after the conquest of Alsace: "When one reads its history," Young says in one of his accounts of his travels, "this does not make so deep an impression. But coming from France, I had first to cross over high mountains and then descend into a plain inhabited by a people differing completely from the French in customs, language, and race, a plain which had been conquered at that time; it made an impression on me." And yet Germany accepted such an insult and negotiated an armistice.

What was there that Louis XIV did not presume to do? I shall not linger over how he abused Genoa or how he sent his ambassador into Rome with an armed force in defiance of the pope. Let us remember that not even his friends were safe. He seized Zweibrücken although it belonged to his old ally, the king of Sweden. Although the Turks were his allies, his admiral bombarded Chios because Tripolitan pirates had fled there. During a period of the best understanding with England, in the midst of peacetime, he seized several forts belonging to the English Hudson's Bay Company. Louis XIV denied the above-mentioned queen of Poland a minor concession to her ambition. After he had acquired friends, either through money or support, he liked to neglect them to show them that he really did not need them, believing that fear of his displeasure alone would keep them in dependence. In every negotiation he wished to have this domination felt. Of one of his foreign ministers he himself said, "I had to remove him. Everything he handled lacked the grandeur and force which one must display when carrying out the orders of a king of France who does not happen to be unfortunate."

We could assume that this attitude was the principal motivation for his wars. It would be hard to call him greedy for land. There was really never any question of widespread territorial conquest, for the campaigns themselves were only part of the activities of the court. One gathers an army and parades it before the ladies; everything is prepared; the attack successful, the king marches into the conquered city, and then hurries back to court. It was chiefly the triumph and splendor of his return, the admiration of his court, in which he delighted. He cared not so much for conquests or for war as for the glory which they shed upon him. No, he did not seek a free, great, and imperishable fame; he cared only for the praises of his entourage, and for him these were both public and posterity.

But this was no less dangerous to the peace of Europe. If there were to be a supremacy, then it ought at least to be a legally determined one. This actually illegal domination which could disturb the peaceful situation at will and at any moment threatened to destroy the foundations of the European order and development. It is not always recognized that European order differs from others which have occurred in world history because of its legal, even juridical, nature. It is true that world disturbances repeatedly destroy this system of law, but after they have passed, it is reconstituted, and every effort aims only toward perfecting it once again.

Nor was this the only danger. It was no less serious that the dominating influence of one nation would make it hardly possible for others to achieve an independent development, especially when this domination was supported by literature. Italian literature had already completed its original course; English literature had not yet attained universal significance; German literature did not exist at the time. But French literature, light, sparkling, and lively, in strictly regulated and yet pleasing form, was comprehensible to everyone, and yet possessed its own national character. It began to dominate Europe. It might be amusing to note that the dictionary of the Académie Française, which set the standards for the language, was particularly rich in expressions which made the rounds of the court. But there is no doubt that French literature corresponded completely with the state, and that one supported the other in the achievement of supremacy. Paris became the capital of Europe. She exercised a domination like no other city's on language, custom, the fashionable world, and the powerful classes, and was the center of the community of Europe. It is remarkable that the French had already begun to praise their constitution to all the world as "the happy condition of well-protected subjection, in which France finds herself under a prince who deserves more than any other to rule the world by his courage and wisdom and to bring it into true unity."

Were we to place ourselves back in that period, in the mind of a contemporary, what an unhappy, oppressed, painful prospect we would see. It might well have happened that the wrong course of the Stuarts would have won out and that English policy would have been chained to the French forever. After the Treaty of Nijmegen negotiations were carried on with the greatest energy to secure the election as king of the Romans for Louis XIV or the Dauphin. Significant supporters were found for Louis' cause, "for only the Most Christian King is capable of restoring to the empire its ancient splendor." Nor was it so impossible that under favorable circumstances such an election might have taken place. What then, if afterward the Spanish monarchy also fell to a prince of this house? If at the same time French literature had been cultivated in the directions of which it was capable, toward Protestant as well as Catholic countries, the state and culture of France would have conquered Europe with irresistible force. If we were to put ourselves back in those times, as we have suggested, how could we believe that such an unfortunate course of events could have been prevented?

Against this growth of power and political domination, the smaller powers could unite. They concluded alliances and associations. Thus was formed the concept of the European balance of power, whereby the union of many other states must serve, to use their expression, to resist the pretensions of an exorbitant court. The forces of resistance gathered around Holland and William III. With common exertion they resisted attack and waged war. But it would have been wrong to consider this a permanent remedy. Despite the European alliance and a successful war, a Bourbon still became king of Spain and America. In the further course of events, the authority of this dynasty was extended even to parts of Italy. In great danger, one can always trust in the guiding Genius which ever protects Europe from a one-sided and forceful dominating tendency. Every pressure from one side is resisted by one from the others, and their connection into a whole, which grows closer and closer from century to century, has happily preserved the freedom and particular development of all. Since the predominance of France depended on the superiority of her military forces, upon her inner strength, it was necessary for the other powers which opposed her either to recover or for the first time to attain inner unity, independent strength, and general importance. Let us review, in a few swift strokes, how this happened.

## ENGLAND, AUSTRIA, RUSSIA

England was the first to awaken to a sense of its strength. This strength, as we have seen, had been restrained, deflected, by Louis XIV, who simultaneously manipulated Charles II and his parliament and knew how to use first the one, then the other, for his own purposes. But with James II, Louis stood in an even more confidential relationship. If by nothing else, they were united in a common religious attitude, a common devotion. The prince who himself so cruelly persecuted Protestants was well pleased by the notable favor shown Catholics by James. Louis poured forth his praise, and the English ambassador could hardly describe sufficiently the heartiness with which Louis offered every conceivable assistance when James took the decisive step and arrested the bishops. But it was just this which turned the popular forces and— since the English church was in danger—even the aristocratic forces against the king and against the French. The movement which overthrew the Stuarts was a religious, a national, movement, and one in the interest of threatened Europe. The leader, William III, had up to then been the soul of all the undertakings against France. The new king and his parliament formed thenceforth a single party. There were disagreements, sometimes strong disagreements, but in the long run, concerning the important things, both perceived that their opposition was too strong for them again to become disunited. The parties, which had previously driven themselves to extremes, in order to attack one another from opposing positions, were directed toward an area of understanding; they still disputed with one another, but they also came to compromises, so that their conflicts became the leavening element in the constitution. It is not without interest to compare this condition with that of France. They had much in common. In France as in England, the aristocratic class possessed the power. Both enjoyed exclusive legal privileges, which they enjoyed by virtue of their religion —the one through its Catholicism; the other, its Protestantism. But there was also a great difference.

In France everything was characterized by uniformity, subjection, and dependence upon a richly developed, but morally spoiled, court life. In England a powerful competition, a political duel between two nearly equally armed parties, took place in a determined, circumscribed arena. In France the forcefully implanted piety was transformed only too soon into its opposite; in England a perhaps more restricted, on the whole manly, and confident religious feeling arose which overcame its opposition. The one was bled by the enterprises of a false ambition; the other's veins were filled to bursting with youthful vigor. It was as if the stream of English national strength emerged for the first time from the mountains in which, as it were, it had long lain in a deep and full but narrow bed, poured forth into the plain to rule it in proud majesty, to bear ships, and to see world cities founded upon its shores. The right to grant taxes, which had brought about most of the disputes between king and parliament, now began instead to unite them. During the quarter-century of his reign, Charles II had raised altogether 43 million pounds; William, in just thirteen years, collected 72 million pounds. These efforts increased enormously afterward, and they rose because they were voluntary, because it could be seen that the proceeds benefited, not the luxury of a few courtiers, but the common need. As a result, the predominance of the English navy did not long remain in doubt. In 1678, the royal fleet appeared in flourishing condition with 83 warships (including fire ships) with a complement of 18,323 men. By contrast, in December 1701, there were (excluding fire ships and smaller vessels) 184 ships from first to sixth class and a complement of 53,921 men. If, as we believe, we may take the income from postal revenue as a measure of internal traffic, we would have to state that this also increased extraordinarily. In 1660 the post yielded 12,000 pounds; in 1699, in contrast, 90,504 pounds sterling.

It was already remarked at the time that the real national motive in the War of the Spanish Succession was the concern that a united

France and Spain might together tear the West Indian trade away from the Dutch and English. Even if the peace which the Whigs so loudly condemned deserves their blame, it nonetheless laid that fear to rest. Nothing indicated the superiority of the English over the Bourbon dynasty so much as the fact that they retained Gibraltar. They secured the best trade with the Spanish colonies for themselves by treaty, while their own colonies expanded with tremendous progress. Just as Calcutta eclipsed Batavia, so the old maritime glory of Holland faded before the English. Frederick the Great was heard to remark that Holland followed its neighbor like a dinghy its ship. The union with Hanover brought still another new, continental, and no less anti-French interest for England. Throughout this historical movement, English literature for the first time attained a European influence, and began to rival the French. Natural science and philosophy, the latter in both its tendencies, created a new and original outlook on the world in which the world-dominating spirit expressed and reflected itself. It would perhaps be too much to assert that the English created perfect, imperishable monuments of poetry or art in this period; but they did have magnificent geniuses even at that time and had long possessed at least one great poet, whose works, understandable and moving in all ages, Europe came to know for the first time. Although the English for a while had not hesitated to copy French models, now the most distinguished Frenchmen were influenced by English science and culture.

In such manner Louis XIV found himself opposed by a rival which he had hoped through politics or the influence of religion to disarm, a more powerful, imposing, and dangerous rival, than he had ever expected. Thereby the maritime balance of power, and the whole condition of Western Europe, were basically changed.

At the same time, the East was also being transformed. I cannot agree that German Austria as we now know her can be called an old power. During the Middle Ages she had little importance without the imperial crown. Thereafter she was at once harnessed to and overshadowed by the Spanish monarchy. By the end of the sixteenth century, religious division and the hereditary privileges of her Estates had deprived Austria of any external respect. At the beginning of the Thirty Years' War, the emperor had to use a German army to reconquer his hereditary lands. Even the splendor which the efforts of Wallenstein cast upon Ferdinand II was only passing, and evoked a powerful reaction. How often were the capitals of the Austrian provinces threatened by the Swedish armies! Yet even at that very time, the House of Austria was building the permanent inner foundations of its power through the destruction of its enemies, the elevation of its dependents, and the final entrenchment of Catholicism. It was the first step toward that prestige which she has had in modern times. But Austria first became an independent and continentally significant power through the reconquest of Hungary. As long as Ofen remained in the hands of the Turks, France could threaten, even endanger, Austria, as often as she pleased, by exercising her influence at the Porte. Although France did not incite Kara Mustapha's campaign of 1683, she was at least aware of it. Her intention was not to destroy Germany or Christendom; she did not go that far; but she wanted to see the Turks take Vienna and press on even as far as the Rhine. This would have made Louis XIV appear as the only savior of Christendom. In the confusion which such events must have produced, he could not have failed to gain control over the German crown, and even, if he wished, take it for himself.

Under the walls of Vienna this plan failed. It was the last great effort of the Turks, and reacted all the more destructively upon them because they had thrown all their force into it, in a barbaric excess of effort. Afterward, the disorderly Turkish horde, which once advanced, according to an Italian observer, "like a strong impenetrable wall," yielded on all sides to the advancing German troops. In vain did an order of the mufti declare that Ofen was the key to the empire, and its defense a duty of faith. It fell too, and all Hungary was reconquered and made into an hereditary kingdom. The discontented inhabitants submitted. Orthodox Serbian settlers were established in the borderlands of lower Hungary to defend it in the future against the Turks.

From that time, Austrian power rested upon a completely different foundation. Up to that period, all the wars in Hungary had been waged by German armies, and it was said that all its rivers had been tinged with German blood. But now the Hungarians were the heart of the Austrian army in its German wars. No longer was it possible for French diplomacy to summon the Turks into the heart of the monarchy on the slightest occasion. Only once again did France get support and aid from the discontented elements. Finally, all was quiet. Thus the emperor founded his power on that very province which previously had endangered it the most.

It is obvious what a transformation in the situation of Eastern Europe must result from such a strengthening of this stable, wealthy, and well-armed power, which had held the Turks in check and whom they feared.

Louis XIV experienced at least the beginnings of still another such change. The conditions in Poland, which made it easy for him always to have a party in this country, and the power of Sweden, which was at least usually bound to him by custom and old alliances, gave him without much effort a decisive hegemony in the North. Charles XII caused no alteration in this. One of his first decisions, as he told his chancellor was "to conclude at any rate an alliance with France and to belong among her friends." It is true that the Northern War and the War of the Spanish Succession, which began about the same time, had no premeditated or negotiated connection as is sometimes suspected. But the success of the Swedish undertaking aided the French. Actually, both events followed the same tendency. While the Spanish succession was supposed to serve to deliver southern Europe into the hands of the Bourbons, their old allies the Swedes were close to bringing the North under their control.

Charles XII had attacked Denmark and dictated peace, had conquered Poland and made himself her king, marched halfway across a Germany whose eastern regions were no better defended than her western—and occupied Saxony. After this he required nothing more to establish his supremacy than to destroy completely the czar, whom he had already defeated once. Thus he set forth from Saxony with a renewed army; the czar, meanwhile, had mobilized his forces with great effort; and the result was the decisive battles of the year 1709.

Once again the two northern heroes, Charles XII and Peter I, faced each other: original offspring of Germanic and Slavic nationality. It was a memorable confrontation. The German, high-minded and simple, blameless in his conduct, completely a hero, true to his word, bold in his undertakings, God-fearing, stubborn to the point of obstinacy and steadfast. The Slav was at once good-natured and cruel, highly active, still half a barbarian but attracted with all the emotion of his alert, eager nature to the studies and progress of the European nations, full of great enterprises and tireless in carrying them out. It is a sublime spectacle to behold the struggle of these two natures. It is open to debate as to which was the superior, but this much is true: the greater prospect for the future lay in the czar's success. While Charles showed little understanding of his nation's true interests, Peter made the development of his country his chief aim, and personally prepared and began it.

He won the victory. In reporting the battle of Poltava to his people, he added the postscript "and thereby the cornerstone of St. Petersburg has been laid." It was the cornerstone of his whole edifice of state, and of his politics. Thereafter, Russia began to lay down the law in northern Europe. It would be wrong to believe that this required a prolonged development; it happened instantly.

How could Augustus II of Poland, who owed his restoration solely to Russian arms, have freed himself from their influence? It was more than that, for he was forced to appeal for help again in dealing with his quarrelsome nobility. Peter I thus became the direct arbiter of Poland, exercising his mastery over both parties. He was the more powerful because the Poles had reduced their army by three-quarters while his was becoming larger, better trained, and more to be feared. The czar, a Venetian noted in 1717, used to take orders from the Poles but now gave them as he wished with unlimited authority.

Necessarily, France's influence in Poland declined increasingly from this time. She was no longer able to promote her candidates for the throne, even when the nobility was on their side. Meanwhile, Sweden was stripped of her powers and reduced by these events. In the last days of his reign, Louis XIV had guaranteed all the possessions of the Swedish crown; nonetheless, a significant portion of them were lost. But the French maintained their influence in Stockholm. There were complaints in 1756 that Sweden was being ruled from Paris, like a French province. But, as we have stated, Sweden had become completely unimportant. French influence could be exercised only on the miserable internal clashes of the Hats and Caps. If France utilized these occasionally to provoke a war with Russia, it was to Sweden's disadvantage, for it only gave Russia the opportunity for new victories and territorial enlargement.

And thus northern Europe passed under a totally different control from that of the French; there a great nation entered into a new and especially a European development. In eastern Europe, French influence did not disappear, but it no longer retained its old significance, despite the weakness of Austria under Charles VI. The sea was in the hands of France's rivals, and the advantage which France had begun to enjoy via Cadiz with Spanish America was either tolerated or interrupted by them at their convenience.

In contrast, in southern Europe, France was able, after a brief interruption, to restore its natural alliance with the Bourbon courts, and to effect common plans. Here, and in Germany, France still maintained a great preponderance.

This was especially true in Germany.

We have a "Considerations" on the state of European politics in 1736 which sketches for us in a lively and concise way the situation, and especially the German situation, on the eve of the War of the Austrian Succession. The author concedes that Charles VI had violated a few articles of his election capitulation through his efforts to increase his power in the empire, and to make its constitution more monarchical by alliance with the Russians, who had already appeared on the Rhine. But he concludes that this constituted no great danger, since the last war had demonstrated the weakness of the imperial court, and the arrogance and ruthlessness with which it sought to carry out its own plans offered its own remedy. Let us rather, he exclaims, guard ourselves against those who seek to enslave us with secret artifice, ingratiating manners, and a feigned benevolence. He maintains that Cardinal Fleury, the French chief minister, despite his guise of extraordinary moderation, was pursuing the plans of a Richelieu and Mazarin. With apparent magnanimity he lulled his neighbors to sleep, while his gentle and calm character lent itself to serving the diplomacy of his court. How shrewdly, without sensation or alarm, had he been able to gain Lorraine for France! For her to gain the desired Rhine frontier required little more than to await the disturbances sure to follow the death of the emperor.

In the year 1740 Charles VI died. Cardinal Fleury allowed himself to dare even bolder measures than had been expected. He frankly declared that he did not wish the husband of Maria Theresa to be her father's heir because he was hostile to France. It was chiefly Fleury who secured the German crown for Charles VII of Bavaria. He conceived the plan to establish four equal-sized states in Germany: the House of Austria, limited nearly to Hungary; Bavaria with Bohemia; Saxony with Moravia and Upper Silesia; and Prussia with Lower Silesia. How simple it would have been for France to have maintained a perpetual domination over four such states, whose very nature would have prevented their mutual agreement.

## PRUSSIA

In this moment of seeming danger to the German fatherland, which then possessed neither powerful states nor distinguished men of action, with no literature, no art or culture of its own with which to resist the domination of its neighbor, Prussia arose. There appeared Frederick II.

This is not the place to discuss either the ruler or the state which he inherited and the state which he created. Nor may we easily venture to tell of the inner power of the man and of the state, and the living, developing reality which they comprised. Let us try only to make clear their position in the world.

We must concede that Frederick's first action was supported by the direction which French policy took upon the death of Charles VI. But should he continue to collaborate closely with it? It was Frederick himself, still, as crown prince, removed from the affairs of state, who was the author of those "Considerations" which I have just tried to describe. They are, we can see, directed completely against French policy. He perceived as clearly as possible the dangers which threatened Germany from this quarter. For this reason he undertook to declare war solely on his own. He wanted the success of his arms to be independent of the French. He explained in great earnest to their ambassador that he was a German prince, and that he would not tolerate their troops on German soil any longer than the treaties provided.

In late 1741 it was not an impossibility that Austria might be completely destroyed. Silesia, Bohemia, and Upper Austria were in enemy hands; Vienna threatened as well as Prague. If this attack had continued forcefully, who can say what would have resulted? I shall not credit Frederick with magnanimity in avoiding this final step. He knew well that it was not to his advantage to relieve France of its ancient opponent. When he saw the queen of Hungary on the brink of ruin, he wished to give her pause to catch her breath; he said so himself. He deliberately paused and concluded an armistice. His intent was to depend neither on France nor on Austria. He wanted to feel free, and took up an independent position, based on his own strength, between the two powers. In this simple purpose lies the key to his diplomacy during the Silesian wars. Never was an acquisition defended with more jealous vigilance than his own. He mistrusted his friends no less than his enemies, keeping himself always well armed and battle-ready. As soon as he believed himself at a disadvantage, or only glimpsed danger afar, he took up arms. Whenever it was to his advantage and he had gained a victory, he offered his hand in peace. It goes without saying that he could not bring himself to further the interests of a foreign power; but he regarded his own without exaggeration or self-deception. His demands were never exorbitant. His intentions were directed only toward his immediate needs. But in these he would remain firm to the very end.

In the meantime, such an unexpected new independence, seized by a bold and defiant attitude, could arouse the displeasure and enmity of his neighbors.

We can understand why Maria Theresa could not immediately recover from the loss of a rich province and why she looked with displeasure on the rise of so successful and able a rival in the empire. But the prestige of Prussia also significantly affected the northern system. It aroused the thorough hatred of several Russian ministers, who believed that their supremacy in the North was threatened by Prussia's conclusion of a very innocent treaty with France and Sweden, which ensured the balance of power in the North. True, the king might all the more easily get the support of France. But the resentment of the court of Versailles was provoked by the fact that he, unlike the Swedish king, could not be controlled and presumed to follow a free, independent policy. Although this court knew very well what it was doing, it decided to alter its whole system and henceforth ally itself with Austria. Public opinion, in one of those sudden outbursts which are so peculiar to France, joyfully greeted the treaty.

Thus the empress managed to join the two great continental powers to herself; lesser states such as her neighbors in Saxony and Pomerania joined their company. An alliance was in the making, not much different from the one against Austria which had formed after the death of Charles VI. Russia's participation would make the present one even stronger. Talk now was of a division of the Prussian lands, just as a division of the Austrian had been earlier. Frederick could find only an ally from across the sea—the same ally which had previously taken Austria's side. But even with this new recruit, he had only a very modest power, insignificant in comparison with the alliance. How would he be able, how would he even dare, to hold his own in such a conflict?

He had, as we know, requested from the court of Vienna a categorical explanation of their armament. "If it were only somewhat satisfactory," he said to one of his ministers, "then we shall not march." Finally the awaited courier arrived. The answer was hardly satisfactory. "The die is cast!" he declared. "Tomorrow we march!" Thus he launched himself bravely into these perils; he sought them out, and practically called them upon himself. But it was only when in the middle of them that he learned their true extent.

If ever an event depended upon a great personality, it was the Seven Years' War. Our contemporary wars are brought to an end by a few decisive battles. Previously they lasted longer, but men fought more over limited demands and claims than about the very being, the existence or non-existence, of their state. The Seven Years' War differed, in that throughout its course the very existence of Prussia was at stake. Conditions were such that amid the general hostility only one single unfortunate day would have been sufficient to have brought about its ruin. Frederick perceived this completely. After the battle of Kollin he exclaimed, "This is our Poltava." And if the prediction was unfulfilled, it was true that he felt himself threatened with disaster at any moment.

I shall not discuss the sources of aid which he drew upon in such a desperate situation: his military genius, the bravery of his troops, the loyalty of his subjects, or chance circumstance. The main thing was that he kept up his courage.

French philosophy had guided him only toward light intellectual exercises, casual poetry, and academic learning. It seemed to invite him more toward the enjoyment of life than to such forceful struggles. But we might say that true genius itself remains unharmed by such false teachings. It is a law unto itself and rests on its own spiritual truth, of which it needs only to become aware. Life and the exertion of a great enterprise provides this awareness, and misfortune ripens it.

Frederick II had long been a great general; the disasters which he sustained made him a hero. His resistance was not only military, but at the same time an inner, moral, spiritual thing. The king conducted the war with continual reflection on the final causes of things, with a grand perspective of the transitory nature of earthly existence.

I do not wish to praise his poems as distinguished works of poetic talent. In that respect they may have many defects. But at least those which were written during the changing fortunes of this war have a magnificent sweep of simple thought. They disclose to us the agitation of a manly soul in distress, struggle, and danger. He saw himself "in the midst of a raging sea; lightning strikes through the storm; thunder bursts above my head; I am surrounded with cliffs. The hearts of the helmsmen are benumbed; the source of our fortune is dried up, the palms have vanished, the laurel is withered."

Occasionally he may have sought support and strength in the sermons of Bourdaloue. More often he turned to ancient philosophy. Yet the third book of Lucretius, which he so often studied, told him only that evil was necessary and that no remedy against it was possible. He was a man who drew exalted thoughts even from this hard and despairing doctrine. He looked death, which he had often wished to find on the battlefield, straight in the eye without flinching. Just as he often liked to compare his enemies with the triumvirate, so he invoked the spirits of Cato and Brutus and was resolved to follow their example. But he was not entirely in the position of those Romans. They had been caught up in the general destiny of the world—Rome was the world—without any considerations but the meaning of their own personal ideals for which they fought. But he had a country to represent and defend. If any special idea worked upon him, we could say that it was the thought of his country, of his fatherland.

We can picture him after the battle of Kunersdorf, as he weighed the extent of his misfortune and the hopelessness of his situation, as he felt the hatred and good fortune of his enemies, and regarded all as lost. He saw only one expedient for his army and his land and resolved to seize it: to sacrifice himself. Then he gradually became aware of the possibility of a revived resistance, and he dedicated himself to this almost hopeless duty. It was impossible for him to leave his country in the situation which it must so long endure, "submerged by its enemies, robbed of its honor, without a source of aid, in clear danger." "To you," he declared, "I will dedicate the rest of my disastrous life. I will not let myself be consumed with fruitless anxiety. I will throw myself once more upon the field of danger." He exclaimed to his troops: "Let us oppose fate, courageous against so many enemies, who conspire together, drunk with pride and arrogance." Thus he continued to hold out, and finally experienced the day of peace. "Steadfastness," he said at the conclusion of his history of this war, "is the only thing which can rescue from danger the great affairs of state."

He had preserved his territory intact, and from the moment he was again master of it made it his principal, his only, concern to heal the wounds which the war had caused. If we consider a great power as one which must be able to maintain itself against all others, even when they are allied, Frederick had raised Prussia to this rank. For the first time since the age of the Saxon emperors and Henry the Lion there had appeared in northern Germany an independent power, relying upon its own resources with no need of allies. It followed that thereafter France was able to do little or nothing in German affairs. An opposition, such as the one which she had aroused or favored in the War of the Austrian Succession was a thing of the past. While Prussia had emancipated herself, Bavaria and Saxony now resumed their ties to Austria.

Nor was an early return of the old situation to be expected. France herself had prevented it by entering into that close alliance with Austria which resulted in the Seven Years' War. I shall not inquire whether that alliance had all the other effects which the French without exaggeration ascribe to it. But it is sure that France herself gave up her previous position, which allowed her to support the German opposition. "From this moment on," it was said in France, "the king of Prussia will become the protector of German liberty, to the disadvantage of French supremacy." Nor can we believe that Austria would have allowed France to exercise its former influence. While he was still co-regent, and from the very beginning, Joseph II declared that "he would regard the rights of the imperial crown as sacred; he insisted that anyone wishing to be on good terms with him not interfere with them." At that time, it was already recognized that the true safeguard of the political independence of Germany lay in a free and solidly established union of both these powers against the outside world.

This great change now achieved full significance because at the same time German literature accomplished its liberation from French models and their false imitation. I do not say that our nation had not previously enjoyed a certain degree of intellectual independence. It lay chiefly in the development of a theological system which had taken hold of all minds and was primarily German in its origin. But it included only a small portion of the nation, while the pure ideal of inner religious experience was forced into a curious scholastic form. We cannot deny the activity and partial success with which work was carried on in many other kinds of learning, but they all had to conform themselves to this same form. They were taught in complicated systems suited for delivery from a professor's lectern and seldom for real intellectual understanding. The universities dominated learning in general, not without narrowness and compulsion. It was thus so much easier for the upper classes of society to become gradually less affected by this system and to let themselves be carried away by French influences.

But from the middle of the century there began a new development of the national spirit. We must not forget that this developed largely from the previous system, though it also contained a certain contradiction to it. Dissatisfied, still tied to the old dogmatic system but no longer so restricted by it, the German spirit attained an enlargement of itself through poetry. Religion was once again brought close to men's hearts, in all of its human implications, and above all without emotionalism. With bold efforts, philosophy courageously embarked upon a new discussion of the ultimate foundations of all knowledge. Side by side there appeared the two tendencies of German philosophy, essentially different, yet closely related, the one more intuitive, the other more analytical, which have since developed next to and with one another, attracting and repelling, but only together able to express the fullness of an original consciousness. Criticism and archaeology broke through the mass of formal scholarship and pressed forward to grasp living awareness.

The national spirit, awakened with one blow and supported by its own thoroughness and maturity, then developed a poetic literature independently and with free experimentation. And thereby it developed a comprehensive world-outlook, which was new, and though caught up in many inner contradictions, was on the whole harmonious. This literature had the inestimable quality of no longer being restricted to part of the nation but embraced the whole and made it aware of its unity for the first time.

If new generations of great poets do not always follow upon the old ones, one should not wonder too much. Great attempts are made and are successful; what there was to say has been said. The true spirit scorns to travel frequented and easy paths. And yet the world of German genius was far from being complete. Its task now was to penetrate into positive science. Many obstacles stood in the way, springing from its own course of development and other influences as well. We can now hope that it will overcome them all, achieve a more complete inner coherence, and then be capable of continuous new creation.

But I shall pause here, for I wished to speak of politics, although these things are most closely related and true politics can be sustained only by a great national existence. This much is certain: that no other phenomenon contributed so much to the self-confidence with which this internal upsurge was accomplished as the life and renown of Frederick II. For a nation must feel itself independent in order to develop freely; and no literature ever flourished save when a great moment of history prepared the way. But it was strange that Frederick himself knew nothing of this, and hardly expected it. He worked for the emancipation of the nation, and German literature worked with him, though he did not recognize his allies. But they knew him well. It made the Germans proud and bold to have had a hero arise from their midst.

It was, as we have seen, a necessity of the seventeenth century that France be restrained. In what manner, surpassing all expectation, had this now occurred! One could not say that a complex system had been artificially constructed for this purpose, as it appeared in form. What essentially happened was that the great powers had arisen through their own strength and that new independent national states with all their original power had taken over the world stage.

Austria, Catholic and German, militarily stable, rich, and containing inexhaustible vitality, was a world in herself. The Graeco-Slavic principle appeared more strongly in Russia than ever before in world history. The European forms which she adopted, far from repressing her original element, penetrated it, enlivened it, and for the first time channeled its own strength. In England the Germanic maritime interests developed a colossal world power which ruled all the seas, and by comparison eclipsed earlier memories of the sea powers. The German Protestant principle found the support which it had so long sought, its representation and expression in Prussia. "Even if one knows the secret," says the poet, "who would have the courage to tell it?"

I shall not presume to grasp the character of each of these states in words. But we can clearly see that they were founded on principles which had grown out of the various important developments of earlier centuries, that they were formed in accordance with these original differences and with varying constitutions, and that they represented those historical demands which were made in the nature of things upon succeeding generations. In their rise and development, which, understandably, could not have happened without a many-sided transformation of their inner conditions, lies the great event of the hundred years which preceded the outbreak of the French Revolution.

## THE FRENCH REVOLUTION

Although this event undoubtedly had its own legitimate significance, we cannot deny that France was thereby restricted and might well regard the success of the other countries as her own loss. She had always energetically opposed them. How often had she attempted earlier to restrain the progress of Austria in Hungary and against the Turks! How often did the best Austrian regiments have to be recalled from the Danube, where they stood against the Turks, to the Rhine to oppose the French! Russia had wrested from France her political influence in the North. When the cabinet at Versailles became aware of the position which Prussia had assumed and sought to maintain in the world, it forgot its American interests in order not only to reduce this power, but even to destroy it totally. How often had the French attempted to favor the Jacobites, to place a Stuart on the English throne, and restore their old relationship. In return they gained the English as their perpetual enemies, whether England stood with Prussia against Austria, or with Austria against Prussia. The French waged their wars upon the continent and sustained their losses at sea. During the Seven Years' War, as Chatham said, they lost America in Germany.

And this France stood nowhere as definitely at the center of the European world as she had a hundred years earlier. She had to witness, without being consulted, the partition of Poland. In 1772, to her deep resentment, she was forced to allow an English frigate to appear at the roadstead of Toulon to observe the stipulated disarmament of her fleet. Even the smaller independent states such as Portugal and Switzerland had opened themselves to other influences.

But at the same time, it must be noted that the situation was not so bad as has been often represented. France still maintained its old influence over Turkey, and through the Family Compact she had linked Spain to her policy. The Spanish fleet and the riches of the Spanish colonies stood at her disposal, and the other Bourbon courts (among whom one could almost include Turin) allied themselves with France. The French faction finally won out in Sweden. But for a nation which had enjoyed the glory of a universal superiority longer than any other, this was not nearly enough. She felt only the loss of claims, which she regarded as rights. She noticed only what others conquered and not what she had kept. She looked with resentment on such strong, well-established powers, for which she was no longer a match.

There has been much talk about the causes of the Revolution and efforts to seek them where they will never be found. One of the most important, I believe, is in this change in France's international situation which brought the government into deep discredit. It is true that the government did not know how to administer the state or to wage war properly. It had allowed the most dangerous abuses to prevail, and the collapse of its European reputation was in large part the result. But the French also blamed their government for everything which was simply the result of this changed world situation. They still lived with memories of Louis XIV's power. All the events which resulted from the rise of other powers with fresh energies, and which deprived them of an influence which they had previously exercised, were blamed on the incompetence of their foreign policy and on the undeniable decline of their internal situation.

Thus it happened that the popular movement in France, which at first had a reform character but was too soon transformed into a revolutionary one, was directed from the very beginning against the outside world.

The American Revolution quickly revealed this two-sided nature. If we did not already know this, it could be seen from Ségur's memoirs what a strange mixture of desire for war and so-called philosophy motivated the youth of the higher French nobility who took part in it. "Freedom," Ségur said, "presented itself to us with all the attraction of glory. While the more mature used the opportunity to put their principles into practice by restricting arbitrary power, we younger ones marched under the banner of philosophy only in order to wage war, to distinguish ourselves, to gain places of honor; we were philosophers out of knightly conviction." These youths gradually became philosophers in earnest. What a curious combination! While they attacked England—and their ambition was to weaken her and strip her of her colonies—they still sought to attain for themselves the independence of an English peer or a member of the House of Commons!

The American War for Independence became a decisive one, not so much because of the alteration in the general balance of power, as because of the indirect results which it brought about. Though the English colonies had been sundered from the mother country, it quickly became apparent that the English had such a well-established state that they did not feel their loss too badly. If the French navy had again attained a certain prestige, England was still victorious in the decisive battles, and had maintained her supremacy over her united opponents.

Not only was there a rise of republican tendencies, but also direct results of the struggle. Turgot had opposed the war with great fervor. Only in peacetime could he hope to restore the deficit-ridden finances by rigid economies, and at the same time carry out the necessary reforms. But even he had to yield to the tide of youthful enthusiasm. War was declared and waged at extravagant cost. Necker, with all the talent of a great banker, knew how to float new loans. But the higher they increased, the higher the deficit rose. As early as 1780, Vergennes informed the king that the condition of the finances was truly disturbing: peace, and an early peace, was essential. In spite of this, peace continued to be delayed, and only after its conclusion was the financial confusion generally realized.

England was no less exhausted and debt-ridden as a result of the American war. But while Pitt in England grasped the evil by the root and restored confidence through strong measures, the French finances passed from one weak hand into still weaker ones, more inexperienced and even more reckless. Thus the bad situation grew worse monthly, and threatened not only to strip the government of its power but to deprive it of all respect.

How strongly this affected foreign relations! France had no more choice: she had to avoid war at any cost. When Austria made demands on Holland, France supplied half the sum of money. Nor would the emperor have suffered much hindrance in his designs upon Bavaria if it had depended upon France alone. As close as the French government was to the so-called patriotic party in Holland, it had to allow Holland to be invaded and defeated by Prussia. Nor do I blame France greatly for this. What could they do in July 1787 when the Prussian declaration against Holland was issued? Shortly afterward, on August 15, came the famous session of the *grand chambre* of the *parlements*, which opened their doors to declare to the assembled crowd that the king might levy no taxes in the future without calling a meeting of the Estates General! At the time when its whole existing system was being called into question, how could France exert any influence in foreign affairs? At just that time the two imperial courts decided to attack Turkey. The French were in no condition to aid their old Turkish ally, which had to seek help from England and Prussia in order to survive.

At any rate, French foreign policy displayed an insignificance and futility which suited neither the natural position of the country nor the interests of Europe itself. If it was undeniably a result of France's internal disorders, the foreign situation itself greatly aggravated it. The policies of Archbishop de Brienne earned the most violent and general censure. He was accused of cowardice and even of disloyalty because he failed to support Holland and neglected this opportunity to restore France's military position on land. It was said that French honor had been so defamed that it would be redeemed only by streams of blood.

If that was an exaggeration, it is impossible to blame the sentiment which underlay the dissatisfaction. The national self-consciousness of a great people demands an appropriate position in Europe. The foreign relations of a kingdom are, not a convenience, but a part of its essential power, and the exterior respect of a state will always depend on the degree to which its own inner power is developed. Every nation will feel aggrieved when it sees itself denied its proper place. How much more was this true of the French, who had so often demanded that they be considered the pre-eminently great nation!

Without going into the variety of causes which led to the further development of the French Revolution, let me remind you that this collapse of France's foreign relations contributed much to it. We have only to think of the role played by an Austrian princess and unfortunate queen, who received all the hatred which the nation had for so long directed at the House of Austria, or of the unfortunate scenes caused by false rumors of an Austrian Committee. It was not enough that the French saw that they had lost their old influence on their neighbors; they went so far as to convince themselves that foreigners were exercising a powerful and secret influence on their state, and they thought that they detected a foreign hand in every decision of their domestic government. It was just this which increased the general indignation and raised the ferment and anger of the crowd.

By remaining with this view of the importance of foreign affairs, we can form the following picture of the Revolution.

Everywhere the national power had been concentrated to an unprecedented degree, in order to achieve greater power. In the process, the many obstacles which the ancien régime afforded had to be cleared away, and old privileges were often violated. This occurred in the different countries with more or less planning and success. It would require a very instructive and lively book to describe how this was attempted and more or less succeeded in various places, and where it led. Finally it was tried in France. Much has been said about the absolute power of earlier French monarchs. The truth is that this power was exercised in some few arbitrary acts, but for the most part had greatly declined. When the government made its attempt, it was already too weak to accomplish it. It acted with unsteady hands, and was unable to overcome the resistance of the privileged classes. To counter this it appealed to the Third Estate—the force of democratic ideas which had already begun to capture public opinion. This proved to be an ally which was far too strong. The government wavered when it recognized the latter's strength, abandoned the path which it had taken, and returned to the privileged classes whom it had wished to attack, offending those whom it had called to its aid. It thereby aroused popular political passions and placed itself in opposition to the ideas and tendencies of the century, and even to its own tendencies. It provoked a movement in which the Third Estate (or rather the violent element which developed within it) took a gigantic step forward and not only overthrew the privileged class, the aristocracy, but the king and throne itself, and destroyed the entire ancien régime.

A policy which had strengthened several, though not all other, governments in France took a course and consequence which led the French into disaster.

But it would be wrong for us to believe that under such ruinous conditions the power and international significance of France could be totally destroyed. The recuperative tendencies of her former power were so great that they not only were not lost under such frightful conditions, but were even strengthened in an unprecedented manner, far beyond the power of similar states. While elsewhere the existing intermediate classes were only restricted in their powers and forced into greater participation in the common weal, in France they were directly destroyed. The clergy and nobility lost not only their privileges, but, in the course of events, their property as well. It was a confiscation on the grand scale, of unheard-of extent. The ideas which Europe had greeted as salutary, humane, and liberating now suddenly were transformed before its eyes into a cruel devastation. The volcanic fires which were expected to offer a life-giving, nourishing earth-warmth now poured forth with a fearful eruption! Yet in the midst of this wreckage the French never abandoned the principle of unity. How much mightier France appeared to the other European states in the confusion of the revolutionary years! We can say that this powerful explosion of its forces was directed outward. Between the old France and the new existed the same difference as between the old aristocracy which governed the state—spirited and naturally brave, but used to court life, effete, pleasure-loving, often snared by petty ambition—and the wild, violent, unrestrained and bloodstained Jacobins who were the new rulers. In the course of events, other states had developed an aristocracy not identical with but similar to that which stood at the head of France. Small wonder that the Jacobins' wild efforts gained for them a preponderance of power! It required only the first victory from an unexpected battle to awaken the revolutionary enthusiasm which seized the nation, and became for a long time its living principle.

We could hardly say that France thereby became stronger than the other great powers put together, or even its closest neighbors, as long as they remained united. We are thoroughly aware of the errors of policy and military strategy which produced such unfavorable results for these countries. They could not at once accustom themselves to abandoning their previous jealousy. Even the one-sided coalition of 1799 was able to liberate Italy and to assume a very powerful military position, until it was divided by unfortunate disagreements. It cannot be denied that the French state, which had been formed in conflict with Europe, was able, by virtue of its centralization of power, to overcome any single continental state. Though it presented the image of always searching for freedom, it marched from revolution to revolution until it became a military despotism, which far exceeded the extent of the other great existing military systems. The successful general awarded himself an imperial crown. He could throw all the available forces of the nation into the field at any moment. In this fashion France recovered her hegemony, and succeeded in excluding England from the continent. In successive wars, Austria was deprived of her oldest provinces in Germany and Italy, and the army and monarchy of Frederick II were overthrown. Russia herself was forced into submissiveness, and saw her inner provinces and ancient capital city invaded. The French emperor required only these battles with the great powers to establish a direct dominance over southern and central Europe, as well as over a great part of Germany. This far exceeded anything which had happened in the time of Louis XIV. How deeply the old liberties of Europe were submerged! Europe seemed about to be absorbed by France. That universal monarchy which had once been regarded only as a remote danger was now nearly realized!

## RESTORATION

But were the energetic forces which had emerged as the great powers to be at once suppressed and destroyed?

War, Heraclitus tells us, is the father of all things. Out of the conflict of opposing forces, in the great moments of danger, disaster, resurgence, and deliverance, new developments proceed most decisively.

France had only been able to attain her supremacy because she was able to keep the feeling of national unity intact in the midst of stormy turbulence, and to strain all her national energy in an extraordinary expansion for the single purpose of the war.

Anyone who wished to resist her or who hoped again to break her dominance could not expect to do so with the same means which had hitherto sufficed. An improved military organization alone would not have helped. It required a more thorough renewal, a concentration of all resources available. It was necessary to decide to wake the slumbering spirits of the nation, which had previously carried on their lives unconsciously, to self-awareness and to action.

It would be a splendid task to investigate this rejuvenation of national spirit in the whole range of European peoples and states; to note the events which again aroused it; the signs which first announced its resurgence; the rich variety of movements and institutions in which it expressed itself; and, finally, the deeds by which it victoriously emerged. But that would be an undertaking so broad and extended that we cannot even touch upon it here.

It is certain that men first began to fight with some hope of success in 1809, as they began to satisfy the demands of world destiny. When in well-ordered kingdoms entire populations left their long-accustomed dwellings to which they were bound even by religion and abandoned them to the flames; when great peoples who had previously been used to a peaceful civic life took up arms; when people at last forgot their inherited feuds and joined together in earnest, then and not before was it possible to defeat their enemy, restore their former freedom, contain France within her boundaries, and drive the over-flooding stream back into its course.

If the main event of the last century before the French Revolution was the rise of the great powers in defense of European independence, the chief event of the period since has been the renewal and fresh drive of the nationalities. They have entered consciously into the state, which cannot exist without them.

It is generally thought that our age possesses only the tendency, the pressure, toward dissolution. Its significance seems to lie in putting an end to the unifying, binding institutions which have remained since the Middle Ages. It strides toward this goal with all the assurance of an innate drive. This is the result of all the great events, the discoveries, of our entire civilization. From this same source comes the irresistible inclination toward the development of democratic ideas and institutions, which of necessity causes the great changes which we are witnessing. It is a universal movement, in which France led the other countries. This opinion can lead only to the most dismal prospects for the future, but we believe that it cannot be maintained against the true facts of the case.

Far from merely satisfying itself with negations, our century has produced the most positive results. It has completed a great liberation, not in the sense of a dissolution, but in a constructive, unifying sense. Not only has it first of all created the great powers; it has renewed the principle of all states, religion, and law; and revitalized the principle of each individual state.

In just this fact lies the characteristic of our age.

In most epochs of world history peoples have been bound together by religious ties. But there have also occasionally been other cases comparable to our own, in which there has been a political system of interconnected monarchies and free states. I shall mention only the period after Alexander in the Macedonian–Greek kingdoms, for it offers many similarities to our own situation. It possessed a very extensive common culture, military science, action and interaction of complicated foreign relations; a great importance of business interests, of finance, of industrial competition, and a flowering of the exact mathematics-related sciences. But these states, which resulted from the enterprise of a conqueror and the dissension of his heirs, neither possessed a particular principle of existence nor managed to create one. They were based on military power and money. For that very reason they were soon dissolved and at last entirely disappeared. It has often been asked how Rome could have overcome them so quickly and completely. It happened because Rome, at least as long as it had significant enemies, maintained its principle of existence with admirable firmness. In our own case, it appeared that only the extent of a state's possessions, its military power, amount of wealth, and its certain share in civilization as a whole were of value to it. If ever there were events suited to destroy such an error, they are the events of our own time. They have restored a universal awareness of the importance of moral strength and sense of nationality for the state. What would have become of our states if they had not received new life from the national principle on which they were based? Is it convincing that they could exist without it?

[And so we cannot say that in these widespread changes which have made all states more or less similar every state would experience the same stages as the French, or that each would be threatened by the same things as the French have experienced. It is clear, if I am not mistaken, that France has affected other states more by the reaction which she has provoked than by the imitation which she has invited. How can we distinguish between the unheaval in France and the transformations which took place in other states? In the former, unrest, after gaining its victory, was made the ruling principle. The state thus limited by its own origins could hardly achieve consistence. Nor were the results of the Revolution ever essentially rejected by the restoration. Rather, they were consolidated under its aegis and continued to exist in permanent contradiction to the legitimate dynasty. But in other countries the ruling powers were associated with the greater freedoms which they conceded, thereby making their own position more independent and more powerful.

We should not allow ourselves to be deceived by a frequent error. In the mid-eighteenth century the European princes seemed to be in league with French philosophy. This was caused by several reasons, but it was also natural in that the philosophers formed an opposition to a regime which pretended to hegemony in Europe. Thus Frederick II, though he was host to French *philosophes*, protected them, and shared their opinions, did not think of reconstructing his state according to their theories. He always vigorously opposed their practical tendency. In the revolutionary state, in contrast, the theories of the Gazette and the Quotidienne and the interests which they championed formed the opposition. It was natural that they should find approval in the rest of Europe. But it was not to be expected that the states which were disposed to these views should become transformed by them. The stability of the hereditary aristocracy of old France was opposed by a freer, greater movement. The incessant, wild disturbance of Modern France found its antithesis in a greater stability. Nonetheless the development of the states took its own course and followed its own principles.

Though the French revolutionary spirit, which was so suddenly resurrected in 1830, spread rapidly, and revived by analogy the actions of the first great universal upheaval, seeking in a thousand ways to revolutionize Europe, one could hardly fear that its movement could bring about another revival of universal change.

It is true that the revolutionary spirit was no ally to be disdained for France's unabandoned pretensions. It gave forceful movement toward every aspect of the previous French hegemony, and exercised a significant influence on the world situation of the moment. But it necessarily found within itself its own resistance. No state can maintain itself with the revolutionary spirit alone; it would be too much for it. Thus we have only to consider what effects followed its first attacks. Did it not serve to awaken and revive a nationality whose existence was hardly believed? Holland, which was completely subjected by the French Revolution, which subsequently formed an insignificant province of the empire, now felt the sense of its ancient fame, unyieldingly and courageously asserted its destiny, and bravely maintained it.

However it could not be achieved without an extraordinary steadfastness by the government and a great liberal feeling by the nation, and a merger of both interests. But precisely this is required for successful resistance. Nothing can be done by negation. Strength must oppose strength.]

World history does not present such an accidental tumult, conflict, and succession of dates and peoples as appears at first sight. Nor is the often dubious advancement of civilization its only significance. There are forces, and indeed spiritual, creative forces, life itself, and there are moral energies whose development we can see. We cannot define them or put them into abstractions but they can be glimpsed and perceived. We can develop a sympathy for their existence. They unfold, capture the world, and express themselves in the greatest variety of forms; contend with, contain, and conquer one another. In their interaction and succession, in their life, their decline or resurrection, which then encompasses an ever greater fullness, higher significance, and wider extent, lies the secret of world history.

[If we are now attacked by a spiritual power, so we must oppose it with spiritual force. The domination which another nation threatens to exercise over us can be countered only by the development of our own nationality. I do not mean an invented chimerical nationality but the actual, essential one which is expressed in the state.

But, people will reply, is not the world now developing into an ever closer community? Will this tendency not be hampered by the contrast between different peoples and their customs, the states with their own principles?

There is, if I am not mistaken, a close analogy here with literature. No one spoke of a world literature at the time when French literature dominated Europe. Only since then has this idea been conceived, expressed, and popularized. Only since then have the leading peoples of Europe developed their own literature independently and often enough in competition with one another. If I may be allowed to compare a trivial situation with a serious one, might I remind you that company does not afford the same pleasure and profit when one person monopolizes and dominates the conversation, or where everyone, at a common level of mediocrity, says the same thing. We are satisfied only when many-sided personalities, themselves well developed, encounter one another on a higher common ground, or indeed create this meeting place by a lively mutual contact and enlargement. It would only be a disagreeable boredom if the different literatures should merge and lose their individuality. No, the union of all depends on the independence of each. They can thus stimulate one another in the most lively and continuing way, without any overpowering or injuring of the others.

It is no different with states and nations. A decisive positive dominance of one over the other would lead to the others' ruin. A merging of them all would destroy the essence of each. Out of separate and independent development will emerge the true harmony.]

# THE EPOCHS OF
# MODERN HISTORY

Ranke's many pupils included not only scholars and bureaucrats, but also several royal princes—among them Maximilian Joseph of Bavaria. Later, as king, Max Joseph carried on a policy of cultural benefaction initiated by his predecessor Ludwig I; but Ludwig's taste freely appreciated poetry, architecture, and beautiful women, and Max more soberly furthered the study of politics and history. In 1853 he wrote to his former professor: "it is my earnest desire to bring you to Munich—my object is the propagation of the historical method, and the foundation of an historical school, in Bavaria like that of north Germany," and signed it, "your old pupil." Ranke after some consideration finally declined the royal offer of a professorship (but he did use the occasion to extract a raise from the Prussian government). He felt too bound to Prussia, where he was on good terms with King Friedrich Wilhelm IV and had been named Royal Historiographer in 1841. But, on his recommendation, the Bavarian government appointed successively two of his students, Sybel and Giesebrecht, to the Munich chair of history. Ranke did accept the presidency of Max Joseph's newly established Historical Commission of the Bavarian Academy of Sciences, which became the major scholarly institution promoting the study of German history, publishing the Acts of the old Imperial Diet, the *Allgemeine Deutsche Biographie*, and the chronicles of the medieval German towns. Max continued to consult with Ranke, and in 1854 invited the Berlin scholar to come to deliver a special series of lectures to him personally.

They were given in a most unusual setting. Max had invited Ranke to his country estate in Berchtesgaden, and scholar and monarch strolled together through the Bavarian mountains, while a stenographer tagged unobtrusively behind. "I had," Ranke tells us, "not the trace of a book with me, and am curious to see what my rhapsodies will look like when they have been written out in clean copy. My history, I believe, has never brought such complete and wholehearted joy to me as at this place."

"The Epochs" take the form of a series of talks by Ranke, followed by questions from the king, and an ensuing discussion. It is a lengthy work, and this selection includes only the first lecture and part of the second. In these, Ranke takes up the prevalent nineteenth-century idea of progress, and argues that it is not demonstrable from history. Each era, notes Ranke, has its own values and must be studied for itself, not

as the antechamber to some later or higher period; "every epoch is immediate to God." The message is at the heart of the historicist position,
since the values of each era are unique, rooted in their own historical
context, and must be studied through history, rather than through present systems of thought. The problem for the historian is, not the relevance of a past period to the present, but rather the difficulty of seeing
each era from an objective universal perspective which approximates
the divine.

"The Epochs" as a whole offer an interesting counterpart to the essay
on "The Great Powers," twenty years later, and present a survey of modern history with Ranke's more mature consideration. Unfortunately,
there has never been an English translation of the whole. The following
selection was translated from the text in Ranke's *Weltgeschichte* IX,
Part 2, pp. 1–13, which was published posthumously by his student
Alfred Dove from Ranke's own copy of the lectures. It was compared
with the new German edition published from the original stenographer's
notes in the Munich archives by Walther Peter Fuchs as Volume II of
*Aus Werke und Nachlass, Über die Epochen der neueren Geschichte*
(Munich, 1971).

THE OBJECT OF THE PRESENT LECTURES requires that we understand two things: first, our starting point; and, secondly, the major
concepts. As far as a starting point is concerned, to place ourselves in
far-distant periods, in wholly remote circumstances, would lead us
too far afield from our purpose. These periods do exercise an influence
upon the present, but only indirectly. We must, in order not to lose
ourselves in purely historical detail, begin with Roman times, in
which we can find a combination of the most diverse historical forces.
Next, we must come to an agreement on the concept of progress in
general, and then on the way in which we can understand the role
played by leading ideas in combination with this concept.

### I. How the Concept of Progress
### Should Be Understood in History

If we wished to agree with many philosophers that the whole of humanity has developed from a given original state toward a positive
goal, we could present the matter two ways: either a general directing
will guides the development of the human race from one point to

another, or humanity contains an onward-marching progression of the spirit which necessarily drives it toward a defined goal. I should prefer to characterize both these ways as neither philosophically tenable nor historically provable. Philosophically, the first case eliminates human freedom and makes involuntary tools out of men. The other requires that mankind be God or nothing.

But these positions are also unprovable from an historical viewpoint. First of all, the majority of humanity still finds itself in its original state, at the very starting point. We may thus ask: "What is progress? Where is this progress of mankind to be seen?" There are elements of great historical development which have established themselves in the Latin and Germanic nations. At least here there is a gradual development of an evolving spiritual force. But one cannot find anywhere in all of history a similar historical pressure of the human spirit. This is a movement originating in early antiquity which has continued with a certain steadiness. But while there is only one system of peoples out of all humanity which took part in this general historical movement, there were, on the contrary, others which were excluded from it. Moreover, we cannot regard the nations included in this movement as enjoying a steady state of progress. For example, if we should look at Asia, we would see that civilization arose there, and that this part of the earth experienced several cultural epochs. But it was there that the tendency, on the whole, was retrogressive, for the most ancient ages of Asiatic culture were the most flourishing; the second and third periods, in which the Greek and Roman element dominated, were already not so significant; and with the invasion of the Mongol barbarians, civilization in Asia came completely to a halt.

An attempt has been made to counter these facts with the hypothesis of a geographical progression, but from the outset I must declare it a worthless position. How could it be maintained, for example, in the case of Peter the Great, that civilization made its progress around the globe, passing from east to west, but then returning again?

A second error to be avoided is the suggestion that all the branches of human experience and knowledge have developed throughout the centuries at the same rate. History shows us—to select only one example from modern times—that art flourished most in the fifteenth century and the first half of the sixteenth. In contrast, it declined most at the end of the seventeenth and during the first three quarters of the eighteenth century. Though even here there are moments when this art really stands out, they in no way justify the assertion that art ascends in the course of centuries to a higher power.

If we exclude any law of geographical, evolutionary determinism, and assume, on the other hand, as history teaches us, that peoples can go into decline, as developments once begun do not continue, we shall come to know better in what the continuous movement of mankind really consists. It refers to the great spiritual tendencies which dominate mankind, which arise alongside one another, and which fall into certain arranged patterns. But in these tendencies there is always one certain direction which prevails over the others and causes them to recede. Thus, for example, in the second half of the sixteenth century the religious element was so overpowering that the literary was forced into the background. By contrast, in the eighteenth century, utilitarian efforts at social and economic improvement occupied such wide territory that the arts and related fields had to yield. In every epoch of humanity certain great tendencies are expressed. Progress consists in this: in every period a certain movement of the human spirit is revealed, by which for the first time one or another tendency becomes pre-eminent and maintains itself in its own way.

To adopt a contrary point of view, asserting that progress consists in each epoch's raising the life of humanity to a higher power, and that every generation is more perfect than the preceding one, with the later always the preferred one, the earlier ones only porters for the following generations, would be a divine injustice. For such a preceding generation would have no significance in and for itself. It would become meaningful only insofar as it became the steppingstone to the next generation, and would not stand in any immediate relation to the divine. I would maintain that every epoch is immediate to God, and that its value consists, not in what follows it, but in its own existence, its own proper self. This value gives to the contemplation of history, and of individual lives in history, a unique delight, so that every epoch must be regarded as something valid in itself, fully deserving of such respect.

Thus the historian must direct his principal attention to the way in which the people of a certain period thought and lived; he will find that, apart from certain unchangeable main ideas, every epoch has its particular tendency and its own ideal. Though every era has its own justification and its own worth, we should not overlook the results which it causes. Secondly, the historian must discover the differences between the individual epochs, in order to consider the inner necessities affecting the way in which they succeed one another. A certain sort of progress in the process cannot be denied. But I would not want to argue that it moves forward in a straight line. It is more like a stream, whose course winds about in its own way. It seems to me—if I may dare the remark—that God, existing in no particular time, gazes over the whole historic humanity in its totality and finds them all equally valuable. Although the idea of the education of humanity has some truth in it, from God's point of view all the generations of mankind have equal rights, and this is the way the historian too must regard them.

We can assume in the areas of material interest an absolute progress, a highly decisive ascent which would require an enormous upset to bring about a decline. But we cannot find a similar progress in moral affairs. We know that moral ideas can make considerable advance; the same is true in cultural matters. Certain great works of art and literature are nowadays enjoyed by a much larger audience than before. But it would be laughably foolish to wish to be a greater epic poet than Homer or a greater writer of tragedies than Sophocles.

## II. What We Should Believe About the So-called Leading Ideas in History

Philosophers, especially those of the Hegelian school, have advanced the idea that the history of mankind proceeds like a logical process, with a thesis, antithesis, and synthesis spinning itself out in positives and negatives. But life becomes lost in Scholasticisms, and we have already rejected this view of history as a process of spirit evolving itself according to different logical categories. Such a position would hold that the idea is the only thing possessing an independent life; people would all be mere shadows or phantoms permeated by the idea. This doctrine, by which the World-Spirit causes events equally by deception and takes advantage of human suffering in order to gain its goal, is based upon an extremely unworthy conception of God and Man. It can lead only to pantheism. Mankind would thus be the evolving God who gives birth to Himself through a spiritual process which is part of His nature.

In contrast, I would apply the term "guiding ideas" to the dominant tendencies in each century. These tendencies can be only described, not ultimately defined in a concept. Otherwise, we should be back at the position which I rejected earlier.

The historian must unravel the great tendencies of the centuries and unroll the history of mankind, which is precisely the whole network of these different tendencies. From the viewpoint of the divine idea, I can think of the matter only this way: humanity contains within itself an endless variety of developments which come to view from time to time, according to laws which are unknown to us, more mysterious, and greater than we can conceive.

## DISCUSSION

KING MAX: You have spoken about moral progress. Did you have the interior progress of the single person in mind?

RANKE: No, I meant the progress of the human race. The individual, on the other hand, must always strive to attain a higher moral level.

KING MAX: But if humanity is composed of individuals, the question arises whether the efforts of individuals to raise themselves to a higher moral plane would not also bring about a progress of all humanity.

RANKE: The individual person dies. He has a temporary existence; humanity, an eternal one. I accept progress in material things, because here one thing begets another; but it is otherwise in connection with morals. I believe that the real moral greatness of any generation is equal to every other's, and that in moral greatness none has a higher power. We cannot, for example, surpass the moral greatness of the ancient world. It often happens in the cultural world that there is an inverse relationship between intensive growth and extensive greatness. One could compare our contemporary literature with the classics.

KING MAX:    But should it be assumed that Providence, without violating the free will of individual persons, sets humanity as a whole toward a certain goal, leading mankind, though not forcefully, toward it?

RANKE:    This is a cosmopolitical hypothesis which cannot be proven by history. We have in its favor the word of Holy Writ, which tells us that there will be one flock and one shepherd. But up to now this has not been demonstrated in the course of world history. We can use for evidence the history of Asia which fell again into barbarism after periods of the greatest flowering of civilization.

KING MAX:    But are there not now a greater number of individuals who have attained a higher cultural development than previously?

RANKE:    I concede that, but not as a principle. For history teaches us that many peoples are not capable of building a civilization, and that early epochs are often more culturally developed than later ones. France in the middle of the seventeenth century was much more moral and more cultivated than at the end of the eighteenth century. As I have said, a greater expansion of moral ideas may assert itself, but only within defined circles. From the overall human point of view, it seems apparent that the idea of humanity, which is historically represented only in the great nations, will gradually come to include all mankind, and that this would be an inner moral progress. History does not oppose this viewpoint, but neither does it prove it. We must be especially careful to avoid making this view a principle of history.

Our task remains: only the study of the object.

## SECOND LECTURE

The concept of progress, with which our introductory considerations are chiefly occupied, is, as we have seen, not applicable to different things. It cannot be applied to the connections between the centuries in general. That means that we may not say that one century is more useful than another. Furthermore, the concept cannot be applied to the productions of genius, in art, poetry, science, and government, for all these have an immediate relation to the divine. They are a part of time, but their real productiveness is independent of what precedes and follows. So, for example, Thucydides, who is the real originator of historical writing, still cannot be surpassed.

Even less can we accept progress in the individual moral or religious existence, since this also has an immediate connection with divinity. One can allow only that earlier moral conceptions were imperfect; but since the appearance of Christianity, and with it true morality and true religion, no further progress can take place in these matters. It is true that the Greeks held certain national ideas, such as the right to take revenge, which were later refined by Christianity. But the essential part of Christianity was not prepared from earlier imperfect conditions, but itself was a sudden divine manifestation. Thus all great productions of genius bear the character of immediate enlightenment. After Plato, there can be no more Plato; and little as I mistake the contribution of Schelling to philosophy, I do not believe that he has surpassed Plato. Plato was unequalled in his language and diction and, above all, in his poetical form. But it cannot be denied that Schelling had a much greater mass of material, inherited from his predecessors, with which to work.

In contrast, we may accept a progress in everything which is related to the knowledge of or control of nature. The former was in its infancy in ancient times; nor can the ancients be compared with us in the latter. This is further related to what we call expansion. The expansion of moral and religious ideas—above all, the idea of humanity —is caught up in an incessant progress, and wherever a central point of civilization exists, it has the tendency to expand outward in all directions. But not in such a way that we could say that progress takes place in every such place without pause. Therefore progress is not determined, in more material connections, by the formation and application of the exact sciences, or by the rise of the different nations or individuals toward the ideas of humanity and civilization.

But it is questionable whether progress actually takes place in the individual humanities such as philosophy and politics. I must confess that for me the most ancient philosophy, as found in Plato and Aristotle, is sufficient. In a formal sense these two have not been superseded, and even in material respects the more modern philosophers continue to turn again to Aristotle. The same is true of politics. The general basic laws were stated with the greatest authority by the ancients, no matter how much the following ages have enriched them with the experience gained in applied politics. Politics, which affects today, rests upon the historically given conditions of our time. Such questions as those about the constitutional or Estate-type monarchy are fully justified, I think. But they depend upon given circumstances. Thus no one could insist that Estates are already included in the idea of monarchy. More modern times have the advantage over previous periods only in this: that they have a greater number of experiences in the political field at their command. So too the question of whether sovereignty is possessed by the prince is, not solved by political science, but determined by party organizations in an historical manner.

What I have said about politics is also true for the writing of history. No one can, as we mentioned, have a pretension to be a greater historian than Thucydides. On the other hand, I have the pretension to attempt to achieve something different from the historical writing of the ancients. For our history flows more deeply, more fully, than theirs, because we seek to draw other powers into history which include the whole life of the people and, in a word, because we seek to comprehend history as a unity. . . .

# V

# Individual Personalities in History: Three Portraits

Although many historians have had the ability to delineate character and to produce in the course of their narratives striking portraits of the historical figures of their period, this kind of biography occupied a special place in Ranke's approach to writing history. Great personalities had an interest for Ranke which extended beyond the particulars of their character. As was noted in the introduction to this collection, the great figures in history became important because they embodied in their life's work the leading ideas which guided the course of history from one epoch to another. As such they were the nodal points of historical change. Acknowledging the influence which the prevailing tendencies of history had upon individuals, Ranke still insisted on personal autonomy: "human freedom is always taken into account; history is performed in scenes of freedom." But not everything in the life of the individual historical figure was of interest to the historian. He distinguished between the private and historical aspects of a personality. "The first consists in the general condition of his life, the family, the special studies and professions to which he is dedicated, the office in which he serves, his inborn temperament. The second is completely different; it consists of the relationship which he assumes toward the great questions of his century as he engages with and acts upon them, and in the effect which he is able to give his chosen ideas; it is the course of his life in the spiritual sphere." For certain individuals this second aspect is historically decisive. As Ranke notes in his *History of England*, "the greatest thing which can happen to a person is that in defending his own interests he defends the universal. Then his personal existence is enlarged into a world historical moment." Ranke once visited Madame Tussaud's wax works in London and found the elaborately dressed replicas of such historical personalities as Elizabeth I, Henry VIII, and Napoleon disappointing. "It is somewhat spectral," he complained. "It looks like history but is really the contrary of history, for only the external life appears before us." For Ranke reality and the object of history remained the spiritual and moral tendencies which were to be discerned within events and between events, but especially in the great personalities of history. They were essential: for "it is not the universal tendencies which determine the progress of history; they always require great personalities to bring them into effect." Thus Ranke's use of biography is highly selective and limited to those aspects of his characters which make them historically significant.

In his portraits we see a quick delineation of character, with a sparseness of detail, and a concentration on those features which reveal their relationship to universal tendencies of their age. Biography is held in tight rein, always subservient to the larger purpose of his historical narrative. Yet these vanished kings and cardinals and ministers illumine his histories with rare flashes of warmth and insight which reveal Ranke's delight in and appreciation of historical persons and institutions for their own sake as well as for their larger role in world history. The admixture produces a unique sort of historical biography, which is sampled in this section.

The first selection is a portrait of Pope Paul IV; the second, a description of the encounter of Emperor Charles V with the German princes at the 1530 Diet of Augsburg; the third, an account of Cardinal Richelieu.

# POPE PAUL IV

Ranke's description of Pope Paul IV is one of many high points in his *History of the Popes*, the chief fruit of his prolonged researches in Italy, published in three volumes between 1834 and 1836. This was the work which made his international reputation; in it we see a full mastery of materials from the archives of Vienna, Florence, Venice, and the great noble families of Rome—for as a Protestant he had been refused access to the resources of the Vatican—combined with a newly attained maturity in his writing and in his analysis of character. It is no accident that the *Popes* should have been composed during the years when he was completing his intellectual formation as an historian, working as editor of the *Historisch-Politische Zeitschrift*, and initiating the historical seminar at the University of Berlin. For Ranke personally, these were years full of creativity and energy, and these same qualities are captured for us in his narration of the *Popes*.

Historians are often fascinated by similar personalities they discover in history; yet it would be hard to find a character more unlike the methodical Ranke than Giovanni Pietro Caraffa, Pope Paul IV. Ranke pictures for us this fiery nature, this contradictory man, indulgent and terrible, burning with zeal for politics and religion. The portrait unfolds the personality but transcends biography. "An Italian or Roman or Catholic would enter into the subject in a spirit very different from mine," Ranke remarked. He was the first not only to attempt to view the papacy from a neutral position, but also to understand it as one of the great historical institutions of Europe. Torn by conflicting loyalties to his family, to his country, and to his Church, Paul IV mirrors the contradictions of the Renaissance papacy which both led to the Reformation and infused the spirit of counter reform. Ranke coins the concept of Counter Reformation in this work, and shows its growth in the work of Paul III, Paul IV, and their successors. Paradoxically, he shows how the efforts of the great zealot Caraffa only furthered the spread of the Protestant faith.

The text in this selection is adapted from Elizabeth Foster's translation of Ranke's *The Popes of Rome: Their Church and State* (London, 1847), pp. 213–36. The German text is available in SW 37:183–202.

FREQUENT MENTION has already been made of this pontiff, who is that same Caraffa, the founder of the Theatines, the restorer of the

Inquisition, and the speaker who so essentially contributed to the confirmation of the ancient doctrines at the Council of Trent. If there were a party whose purpose it was to reinstate Catholicism in all its strictness, not only was it a member, but the founder and chief, of that party who now ascended the papal throne. Paul IV had already completed his seventy-ninth year, but his deep-set eyes still retained all the fires of youth; he was extremely tall and thin, walked with rapid steps, and seemed all nerve and muscle. His personal habits were subjected to no rule or order; frequently he spent the night in study, and slept during the day—woe then to the servant who should enter his apartment before his bell had rung. It was his custom in all things to follow the impulse of the moment; but this impulse was regulated by a mood of mind formed by the practice of a long life, and had become second nature. He seemed to acknowledge no duty, no occupation, other than the restoration of the Catholic faith to its primitive authority. Characters of this description arise from time to time and are occasionally to be seen even in the present day. Their perceptions of life and the world are gained from a single point of view; the peculiar disposition of their mind is so powerful that all their opinions are tinctured and governed by it; indefatigable speakers, they derive a certain freshness in their manner from the earnestness of their souls, and the system of thought which, as by a kind of fatality, informs and rules their whole being is poured forth in an inexhaustible stream. How powerfully such men act on all around them, when they are placed in a position in which their activity is in perfect harmony with their views and sentiments, and the power to act is coupled with the will! What might men not expect from Paul IV, whose views and opinions never had endured either concession or compromise, but were ever carried out eagerly to their utmost consequences, now that he was raised to the supreme dignity! He himself was amazed that he had reached this point—he who had in no manner conciliated a single member of the conclave, and from whom nothing was to be expected but the extreme of severity. He believed that his election had been determined, not by the cardinals, but by God Himself, who had chosen him for the accomplishment of His own purposes.

"We do promise and swear," he said in the bull which he published on the occasion of his accession to the Holy See, "to make it our first concern that the reform of the universal Church, and of the Roman Court, be at once begun." The day of his coronation was highlighted by the promulgation of edicts respecting monasteries and the religious orders. He sent two monks from Monte Cassino to Spain, with instructions to re-establish the discipline of the convents which had become lax and neglected. He appointed a congregation for the promotion of reforms in general; this consisted of three classes, in each of which were 8 cardinals, 15 prelates, and 50 learned men of different ranks.

The articles which they were to discuss, in relation to the appointments to clerical offices and collations to benefices, were submitted to the universities. It is obvious that the new pope proceeded with great earnestness in the work of reform. The spiritual tendency which had hitherto affected only the lower ranks of the hierarchy now seemed to gain possession of the papal throne itself, and promised to assume the exclusive guidance of all affairs during the pontificate of Paul IV.

But now came the question of the part which he would take in relation to the general movements of the political world.

The principal direction which is once given to a government, and which gradually identifies itself with its very existence, is not readily susceptible of change.

A desire to deliver themselves from the heavy preponderance of Spain must always have been uppermost in the minds of the popes; and at the accession of Paul the moment seemed to have come when this wish appeared to be within the possibility of realization. The war proceeding, as we have seen, from the movements of the Farnesi was the most unfortunate one ever undertaken by Charles V. He was closely pressed in the Netherlands; Germany had deserted his interests; Italy was no longer faithful to him; he could not rely even on the Houses of Este and Gonzaga; he himself was ill, and weary of life. I question whether any pontiff, not immediately attached to the imperial party, could have found strength to withstand the temptations presented by this state of things.

In the case of Paul IV they were more than commonly powerful. Born in the year 1476, he had seen his native Italy in all the unrestrained freedom of her fifteenth century, and his very soul clung to this remembrance. He would sometimes compare the Italy of that

period to a well-tuned instrument of four strings—these being Naples,
Milan, Venice, and the Papal States. He would then utter maledic-
tions on the memory of Alfonso and Louis the Moor: "Lost and un-
hallowed souls," as he said, "whose discords had disturbed that
harmony." That from their time the Spaniard should have become
master in the land was a thought which he could in no way learn to
bear. The House of Caraffa, whence he derived his birth, was allied
with the French party, and had frequently taken up arms against the
Castilians and Catalonians. In 1528 they again joined the French;
and it was Giovanni Pietro Caraffa who advised Paul III to seize Naples
in 1547. To this party spirit came other causes in aid: Caraffa had
constantly affirmed that Charles favored the Protestants out of jealousy
of the pope, and that "the successes of those heretics were attributable
to none other than the emperor." Charles knew Caraffa well: he once
expelled him from the council formed for the administration of affairs
in Naples, and would never permit him to hold peaceful possession
of his ecclesiastical employments within that kingdom; moreover, he
had made earnest remonstrance against Caraffa's declamations in the
consistory. All these things, as may readily be supposed, did but increase the virulence of the pope's enmity. He detested the emperor as
a Neapolitan and an Italian, as a Catholic and as pope: there existed
in his soul no passions other than his zeal for reform of the Church
and his hatred of Charles.

Paul's first act was to lighten various imposts and to permit the
importation of wheat. A statue was erected to him for these benefits,
and it was not without a certain sense of self-complacency that he
viewed this; while in the midst of his splendid court, and surrounded
by a glittering body of Neapolitan nobles, proffering him the most
obsequious obedience, he received the homage of ambassadors who
came crowding from all countries to his presence. But scarcely had he
felt himself well-seated on the pontifical chair than he began a series
of disputes with the emperor. The monarch had complained to the
cardinals of his party that a pope so inimical to himself had been
chosen; his adherents held suspicious meetings; some of them even
carried off certain ships from Cività Vecchia which had previously
been taken from them by the French. The pope at once breathed
fire and flames. Such of his vassals, and the cardinals, as were imperial-

ists, he arrested instantly, confiscating the whole property of those who fled. Nor was this enough. That alliance with France which Paul III could never resolve on completing was entered into with little hesitation by Paul IV. He declared that the emperor designed to "finish him by a sort of mental fever," but that he, Paul, was "determined on an open fight. With the help of France he would yet free this poor Italy from the tyrannies of Spain, and did not despair of seeing two French princes ruling in Naples and Milan." He would sit for long hours over the thick black fiery wine of Naples, his usual drink (it was of a sort called mangiaguerra, champ-the-war), and pour forth torrents of stormy eloquence against those schismatics and heretics, those accursed of God, that evil generation of Jews and Moors, that scum of the world, and other titles equally complimentary, bestowed with unsparing liberality on everything Spanish; but he consoled himself with the promise that "Thou shalt tread upon the lion and adder; the young lion and the dragon shalt thou trample under foot." The time had now come when Emperor Charles and King Philip should receive the punishment due their iniquities. He, the pope, would inflict it, and would free Italy from their grasp. If others would not listen to or support him, the future world should at least have to tell how an old Italian, so near his grave, and who would rather have been employed in preparing for it, had entertained these lofty purposes. We shall not enter into the details of the negotiations which he carried on under the influence of these feelings. When the French concluded a truce with Spain, unmindful of an agreement which they had entered into with him, Paul sent his nephew, Carlo Caraffa, to France, where the different parties contending for power in that country were gradually gained over to his interests. The Montmorencies and the Guises, the wife of the French king and his mistress, were equally persuaded to aid the pontiff in promoting a new outbreak of hostilities. Paul secured a vigorous Italian ally as well in the Duke of Ferrara; nothing less was talked of than completely revolutionizing Italy. Neopolitan and Florentine exiles filled the Curia; their restoration to their homes now seemed imminent; the papal fiscal instituted a legal process against Emperor Charles and King Philip, in which the excommunication of those princes, and the release of their subjects from their oaths of allegiance, were roundly threatened. The Florentines always declared that they held positive evidence of a design to include the House of the Medici in the downfall of Spanish power. Everywhere active preparations were made for war, and the entire character of the century appeared about to undergo change, and to become matter of question.

But meanwhile how different a position was this pontificate assuming from that which it had been expected to take up! All purposes of reform were set aside for the struggles of war, and these last entailed consequences of a totally opposite character.

The pontiff, who, as cardinal, had most sternly opposed the abuses of nepotism, and had denounced them, even to his own peril, was now seen to abandon himself entirely to the weakness. His nephew, Carlo Caraffa, who had passed his entire life amid the excesses and license of camps, was now raised to the rank of cardinal, though Paul himself had often declared of him that "his arm was dyed in blood to the elbow." Carlo had found means to win over his superannuated relative; he contrived occasionally to be surprised by him in seeming prayer before the crucifix and apparently suffering agonies of remorse. But the uncle was further propitiated by the virulent enmity of his nephew toward the Spaniards; this was their true bond of union. Carlo Caraffa had taken military service with the emperor in Germany, but complained that he had met only with neglect as his reward. A prisoner, from whom he had expected a large ransom, had been taken from him; nor had he been allowed to hold possession of a priory belonging to the order of Malta, to which he had been nominated. All these things had awakened his hatred and made him thirst for vengeance. This state of feeling Paul allowed to stand in the place of all the virtues Carlo was lacking; he could find no words eloquent enough to praise him, declaring that the papal seat had never possessed a more efficient servant; he made over to him the greater part, not only of the civil, but even of the ecclesiastical, administration, and was perfectly satisfied that he be regarded as the author of whatever acts of favor were received from the court.

On his other nephews the pontiff would not for some time bestow a glance of kindness; it was not until they had indicated their participation in his anti-Spanish mania that they were received into his grace. Never could anyone have anticipated what he did next. Declaring that the Colonnas, "those incorrigible rebels against God and the Church," however frequently deprived of their castles, had always managed to regain them, he now resolved that this should be amended: he would give those fortresses to vassals who would know how to hold them. Thereupon he divided the possessions of the House of Colonna between his nephews, making the elder Duke of Palliano and the younger Marquis of Montebello. The cardinals remained silent when he announced these purposes in their assembly; they bent their heads down and fixed their eyes to the earth. The Caraffas now indulged in the most ambitious project: the daughters of their family would marry into the family of the French king, or at least into the ducal House of Ferrara; the sons thought of nothing less than the possession of Siena. To one who spoke jestingly concerning the jeweled cap of a child of their house, the mother of the nephews replied, "We should be talking rather of crowns than of caps."

And indeed everything was now dependent on the events of the war which then broke out, but which certainly assumed no very promising aspect even from the beginning.

After the act of the fiscal alluded to earlier, the Duke of Alva had pressed forward from the Neapolitan territory into the Papal States. He was accompanied by the Roman vassals, whose confederates also bestirred themselves. The papal garrison was driven out of Nettuno, and the troops of the Colonnas recalled. Alva seized Frosinone, Agnani, Tivoli in the mountains, and Ostia on the sea. Rome was thus invested on both sides.

The pope had placed his reliance first on his Romans and reviewed them in person. They marched from the Campofiore, 340 columns armed with harquebuses, 250 with pikes. In each rank stood nine men admirably appointed, presenting a most imposing aspect, and commanded by officers who were exclusively of noble birth. These troops passed before the Castel Sant' Angelo, which saluted them with its artillery, to the Piazza San Pietro, where the pontiff had stationed himself at a window with his nephews, and as each *caparione* and standard-bearer passed, His Holiness bestowed his blessing. All this made a very impressive show, but these were not the men by whom the city was to be defended. When the Spaniards approached near the walls, a false alarm, occasioned by a small body of horse, was sufficient to throw them into such perfect confusion that not one man was found remaining by his colors. The pope saw that he must look elsewhere for effective aid, and after a time Pietro Strozzi brought him the troops who were serving before Siena. With these he succeeded in recovering Tivoli and Ostia, thus averting the most imminent danger.

But what a war this was!

There are moments in the history of the world when it would seem that the actions of men are influenced by motives in direct opposition to the principles and ideas which usually govern their lives and conduct.

The Duke of Alva might, in the first instance, have conquered Rome with very little difficulty; but his uncle, Cardinal Giacomo, reminded him of the unhappy end to which all had come who had taken part in the conquest under Bourbon. Alva, being a good Catholic, conducted the war with the utmost discretion; he fought the pope, but did not cease to pay him reverence; he would fain take the sword from His Holiness, but had no desire for the renown of a Roman conqueror. His soldiers complained that they were led against a mere vapor, a mist and smoke which annoyed them, but which they could neither lay hold of nor stifle at its source.

And who were those who defended the pope against such good Catholics? The most effective among them were Germans, and Protestants to a man! They amused themselves with the saintly images on the highways; they laughed at the Mass in the churches, utterly disregarded the fast days, and did innumerable things for which, at any other time, the pope would have punished them with death. I find that Carlo Caraffa even established a very close intimacy with that great Protestant leader, the Margrave Albert of Brandenburg.

Contradictions more perfect, a contrast more complete, than those displayed by these circumstances, could scarcely be imagined. On the one side, we have the most fervent spirit of Catholicism, which was at least exemplified in the leader (how different his proceedings were from those of the old Bourbon times!); on the other, that secular tendency of the papacy, by which even Paul IV, however earnestly he condemned it, was seized and borne forward. Thus, it came to pass that the followers of his faith were attacking him, while it was by heretics and seceders that he found himself defended! But the former preserved their allegiance, even while opposing his power; the latter displayed their hostility to and contempt for his person even while bearing arms to defend him.

It was not until the French auxiliaries crossed the Alps that the contest really began; these consisted of 10,000 foot and a less numerous, but very brilliant, body of cavalry. Their leader would most willingly have directed his force against Milan, which he believed to be unprepared for defense, but he was unable to resist the impulse by which the Caraffas forced him toward Naples. The Caraffas were fully confident of finding numberless adherents in their own country, counted on the assistance of the exiles, and hoped for the rising of their party—if not throughout the kingdom, yet certainly in the Abruzzi and around Aquila and Montorio, where their ancestors, on both the paternal and the maternal side, had always exercised an important influence.

It was clear that matters must now arrive at a crisis, in whatever manner this might terminate. The papal power had too often been excited into hostility against the Spanish predominance not eventually to burst forth without restraint.

The pope and his nephews were determined that matters should proceed to a climax. Caraffa had not only accepted the aid of the Protestants; he had even made proposals to Suleiman I. These were to the effect that the Turkish sovereign should abstain from prosecuting his wars in Hungary, and throw himself with all his force on the two Sicilies. Thus a pontiff was entreating the help of infidels against a Catholic monarch.

In April 1557, the papal troops crossed the Neapolitan frontier; Holy Thursday was highlighted by the conquest and atrocious pillage of Compli, which was full of treasure, part belonging to the town, but also much carried there for safety. This done, Guise also crossed the Tronto, and besieged Civitella.

But he found the kingdom fully prepared to baffle his efforts. Alva knew well that there would be no insurrection among the people so long as he should retain the upper hand in the country; he had received a large grant of money from a parliament of the barons. Queen Bona of Poland, of the ancient family of Aragon, and a bitter enemy of the French, who had shortly before arrived in her duchy of Bari with much treasure, supplied him with half a million scudi. The ecclesiastical revenues which should have been sent to Rome he poured into his military chest instead, seizing even the gold and silver of the churches, and the bells of the city of Benevento—all appropriated to his own purposes. Thus furnished, he proceeded to fortify the towns of the Neapolitan frontier, as well as those of the Roman territory which still remained in his hands. His army was composed in the usual manner of Germans, Spaniards, and Italians, but was an extremely formidable one. He also raised Neapolitan centuries under the command of the native nobles. Civitella was bravely defended by Count Santafiore, who had succeeded in rousing the inhabitants to cooperate actively, and even to repel an attempt to take the place by storm.

While the Kingdom of Naples thus held firmly to King Philip, and displayed only devotion to his service, the assailants were weakened by animosities and dissensions. French and Italians, Guise and Montebello—all were in the utmost discord. Guise complained that the pope did not fulfill his part in the contract between them, and neglected to send him the promised supplies. When the Duke of Alva appeared with his army in the Abruzzi, toward the middle of May, Guise found it advisable to raise the siege, and to retreat across the Tronto; operations were then again transferred to the Roman territories. And now was seen a war in which both sides advanced and then retreated, and invested towns only to resign them—in short, made great movements, but on one occasion only did they come to a serious engagement.

Marc Antonio Colonna made demonstrations against Palliano, which had been taken from him by the pope; seeing this, Giulio Orsini hurried to its relief with provisions and troops; 3,000 Swiss had arrived in Rome under the command of a colonel from Unterwalden. The pope received them with great delight, decorated their officers with gold chains and knightly titles, and declared that they were a legion of angels sent by God on his behalf. These were the troops who, together with a few companies of Italian cavalry and infantry, marched under the command of Giulio Orsini. They were met by the forces of Marc Antonio Colonna, and once more there ensued one of those bold battles in the manner of the Italian wars of 1494–1531, the papal troops against those of the empire, a Colonna opposing an Orsini; the German *Landsknechts*, under their distinguished leaders, Caspar von Feltz and Hans Walther, stood face to face, as they had so often, with their ancient antagonists the Swiss. Once again the combatants on both sides arrayed themselves for a cause in which neither felt the slightest interest, but for which they nonetheless fought with determined bravery. Hans Walther at length—"tall and strong," the Spaniards said, "as a giant"—threw himself into the midst of a Swiss company. With a pistol in one hand and his naked sword in the other, he rushed upon the standard-bearer, whom he brought down, shooting him in the side, at the same moment as he dealt him a fatal blow on the head. The entire troop fell upon him, but his *Landsknechts* were already at hand for his support. The Swiss were completely broken and dispersed, their banners, on which had been inscribed in large letters "Defenders of the Faith and of the Holy See," were trampled in the dust, and of the eleven captains who went forth, their commander led only two back to Rome.

While this miniature war was in progress here, the great armies were in action on the frontier of the Netherlands. The battle of St. Quentin ensued, in which the Spaniards gained a complete victory. In France men even wondered that they did not at once press forward to Paris, which at that moment they might certainly have taken.

Hereupon Henry II wrote to Guise: "I hope," he remarked, "that the pope will do as much for me in my need as I did for him in his straits." So little could Paul now hope from the aid of the French that it was he, rather, who was called on to help them. Guise declared "that no chains would now avail to keep him in Italy," and he instantly hurried with all his forces to the aid of his embarrassed sovereign.

No force remaining which could pose any obstacle to the imperialists and troops of Colonna, they advanced toward Rome, whose inhabitants once more saw themselves threatened with conquest and plunder. Their condition was all the more desperate since they had little less to fear from their defenders than from their enemies. For many nights they were compelled to keep lights burning in every window and through all the streets. A skirmishing party of Spaniards which had reached the gates was frightened back by this demonstration, which was, however, a mere precaution against the papal troops; everyone murmured. The Romans wished their pope in his grave a thousand times, and demanded that the Spanish army be admitted by a formal capitulation.

So far did Paul IV permit his affairs to come. It was not until every enterprise had completely failed, until his allies were beaten, his States for the most part invested by the enemy, and his capital a second time menaced with ruin, that he would humble himself to sue for peace.

This was accorded by the Spaniards in the same spirit in which they had acted throughout the war. They restored all the fortresses and cities of the Church which had been taken, and even promised compensation for Palliano, which the Caraffas had lost. Alva came to Rome; with the most profound reverence he now kissed the foot of his conquered enemy, the sworn adversary of his king and nation, and was heard to say that never had he feared the face of man as he had that of the pontiff.

This peace seemed in every way favorable to the papal interest; it was, nevertheless, utterly fatal to all the projects hitherto cherished by the papacy. Any further attempt to throw off the Spanish yoke must now be abandoned, and, accordingly, none such has ever (in the old sense and manner) been brought forward again. The influence of the Spaniards in Milan and Naples proved unassailable. Their allies were more powerful than ever. There had been hope among the Caraffas of expelling Duke Cosmo from Florence; but this prince not only had held firm his grasp, but had seized Siena, and was now the possessor of an important sovereignty. By the restitution of Placentia, the Farnesi had been gained over to Philip II. Marc Antonio Colonna had earned himself a brilliant reputation, and had fully restored the ancient luster of his family. For the pontiff there was nothing left but to resign himself to his position of affairs. Bitter as this was for Paul IV, he yet felt that he must submit—with what feelings it is not difficult to imagine. When Philip II was on some occasion called his friend, he replied, "Yes, my friend who kept me beleaguered, and who thought to have my soul!" It is true that in the presence of strangers he compared Philip to the prodigal son of the Gospel, but in the circle of his intimates he took care to mark his estimation of those pontiffs who had designed to raise the kings of France to the imperial throne; for others he had no praise. His sentiments were what they had always been, but the force of circumstances controlled him. There was nothing more to be hoped for, still less to be undertaken; he dared not even bemoan himself, unless in the closest secrecy.

Once an event is indeed accomplished, it is altogether useless for a man to struggle against its consequences. Even Paul IV realized this, and after a certain time his thoughts took another direction; he experienced a reaction which was of most effective importance, whether in regard to his own administration or to the general transformation brought about in the papal position and system.

Other pontiffs had promoted and favored their nephews because of family affection or mere selfish ambition to elevate the House they sprang from. Paul's nepotism had a totally different origin. His nephews were favored because they assisted his efforts against Spain, and because in this contest he considered them his natural allies; once that was over, the utility of the nephews was at an end. It is only by success that a man is maintained in a position of great eminence, more especially if it is not acquired in a manner altogether legitimate. Cardinal Caraffa had undertaken an embassy to King Philip, principally to promote the interests of his own House, for which he desired to receive the compensation promised in lieu of Palliano. He returned without having accomplished any material purpose, and from that time on the pope became ever colder and colder toward him. The cardinal soon perceived that he could no longer decide, as he had hitherto, who should or should not be about the person of his uncle; no more could he exclude those who were inimical to himself; and rumors reached the pontiff, by which his unfavorable impressions of former days were revived. A serious illness seized the cardinal once, and on this occasion his uncle paid him an unexpected visit, and found certain persons with him whose reputation was of the worst possible character. "Old people," Paul said, "are mistrustful, and there I saw things which opened a wide field before me." It is obvious that only very slight provocation was needed to arouse the storm within him, and this was presented by an occurrence otherwise of little importance. In the New Year's night of 1559, there was a tumult in the streets, in which the young Cardinal Monte, that favorite of Pope Julius's mentioned before, drew his sword. This was related to the pontiff the very next morning, and he felt greatly offended with Cardinal Caraffa for not bringing the matter to his attention himself. The pope waited some days, but finding no word said, he then expressed his displeasure. The court, ever delighted with change, caught eagerly at this mark of disgrace. The Florentine ambassador, on whom the Caraffas had in-flicted mortifications innumerable, now made his way to the pope's presence, and uttered the most bitter complaints. The Marchese della Valle, a member of the pontiff's family, but one who had never been allowed access to him, found means to get a note placed in his breviary, in which certain of his nephew's misdeeds were described; "if His Holiness should desire further explanations," said this paper, "he has but to sign his name." The pope gave the required signature, and the promised information did not fail to appear. Thus, well provided with causes for resentment, Paul appeared on January 9 at the assembly of the Inquisition. He spoke first of that nocturnal riot, reproved Cardinal Monte with extreme severity, and repeatedly thundered forth "Re-form! Reform!" The cardinals, usually so silent, this time had the courage to speak. "Holy Father," said Cardinal Pacheco, interrupting the sovereign, "reform must first of all begin among ourselves!" The pope was silenced. Those words struck him to the heart, and the half-formed convictions which had gradually been gaining power within him were at once changed into palpable certainty; he said nothing more of Cardinal Monte's offenses, but shut himself up in his apartment, burning with rage, and thinking only of his nephews. Giving immedi-ate direction that no order proceeding from Cardinal Caraffa should be complied with, he sent to demand that minister's papers. Cardinal Vitellozzo Vitelli, who was believed to be in possession of all the Caraffa secrets, was immediately summoned, and compelled to swear that he would disclose all he knew. Camillo Orsini was called from his palace in the Campagna, for the same purpose. Those of the more austere party, who had long remarked the proceedings of the nephews with disapproval, now made themselves heard. Don Geremia, the old Theatine, who was held to be a saint, passed long hours with His Holiness, who was made acquainted with circumstances which he had never suspected, and which excited equally his detestation and horror. He fell into a state of pitiable agitation, could neither eat nor sleep, and passed ten days consumed by fever, resulting from distress of mind. At length he was resolved; and then was seen to occur an event forever memorable: a pope, with self-inflicted violence, tearing asun-der the ties which bound him to his kindred. On January 27 a consistory was summoned, in which the evil lives of his nephews were denounced with passionate emotion by the grieving pontiff, who called God and the world to bear witness that he had never known of these misdoings, but been constantly deceived by those around him. He deprived the accused of all their offices, and condemned them to banishment, together with their families. The mother of the nephews, 70 years old, bent with age, and sinking beneath her infirmities, entreated for them, throwing herself at the pope's feet as he entered the palace; but, though she herself was blameless, he passed her by with harsh words. The young Marchesa Montebello arrived in Rome from Naples at this time; she found her palace closed against her; at the inns they refused to receive her; she went from door to door in the rainy night, and could find no shelter, until in a remote quarter, to which no order had been sent, an innkeeper was found who permitted her to take refuge beneath his roof. Cardinal Caraffa vainly offered to constitute himself the pope's prisoner, and demanded to have his conduct investigated. Paul commanded the Swiss guard to repel not only him, but all who, having been in his service, should venture to approach the palace. He made but one exception: this was in favor of the young man, the son of Montorio, whom he loved greatly and made cardinal in his eighteenth year. This youth he permitted to remain about his person, and to take part in his devotional exercises; but he was never allowed to name his banished family, still less to implore their forgiveness; he dared hold not even the slightest intercourse with his father. The misfortunes of his House affected him all the more painfully from this restraint, and the suffering which he was not permitted to express in words was yet manifest in his face, and legible in his whole person.

And would it not be supposed that occurrences of this character must react on the mind of the pontiff?

He proceeded as though nothing had happened. Immediately after having pronounced sentence against his kindred with stormy eloquence in the consistory, he betook himself to other business, and while most of the cardinals were paralyzed in fear and astonishment, the pontiff betrayed no emotion. The foreign ambassadors were amazed by the coolness of his demeanor. "In the midst of changes so unexpected and so complete," they remarked, "surrounded by ministers and servants all new and strange, he maintains himself steadfastly, unbending and imperturbable; he feels no compassion, and seems not even to retain a remembrance of his ruined House." Henceforth it was to a totally different passion that he surrendered the guidance of his life.

This change was most certainly of the highest importance and of ever memorable effect. His hatred of the Spaniards, and the hope of becoming the liberator of Italy, had hurried even Paul IV into designs and practices utterly worldly, led him to the endowment of his kinsmen with the lands of the Church, caused the elevation of a mere soldier to the administration even of ecclesiastical affairs, and plunged him into deadly feuds and sanguinary hostilities. Events had compelled him to abandon that hope, to suppress that hatred, and then his eyes were gradually opened to the reprehensible conduct of those about him. Against these offenders, after a painful struggle with himself, Paul and his stern justice prevailed. From that hour his early plans of reformation were resumed. He began to reign in the manner which had at first been expected from him. And now, with that impetuous energy which he had previously displayed in his enmities and in the conduct of his wars, he turned to the reform of the State and, above all, to that of the Church.

All secular offices, from the highest to the lowest, were transferred to other hands. The existing podestas and governors lost their places, and the manner in which this was effected was occasionally very singular. In Perugia, for example, the newly appointed governor arrived during the night; without waiting for daylight, he caused the *anziani* to be called together, produced his credentials, and commanded them forthwith to arrest their former governor, who was present. From time immemorial, there had been no pope who governed without nepotism: Paul IV now showed this example. The places hitherto monopolized by his kinsmen were bestowed on Cardinal Carpi, on Camillo Orsini, who had held so extensive a power under Paul III, and on others. Nor were only the persons changed; the whole system and character of the administration were changed as well. Important economies were made, and taxes proportionately remitted; the pontiff established a chest, of which only he held the key, for the purpose of receiving all complaints that any man should desire to make; he demanded a daily report from the governor. The public business in general was conducted with great circumspection, and none of the old abuses were permitted to remain.

Amid all the commotions of the early part of his pontificate, Paul IV had never lost sight of his reforming projects; he now resumed them with earnest zeal and undivided attention. A more severe discipline was introduced into the churches: all begging was forbidden; even the collection of alms for Masses, hitherto made by the clergy, was discontinued; and such pictures as were not, by their subjects, appropriate to the Church, were removed. A medal was struck in his honor, representing Christ driving the money-changers from the temple. All monks who had deserted their monasteries were expelled from the city and the Papal States; the court was enjoined to keep the regular fasts, and all were commanded to solemnize Easter by receiving Holy Communion. The cardinals were even compelled to occasional preaching, and Paul himself preached! Many abuses which had been profitable to the Curia he did his best to correct. Of marriage dispensations, or of the resources which they furnished to the treasury, he would not even hear mention. A host of places which, up to his time, had been constantly sold, even those of the clerks of the chamber (*chiericati di camera*), he would now have disposed of according to merit only. Still more rigidly did he insist on the worth and clerical endowments of all on whom he bestowed the purely ecclesiastical employments. He would no longer endure those compacts by which one man had hitherto been allowed to enjoy the revenues of an office, while he had made over its duties to another, by whom, for some mean hire, they were performed, well or ill, as might chance. He had also formed the idea of reinstating the bishops in many rights which had been wrongfully withheld from them; and considered it highly culpable that everything should be absorbed by Rome which could in any way be made to yield either profit or influence.

Nor were Paul's reforms confined merely to the abolition of abuses. Not content with a negative effect only, he proceeded to practical amendments. The services of the Church were performed with increased pomp; it is to him we are indebted for the rich ornaments of the Sistine chapel, and for the solemn representation of the Holy Sepulchre. There is an ideal of the modern Catholic service of the altar, full of dignity, devotion, and splendor: this it was which floated before the eyes of Paul, and which he would fain have realized.

He permitted no day to pass, as he boasts, without the promulgation of some edict tending to restore the Church to its original purity. Many of his decrees present the outlines of those ordinances which were afterward sanctioned by the Council of Trent.

In the course which he now adopted, Paul displayed, as might have been expected, all that inflexibility of nature peculiar to him.

Above all other institutions he favored that of the Inquisition, which he himself had re-established. The days appointed for the *segnatura* and the consistory he would often allow to pass unnoticed; but never did he miss the Thursday, which was the day set apart for the congregation of the Inquisition, and when it assembled before him. The powers of this office he desired to see exercised with the utmost rigor. He subjected new classes of offense to its jurisdiction, and conferred on it the barbarous prerogative of applying torture for the detection of accomplices. He permitted no respect of persons. The most distinguished nobles were summoned before this tribunal; and cardinals, such as Morone and Foscherari, were now thrown into prison, because he entertained certain doubts about the soundness of their opinions, in spite of the fact that these very men had formerly been appointed to examine the contents, and decide the orthodoxy, of important books—the *Spiritual Exercises* of Ignatius Loyola, for example. It was Paul IV who established the feast of St. Dominic, in honor of that great inquisitor.

Thus a rigid austerity and an earnest zeal for the restoration of primitive habits became the prevailing tendency of the papacy.

Paul IV seemed almost to have forgotten that he had ever pursued purposes other than those which now occupied him; the memory of past times seemed extinguished. He lived and moved in his reforms and his Inquisition, gave laws, imprisoned, excommunicated, and held *autos-da-fé*; these occupations filled up his life. At length, when laid prostrate by disease, such as would have caused death even to a younger man, he called his cardinals about him, commended his soul to their prayers, and the Holy See with the Inquisition to their earnest care. Once more he would fain have collected his energies: he sought to raise himself, but the disease prevailed; his strength had failed him —he fell back and died (August 18, 1559).

In one respect, at least, are these determined and passionate characters more fortunate than men of feebler mold; they are, perhaps, blinded by the force of their feelings—the violence of their prejudices

—but they are also steeled by his force, this violence, which renders them invincible.

The Roman people did not forget what they had suffered under Paul IV so readily as he had—they could not forgive him for the war which he had brought on the State; nor, though his nephews were abhorred, did their disgrace suffice to the resentment of the multitude. At the news of his death, large crowds assembled in the capital, and resolved that, since he had not deserved well either of Rome or of the world, they would destroy his monuments. Others attacked the buildings of the Inquisition, set fire to them, and roughly handled the servants of the Holy Office; they even threatened to burn the Dominican convent of Santa Maria alla Minerva. The Colonnas, Orsini, Cesarini, Massimi, and other nobles whom Paul had mortally offended, took part in these tumults. The statue which had been erected to this pope was torn from its pedestal and broken to pieces, and the head, bearing the triple crown, was dragged through the streets.

It would, nevertheless, have been fortunate for the Papal See had it met with no more serious reaction against the enterprise of Paul IV than was intimated by this outbreak. . . .

It will have become obvious to the reader that the earlier dissensions between the papacy and the imperial or Spanish power had contributed more than any other external cause to the establishment of Protestantism in Germany. Yet a second breach was not avoided, and this produced results still more comprehensive and important.

The recall of the papal troops from the imperial army by Paul III and his transfer of the council from Trent to Bologna may be considered as the preliminary steps. Their importance was at once made evident: there was no impediment to the subjugation of the Protestants so effective as that presented by the policy, active and passive, of Paul III at that period.

But the great and permanent results were not obvious until after the death of the pontiff. That connection with France, into which he led his nephews, occasioned a universal war; and in this the German Protestants not only achieved that memorable victory by which they secured themselves forever from the pope, emperor, and council, but also gained important progress for their opinions by the contact into which the Protestant soldiers, who fought on both sides, were forced with those of France and the Netherlands. This contact caused the extensive acceptance of the new doctrines in those countries, their introduction being favored by the prevalence of a confusion, occasioned by the war, which rendered vigilant precaution impossible.

Paul IV ascended the papal throne. It was for him to have taken a clear view of things as they existed before his eyes, and, above all, his first efforts should have been turned to the restoration of peace: but with all the blindness of passion, he plunged himself into the tumult, and thus it came to pass that he, the most furious of zealots, was in fact a more effectual promoter of that Protestantism which he so abhorred and prosecuted than any one of his predecessors.

# CHARLES V
# AT THE DIET
# OF AUGSBURG

Among Ranke's major histories, the *History of the Reformation in Germany* holds a special place. Not only was it his most popular work; but it was also very close to his heart. "In reading the earlier works," his pupil Sybel remarked, "my enjoyment is exactly the same as in visiting a gallery of excellent pictures and statuary. Very different is my feeling when I open the *Reformation* which is impregnated with the enthusiasm of a German patriot for the greatest act of the German spirit." Nor was this warmth entirely surprising. Ranke's own transition in interest from classics to modern history had started during the anniversary year of 1817 when he began to study Luther's writings, with an eye toward composing a biography of the reformer. The unfinished fragments of the Luther work in the Ranke papers display his early effort to rely almost exclusively on primary sources, as well as his interest in Luther as a religious figure, as a person in whom certain ideas are embodied and brought to historical achievement.

But Ranke, throughout his career, as Fritz Hartung has pointed out, was also influenced greatly by opportunity. On the completion of his *Popes*, we know that he had discovered in Frankfurt a complete series of Relations by that city's representatives to the Imperial Diet for the Reformation era. By supplementing these with other archival sources, he was able to write his new work, giving a detailed and authoritative history of the Reformation. It has largely stood the test of time, though later writers have probed the theological issues more subtly, and such social issues as the Peasant's Revolt much more thoroughly, than Ranke did.

In this selection, we meet the Emperor Charles fresh from nine years of hard-fought and triumphant warfare with his adversary Francis I of France, and a host of allies, including the pope. During Charles' absence, since the Diet of 1521 which heard and condemned Luther, his brother Ferdinand has been in charge of Germany, with only a loose rein over the princes; despite the condemnation of Luther, several of the princes and many of the cities have adopted Protestantism, and on Charles' return either a compromise or a confrontation must result. Immediately before Charles' arrival in Germany, the reconciled pope and emperor met in Bologna, where the pontiff placed the crown of the

Holy Roman Empire on the emperor's head. The passage shows us Ranke's skill at sketching portraits of Charles, of Luther, of Elector John of Saxony, and of many lesser figures. The intricate way in which politics shaped the decision on a religious settlement also emerges. Through it we can sense the detachment, but also the commitment, of Ranke to his Protestant cause, and, above all, his sympathy for Luther.

The following translation is based on that of Sarah Austin, *History of the Reformation in Germany*, first published in London, between 1845 and 1847; and is cited from pp. 594–629 of the 1905 New York edition.

THE WORLD thus once more beheld an emperor in the plenitude of power; but the bases on which this power rested were new; the old imperial office and dignity were gone.

Least of all could the German nation boast that the German empire had recovered its ancient character and powers.

The Electors complained that they were neither summoned to the coronation nor invited to share in the treaties which the emperor had concluded with the Italian powers. They registered a formal protest, that if anything should have been agreed to in these treaties which might now or hereafter prove detrimental to the Holy Roman Empire, they had in no wise assented or consented to it.

The emperor had already been reminded that the conquered provinces of Italy belonged, not to him, but to the empire; and had been required to restore to the empire its finance chambers [*Kammern*], especially those of Milan and Genoa; for which the imperial government would appoint a *gubernator*, and from which it would appropriate the surplus revenues for the maintenance of tranquillity and law. But such were not the notions of the emperor or of his Spanish captains. The Duke of Brunswick affirmed that obstacles had intentionally been thrown in his way, during his Italian campaign in the year 1528, by Antonio Lieva; the Spaniard, he said, would endure no German prince among the Milanese. And now this same Lieva had received Pavia in fief, and held the supreme command over an army in the field. German influence had been destroyed.

Under these circumstances the emperor, no longer the perfect representative of the national power, made his way over the Tridentine Alps to Germany (May 1530).

If we inquire what his own views were toward Germany, we discover that none but the most immediate presented themselves with any distinctness to his mind.

He had promised his brother—whose fidelity to him through all the complications of his Italian affairs had been unshaken; who, feeble as his resources were, was ever ready to come to his aid; and who had been his most useful ally—to confer upon him the dignity of king of the Romans. The attempts to transfer this dignity to another House—attempts constantly renewed and not without danger—must, he said, be ended. The fitting moment had now arrived; they must take advantage of this full tide of power and victory.

It had also become absolutely necessary to take effective measures against the Turks. Recent events had shown the Germans that not only Hungary, but their own fatherland, was at stake; the imminence of the danger would render them more compliant. This was an indispensable condition to the stability of the House of Austria.

Yet he distinctly felt that this state of things would not be permanent.

During his stay in Italy, a pacific demeanor—not indeed at variance with his disposition, which rather inclined that way, but contrary to his original intentions—had been imposed upon him by the state of things. But the warlike schemes of his youth, though suspended, were not abandoned. When he turned his eyes toward Germany, as he tells his brother in a letter, he wished to confer with him about many things, and especially about their future conduct toward that nation: whether they should remain at peace or engage in any warlike expedition; whether they should join immediately in a common effort against the Turks, or wait for some great occasion which might justify their enterprise.

Everything depended on the course of religious affairs, and these had already occupied his deliberate attention.

## DIET OF AUGSBURG, 1530

By the Treaty of Barcelona the emperor had bound himself to endeavor, in the first place, to bring the dissidents back to the faith; and if that attempt should fail, then to apply all his power "to avenge the insult offered to Christ."

I do not doubt that this engagement was entirely in accordance with his intentions.

As revolting and arbitrary as the opinion delivered to him by his companion, the papal legate Campeggio, appears to us, it is in fact founded on the same ideas. Campeggio begins by suggesting the means by which the Protestants might be reclaimed: promises, threats, and alliances with the states which remained true to Catholicism. But in case all these should be unavailing, he insists most strongly on the necessity of resorting to force—to fire and sword, as he expresses it; he declares that their property should be confiscated, and Germany be subjected to the vigilance of an inquisition similar to that established in Spain.

All that has come down to us of the correspondence of the emperor with his brother breathes the same spirit and same purposes.

Ferdinand had, as we know, entered into negotiations with Elector John of Saxony; but he assures the emperor that he does this only to gain time. "You may think," he adds, "that I concede too much, and that you may thus be hindered from proceeding to the work of punishment. Monseigneur, I will negotiate for as long as possible and will conclude nothing; but even should I have concluded, there will be many other pretexts for chastising them—reasons of state—without your needing to mention religion; besides, they have played so many bad tricks that you will find people who will willingly help you in this matter."

This, therefore, was the design: to see first whether the Protestants could be brought back by fair means to the unity of Latin Christendom, which was now restored to peace, and to the imposing aspect of a great system; but if this did not succeed, the application of force was seriously contemplated, and the right to apply it carefully reserved.

It would not have been prudent, however, to irritate the antipathies of offended self-love by threats. Clemency ceases to be clemency if future severity is seen lurking in the background. It was therefore determined at present to turn only the fair side to view.

The emperor's convocation of the Diet breathed nothing but peace. He announced his desire "to allay divisions; to leave all past errors to the judgment of our Saviour, and, further, to give a charitable hearing to every man's opinions, thoughts, and notions; to weigh them carefully; to bring men to Christian truth; and to dispose of everything which has not been rightly explained on both sides." This proclamation was dated from the palace in which the emperor was living with the pope. The pope left the emperor's hands free; and, indeed, he too would have rejoiced if these lenient measures had been successful.

But whatever moderation might appear in the emperor's language, the orthodox princes were sufficiently informed of the temper of the imperial court, and of its connection with that of Rome, not to conceive the liveliest hopes on its arrival. They hastened to draw up a statement of all their grievances, and to revise all the old judgments and orders in council for the suppression of the Lutheran agitation. "It pleases us much," said the administrator of Regensburg, in the instructions to the envoys to the Diet, "that the innovations against the excellent and long-established usages of the Church should be rooted out and abolished." The emperor at first held his court at Innsbruck, in order, with the aid of his brother's advice, to secure a favorable result of the proceedings of the Diet. The nature of these proceedings may be inferred from a single fact: that the Venetian ambassador saw an account from which it appeared that, between the time of its departure from Bologna and July 12, 1530, the imperial court had expended 270,000 gulden in presents. Prosperity and power, in themselves sufficiently imposing and attractive, were now, as for centuries in Germany, aided by all the influence of largesse and favor. All who had anything to expect from the court now flocked there, and it was almost forgotten that the Diet ought long ago to have opened: every man was intent on getting his own business settled without delay.

It soon appeared from one example how great an influence the emperor's presence would exercise on religious affairs. His brother-in-law, the exiled King Christian of Denmark, who had hitherto adhered to Luther, constantly corresponded with him, and openly declared himself a convert to his doctrines, was induced in Innsbruck to return to the old faith. The pope was overjoyed when he heard it. "I cannot express," he writes to the emperor, "with what emotion this news has filled me. The splendor of your majesty's virtues begins to scare away the night; this example will work upon countless others." He granted Christian absolution, and imposed upon him a penance which he was to perform after his restoration to his kingdom. The emperor himself hoped that, since he had succeeded, contrary to his expectations, in purifying Italy from heresy, he should not fail in Germany. In Rome everything was expected from the lucky star which seemed to preside over all his proceedings.

Circumstances did indeed appear extremely favorable to his designs.

The emperor's convocation had been favorably received by the Protestants. The prince whose dispositions and conduct were the most important—the Elector of Saxony—was the first to arrive at Augsburg. He went without delay to offer his congratulations to the emperor (who had crossed the Alps at the same time) on his arrival in the empire, of which he had learned "with loyal joy"; he would await the pleasure of his majesty, his own chief and lord, in Augsburg. He had invited his allies to follow him; for the Diet of Augsburg seemed to be the national council which had been so long expected, so often and so vainly demanded, and which now afforded a hope of the reconciliation of religious differences.

The negotiations of the Elector with King Ferdinand had, as may be presumed from what we have just stated, led to no conclusion; but they were by no means broken off. Elector John also had various other affairs to discuss with the imperial court, to arrange which he had sent an ambassador to Innsbruck. The question whether it might not be possible to win him over presented itself, and an attempt was made to prevail upon him to come to Innsbruck. The emperor sent him word that he might rely on all possible friendship from him, and invited him to come to his court, as many other princes had done. "He intended to unite with him in the settlement of affairs, which might be arranged by themselves in person."

But here, too, Charles had a proof of the kind of resistance which he would have to encounter in Germany. The Elector was offended that the emperor had urged him, through the ambassador of another power, to impose silence on the preachers whom he had brought with him. This demand appeared to him an unauthorized attempt to prejudge the very question to be inquired into; and he was persuaded that the compliance which he refused in Augsburg would be extorted from him in Innsbruck if he appeared there. He saw, too, that the court was already filled with his personal adversaries. Nor did he think it expedient to enter upon the business of the Diet at any place other than the one appointed. In short, he adhered to his declaration that he would wait the emperor's coming in Augsburg.

The imperial court was generally unprepared for the bearing exhibited by the Protestants assembled in Augsburg, for the approbation which the preachers received in that city, and the popularity which they enjoyed throughout Germany. In Italy it had been thought that at the first mutterings of the tempest the Protestants would disperse, like a flock of doves when the hawk pounces down in their midst. Chancellor Gattinara first remarked that the court would find more difficulties than he himself had anticipated. Gattinara, an old opponent of the papal policy, and without question the most adroit politician the emperor possessed, would perhaps have been the man to modify the views of the court so as to render them attainable; even the Protestants relied upon him. But at exactly this moment he died in Innsbruck. The state of things excited no such serious misgivings in the others: what did not succeed in Innsbruck, they hoped to accomplish, by some means or other, in Augsburg.

On June 6, the emperor set out for that city. He visited Munich en route, where he was magnificently received. Accompanied by the temporal and spiritual princes of Austria and Bavaria—the same ones who had concluded the Regensburg League—he reached the bridge over the Lech, before Augsburg, on the evening of the 15th.

The most brilliant assemblage of princes of the empire which had been witnessed for a long time had already been waiting for some hours to receive him: sovereigns, spiritual and temporal, from Upper and Lower Germany, and a very numerous body of young princes who had not yet attained to sovereignty. As soon as the emperor approached, they dismounted and advanced to meet him. The emperor also dismounted, and put out his hand to each of them in a courteous and friendly manner. The Elector of Mainz greeted him in the name of all these "assembled members of the Holy Roman Empire." Thereupon they all prepared to make their solemn entry into the imperial city. Since we have just contemplated the imperial coronation, in which Germany had hardly any share, we must pause a moment over the still essentially German ceremony of the solemn entry.

Foremost marched two companies of *Landsknechts*, to whom the emperor entrusted the guard of the imperial city, as whose newly-arrived lord he wished to be regarded. They had just been recruited, and did not have that military air which is required in Germany; but there were many among them who had served in the Italian wars, and some who had become rich there. The most prominent figure was Simon Seitz, an Augsburg citizen, who served the emperor as military secretary, and who now, magnificently clad in gold, and mounted on a brown jennet with embroidered housings, returned to his native town with an air of splendid arrogance.

The mounted guard of the six Electors followed. The Saxons, according to ancient custom, headed the procession; about 160 horsemen, all habited in liver color, with matchlocks in their hands. They consisted partly of the people about the court: princes and counts having one, two, or four horses, according to their dignity; partly of the councilors and nobles summoned from the country. People remarked the electoral prince, who had negotiated the first alliance with Hesse. Then followed the horsemen of the Palatinate, Brandenburg, Cologne, Mainz, and Trier, all in their proper colors and arms. According to the hierarchy of the empire, the Bavarians did not belong there; but before they could be prevented, they had taken their place, and they at least filled it magnificently. They were all in light armor, with red surcoats; they rode in fives, and were distinguishable, even from a distance, by their waving plumes. There might have been 450 horses in all.

People were struck with the difference, when, after this most warlike pomp, the courts of the emperor and the king made their appearance: foremost, the pages dressed in red or yellow velvet; then the Spanish, Bohemian, and German lords, in garments of silk and velvet, with large gold chains, but almost all unarmed. They were mounted on the most beautiful horses, Turkish, Spanish, and Polish, and the Bohemians did not fail to display their gallant horsemanship.

This escort was followed by the two sovereigns in person.

Their coming was announced by two rows of trumpeters, partly in the king's colors, partly in the emperor's, accompanied by their drums, pursuivants, and heralds.

Here then were all the high and mighty lords who ruled almost without control in their wide domains, and whose border quarrels were wont to fill Germany with tumult and war. Ernest of Lüneburg and

Henry of Brunswick, who were still in a state of unappeased strife over the Hildesheim quarrel; George of Saxony and his son-in-law Philip of Hesse, who had lately come into such rude collision in consequence of Pack's plot; the dukes of Bavaria, and their cousins, the counts palatine, whose short reconciliation now began to give way to fresh misunderstandings; near the princes of the House of Brandenburg, the dukes of Pomerania, who, in spite of them, hoped to receive, at the coming Diet, infeudation as immediate lords. All these now acknowledged the presence of one above them all, to whom they paid common homage and deference. The princes were followed by the Electors, temporal and spiritual. Side by side rode John of Saxony and Joachim of Brandenburg, between whom there was no slight grudge, sufficiently accounted for by the troubles caused by the flight of the margrave's wife. Elector John once more bore the drawn sword before his emperor. Immediately after the Electors came their chosen and now crowned chief, mounted on a white Polish charger, under a magnificent three-colored baldachin, borne by six councilors of Augsburg. It was remarked that he who formed the center of this imposing group was the only one who looked a stranger to it; he was dressed from head to foot in the Spanish fashion. He had expressed a wish to have his brother on one side of him, and on the other, the legate, to whom he wished to pay the highest honor; he even wanted the ecclesiastical Electors to yield precedence to him, but on this point they were inflexible. They thought that they had done Campeggio honor enough when the most learned of their College, Elector Joachim, who spoke Latin with considerable fluency (better at least than any of its spiritual members) offered him their congratulations. King Ferdinand and the legate accordingly rode together, outside the baldachin; they were followed by the German cardinals and bishops, the foreign ambassadors and prelates. Conspicuous among them was the emperor's haughty confessor, the Bishop of Osma.

The procession of princes and lords was again succeeded by mounted guards: those of the emperor clad in yellow, those of the king in red; with them, vying in gallant equipments, the horsemen of the lords spiritual and temporal, each troop in its proper colors, all armed either with breastplate and lance or with firearms.

The militia of Augsburg, which had marched out in the morning to receive the emperor, foot and horse, paid troops and citizens, ended the procession.

This was in accordance with the whole import of the ceremony, viz., that the empire fetched home its emperor. Near St. Leonard's Church he was met by the clergy of the city singing "Advenisti desiderabilis"; the princes accompanied him to the cathedral, where the "Te Deum" was sung, and the benediction pronounced over him; nor did they leave him until they had reached the door of his apartment in the palace.

But even here, at their very first meeting—in the church too—the great and all-dividing question which was to occupy this august assembly presented itself in all its abruptness.

The Protestants had joined in the religious, as well as the civil, ceremonies; and the emperor was perhaps encouraged by this to take advantage of the first moment of his presence, the first impression made by his arrival, to prevail upon them to make some material concessions.

Allowing the remaining princes to depart, the emperor invited the Elector of Saxony, the Margrave George of Brandenburg, Duke Francis of Lüneburg, and Landgrave Philip, to attend him in a private room, and there, through the mouth of his brother, requested them to put an end to the preachings. The elder princes, startled and alarmed, said nothing; the imperious landgrave broke the silence, and sought to justify his refusal on the ground that nothing was preached but the pure word of God, just as St. Augustine had enjoined—arguments consummately distasteful to the emperor. The blood rushed into his pallid cheeks, and he repeated his demand in a more imperious tone. But here he had to encounter a resistance of a very different nature from what he had experienced from the Italian powers, who contended only for the interests of a disputed possession. "Sire," said the old Margrave George, now breaking silence, "rather than renounce God's word, I will kneel down on this spot to have my head cut off." The emperor, who wished to utter none but words of mildness, and was naturally benevolent, was alarmed at the possibility thus presented to his mind by the lips of another. "Dear prince," replied he to the margrave, in his broken Low German, "not heads off" [*nicht Köpfe ab*].

The next difficulty was that the Protestants declined to take part in the procession of Corpus Christi on the following day. Had the emperor required their attendance as a court service, they probably would have given it, "like Naaman, in the Scriptures, to his king," as they said; but he demanded it "in honor of Almighty God." To attend on such a ground appeared to them a violation of conscience. They replied that God had not instituted the Sacrament that man should worship it. The procession, which had no longer in any respect its ancient splendor, took place without them.

As far as the preaching was concerned, they did at length yield, but not until the emperor had promised to silence the other party as well. He himself appointed certain preachers, but they were to read only the text of Scripture, without any exposition. Nor would it have been possible to bring the Protestants to yield even this point had they not been reminded that the Recess of 1528, to which they had always appealed, and which they would not suffer to be revoked, authorized it. The emperor, at least as long as he was there in person, was always regarded as the legitimate supreme authority of every imperial city.

It is evident, therefore, that the Protestants did not allow themselves to be driven back one step from their convictions or from their rights. The requests of the emperor when present made no more impression on them than his demands when absent had. If the emperor had counted on compliance, these were no flattering omens of future success.

At length, on June 20, the business of the Diet was opened. In the Proposition, which was read that day, the emperor insisted, as was reasonable, most urgently on an adequate armament against the Turks; at the same time he declared his intention of putting an end to the religious dissension by gentle and fair means, and reiterated the request contained in the convocation: that everyone would give him, to that end, his "thoughts, judgment, and opinion" in writing.

Since the council of the empire resolved to proceed first to the consideration of religious affairs, the grand struggle began immediately.

## THE AUGSBURG CONFESSION

The Protestants hastened immediately to draw up a written statement of their religious opinions, to be laid before the states of the empire.

This statement is the Augsburg Confession, and its origin is as follows:

Immediately after the receipt of the emperor's proclamation, the Saxon reformers deemed it expedient to set forth in writing, and in a regular form, the belief "in which they had hitherto stood, and in which they persisted."

Similar preparations had been made in various areas in anticipation of the national assembly which was to be held in the year 1524; and something of the same kind was, at this moment, taking place on the other side, e.g., in Ingolstadt.

The Wittenberg reformers took, as the basis of their creed, the Schwabach articles, in which, as we may remember, the points of difference between the Lutheran theologians and those of the Oberland were defined. It is very remarkable that, in the framing of this confession, the feeling of the differences which separated them from a party so nearly akin was, to say the least, no less strong than that of the original dissent which had caused the first great movement. The separation now appeared the wider, since Zwingli and his followers had, in the meantime, recanted some admissions which they had made in Marburg and which had found their way from the Marburg convention into the Schwabach articles.

These articles were now revised and redrawn by Melanchthon, in that sound and methodical spirit peculiar to him, and in the undeniable intention of approximating as closely as possible the Catholic doctrines. The expositions of the doctrine of free will and of justification by faith which he added were extremely moderated; he defined at greater length the heretical errors (errors rejected also by the Church of Rome) which were condemned by the articles; he sought to establish these articles, not only on the authority of Scripture, but also on that of the Fathers, and especially of St. Augustine; he did not entirely forbid the honors paid to the memory of the saints, but only endeavored to define their extent more accurately; he insisted strongly on the dignity of the temporal power, and concluded with the assertion not only that these doctrines were clearly established in Scripture, but also that they were not in contradiction with those of the Church of Rome, as understood from the writings of the Fathers, from whom it was impossible to dissent, and who could hardly be accused of heresy.

And indeed it cannot be denied, I think, that the system of faith set forth here is a product of the vital spirit of the Latin Church; that it keeps within the boundaries prescribed by that Church, and is, perhaps, of all its offspring, the most remarkable, the most profoundly significant. It bears, as was inevitable, the traces of its origin; that is, the fundamental idea from which Luther had proceeded in the article on justification gives it somewhat of an individual stamp: this, however, is inherent in all human things. The same fundamental idea had arisen more than once in the bosom of the Latin Church, and had produced the most important effects; the only difference was that Luther had seized upon it with all the energy of religious aspiration; and in his struggle with opposing opinions, and in his expositions to the people, had established it as an article of faith of universal application; no human being could say that, so explained and understood, this idea had anything sectarian in it. Hence, the Lutherans steadily opposed the more accidental dogmas which have sprung up in later ages; though not disposed to ascribe to the expressions of a Father of the Church absolute and demonstrative authority the reformers were conscious that they had not departed widely from his conception of Christianity. There is a tacit tradition, not expressed in formulas, but contained in the original nature of the concept, which exercises an immense influence over all the operations of the mind. The reformers distinctly felt that they stood on the old ground which Augustine had marked out. They had endeavored to break through the minute observances by which the Latin Church had allowed itself to be fettered in the preceding centuries, and to cast away those bonds altogether; they had returned to Scripture and adhered to the letter of it. But they did not forget that it was this same Scripture which had been so long and so earnestly studied in the Latin Church, and regarded as the standard of her faith; nor that much of what that Church received was really founded on Scripture. To that they adhered; the rest they disregarded.

I do not venture to assert that the Augsburg Confession dogmatically determines the contents and import of Scripture; it does no more than to bring the system which had grown up in the Latin Church back to a conformity with Scripture, or to interpret Scripture in the original spirit of the Latin Church. But that spirit had wrought too imperceptibly to produce any open manifestation which could have served as a bond of faith. The confession of the German Lutheran church is itself its purest manifestation, and the one the most immediately derived from its source.

It is hardly necessary to add that its authors had no intention of imposing this as a permanent and immutable standard of faith. It is simply the assertion of the fact: "our churches teach," "it is taught," "it is unanimously taught," "such and such opinions are falsely imputed to us." These are the expressions Melanchthon uses, and his intent is simply to state the belief which already exists.

And in the same spirit he wrote the second part, in which he enumerates and explains the abuses which had been removed.

How wide a field was opened here for virulent polemical attack! What might not have been said (especially during the sitting of the Diet, whose antipathies might thus have been appealed to) about the encroachments of the papal power or about the degeneracies of a corrupt form of worship—and, indeed, we find a long register of them among the rough drafts of the work; but it was thought better to omit them. Melanchthon confined himself strictly to a justification of the ecclesiastical organization to which the reformers had gradually attained. He explained the grounds on which the Sacrament under both species and the marriage of the clergy had been permitted, vows and private Masses rejected, and facts and confession left to the will and conscience of each individual; he sought to show in general how new and dangerous the contrary practices were, and how much at variance even with the old canonical rules. With wise discretion he was silent concerning the divine right of the pope, the *character indelibilis*, or even the number of the sacraments; his object was, not to convert, but simply to defend. It was sufficient that he insisted upon the distinction between the spiritual calling of the bishops and their temporal power; while defining the former in accordance with the tenor of Scripture, he wholly refrained from attacking the latter. He maintained that, on this point also, the evangelical party had not deviated from the genuine principles of the Catholic Church, and that, consequently, the emperor might well consent to tolerate the new organization of the church.

It may be questioned whether the Protestants would not have done better if, instead of restricting themselves so entirely to defense, they had once more acted on the offensive, and appealed to all the strong reforming sympathies then afloat.

But we must acknowledge that from the moment they had decided to refuse to admit the adherents of Zwingli into their community, this was impossible. They found themselves almost eclipsed by the popularity of Zwingli's doctrines, which the majority of the inhabitants of Augsburg espoused; and nothing was more a topic of conversation than a union of Upper Germany and Switzerland, in order to overthrow the entire hierarchy of the empire. Even one of the most eminent of the reforming princes, Landgrave Philip of Hesse, seemed from his conversation to lean to the side of Zwingli. A special admonition from Luther was required to induce him to subscribe to the Confession.

Nor could the Lutherans entertain the least hope of gaining over the majority of the states of the empire, who had already taken too decided a part with their adversaries.

They wished for nothing but peace and toleration; they thought they had proved that their doctrines had been unjustly condemned and denounced as heretical. Luther brought himself to entreat his old antagonist, the archbishop of Mainz, who now seemed more peaceably disposed, to lay this to heart. Melanchthon addressed himself in the name of the princes to the legate Campeggio, and pleaded with him not to depart from the moderation which he thought he perceived in him, since each new agitation might occasion an immeasurable confusion in the Church.

In this spirit of conciliation, in the feeling of still unbroken ties, in the wish to give force to that similarity which not only lay at the bottom of both religions but was obvious in many particulars, this Confession was conceived and drawn up.

On the afternoon of June 25, 1530, it was read aloud in the assembly of the empire. The princes prayed the emperor to allow this to be done in the larger hall, to which strangers were admitted—in short, in a public sitting; but the emperor chose the smaller hall, the chapter-room of the bishop's palace, which he inhabited; to this only the members of the assembly of the empire had access. For a similar reason he wished the Latin version of the document to be read, but the princes reminded him that on German ground his majesty would be pleased to permit the use of the German language. Thereupon the young chancellor of Saxony, Dr. Christian Baier, read the Confession in German, with a distinctness of voice and utterance which well accorded with the clearness and firmness of the belief which it expressed. The number of the spiritual princes present was not great; they thought they should be compelled to listen to too many inconvenient reproaches. Those in favor of it rejoiced that they had made this progress, and were delighted both with the matter of the Confession and the manner in which it had been recited. Some took advantage of the opportunity to write down the main points. As soon as it was finished, the two copies were handed to the emperor: the German he gave to the chancellor of the empire; the Latin he kept in his own hands. Both were signed by the Elector and the electoral prince of Saxony, Margrave George of Brandenburg, the dukes Francis and Ernest of Lüneburg, Landgrave Philip, Prince Wolfgang of Anhalt, and the delegates of the cities of Nuremberg and Reutlingen.

### CONFUTATION—THREATS

The evangelical princes expected that their adversaries would come forward with a similar declaration of faith, and that the emperor would then endeavor to mediate between them. This expectation was held out by the Proposition, and, in still more distinct terms, by the convocation in virtue of which they were now assembled.

It is highly probable that this was actually the emperor's intention; he indeed had wished that the Catholic party had brought forward a distinct charge against the reformers, in which case he would have undertaken the part of an umpire between them. At the meeting of the states, Ferdinand had once made a proposal to that effect.

But the two brothers were not sufficient masters of the assembly to accomplish this.

The majority which had been formed in Speyer, and had acquired greater compactness in Augsburg, regarded itself as the legitimate possessor of the authority of the empire. Though the Catholic zeal of the two brothers was most agreeable to its wishes, it found many things to object to in them. Ferdinand had obtained papal concessions of ecclesiastical revenues, a thing which, though permitted in Spain, was unheard of in Germany. This excited universal disgust and resistance among the clergy. The majority declined, constituting themselves a party, and acknowledging the emperor as judge between them and the Protestants. They declared that they had nothing new to propose; they had simply adhered to the imperial edict. If the emperor was in want of a charge to bring against the reformers, let him resort to that of contravention of his edict. Nay, more: since it had been the custom from time immemorial for the emperor to accede to the sentiments of the assembly of the empire, they were of opinion that he should now adopt their cause as his own. This was, in fact, a request to him to use his imperial power in the affair, with the advice of the Electors, princes, and Estates of the empire. It was a matter of complete indifference to them that this was at variance with the express words of the convocation, since they were not the authors of it. The emperor was, in fact, compelled to relinquish his idea of a judicial mediation.

It has usually been asserted that traces are to be found of personal and independent negotiations between the emperor and the Protestants at this Diet. But the fact is that from this moment on the whole business was conducted by the majority of the states. Concerning even the minutest point—the communication of a document, for example—the emperor was compelled to hold a consultation with them; he acted at last only as they deemed expedient.

It is much to be regretted that we have no protocols of the sittings of the Catholic majority; we do not even know whether any were drawn up. Nor have any full and accurate reports come to light— though they are hardly to be expected, since the most considerable princes were present, and the delegates from the cities did not take part in the sittings.

All that we know is that there was a division of opinion among the majority itself. One party thought that the emperor ought to take up arms at once to enforce the execution of his earlier edict. The archbishop of Salzburg said, "Either we must put an end to them, or they will put an end to us; which of the two suits us best?" An equally violent member of the assembly was heard to remark, in jest, that the Confession was written with black ink. "Were we emperor," said he, "we would put red rubrics to it." "Sir," rejoined another, "only take care that the red does not spurt up in your faces." All, as this answer shows, were not equally hostile. The archbishop of Mainz, in particular, pointed out the danger which would arise from a Turkish invasion in the event of an open breach with the Protestants. It was at length determined to advise the emperor above all things to authorize a confutation of the Confession; meanwhile, an attempt might be made to settle the differences between the temporal and spiritual Estates. The emperor acted on this advice. He gave himself up to the hope that the settling of these differences and the confutation of the Confession would, together, produce such an effect on the Protestants as to induce them to yield.

The situation of the Protestants was thus changed greatly for the worse.

Up to this point they had expected from the emperor's exalted position a fair appreciation of their conduct, and mediation between them and their adversaries; but they very soon perceived that he did not give, but receive the impulse; the old and bitter enemies with whom they had so long striven now constituted a majority, and were directing all the measures of the imperial authority.

The confutation was set about with the utmost zeal. There was no want of laborers. Not only the reforming theologians, but their opponents, had repaired to the Diet with their respective princes; Faber, from Vienna, who had now become the prebendary of Ofen; Eck, from Ingolstadt; Cochlaeus, from Dresden; Wimpina, from Frankfurt on Oder. With the prince bishops came their vicars, or learned officiating bishops; there were some eminent monks—Capuchins, Carmelites, and especially Dominicans: Paul Haug, the provincial; John Burkhard, the vicar; and the prior, Conrad Colli, who had written against Luther's marriage. It is not surprising that a man like Erasmus (who was also invited) felt no inclination to have his name associated with such as these. The men who were there to conduct the discussion were the representatives of the Aristotelian Dominican system, which for so long had ruled the schools of Europe, and which he himself had combated. With the literary weapons which they had hitherto wielded they had accomplished little. Their whole strength lay in their connection with power. They were now no longer private men; they were to speak and write in the name of the empire.

They were not, it is true, left at absolute liberty. People dreaded their violence and their diffuseness, for each of them brought his old animosities and his old refutations of Lutheran opinions, which were not now in dispute. Their first draft was peremptorily returned to them by the assembly of the empire, with the admonition that they confine themselves entirely to the articles of the Confession. A second, shorter, draft, which was presented next, was submitted, article by article, to minute discussion by the assembly. It was August 3 before the confutation was prepared and could be read aloud in the aforementioned hall of the bishop's palace.

Like the Confession, it consists of two parts: the one treating of belief; the other, of practice.

In the former, the contested question already approached the point at which it has since remained stationary. It was no longer maintained that the sacrament, the mere performance of the act, the *opus operatum*, merited grace. It was no longer taught that a good word done without grace was of the same nature as one done with grace, and that the difference between them was only one of degree. Those were the doctrines against which Luther had contended. A nearer approach was made to the more profound concept of justification through Christ which has since been almost universally adopted. If the Catholics strove to retain the doctrine of the necessity of good works, it was in a different sense from that heretofore affixed to it.

This was, however, the only modification to which they consented. On the other points they remained faithful to the established system. They demanded the admission of the doctrine of transubstantiation, the seven sacraments, and the invocation of the saints; they persisted in the denial of the cup and the injunction of celibacy; they even made an attempt (which, indeed, was certain to fail) to deduce these doctrines from passages of Scripture, or from the usage of the earliest ages of the Church, and in this attempt they stumbled again on the false decretals; they would not give up the sacrifice of the Mass; and, above all, they adhered firmly to the idea of the Latin as the universal church. They defended the use of the Latin ritual in the Mass on the ground that the officiating priest belonged far more to the whole Church than to the particular congregation by which he happened to be surrounded.

In short, if, on the one side, the Protestants were driven by the misinterpretation of doctrines, and by abusive practices, to have recourse directly to Scripture (understanding it in a sense corresponding with the fundamental notions of the promitive Latin Church, but ir-reconciliable with the ideas and fictions of recent historical times), their antagonists, on the other, now consented to relinquish some of the most flagrant excrescences in doctrine and to take into considera-tion the removal of the abuses which had already caused so many disputes between spiritual and temporal princes; yet they persisted in affirming that the entire hierarchical system was of immediate divine origin. We see them in search of a method—for they had as yet found none—by which to prove the conformity of their own system with Scripture.

This would not have been of so much importance had they aimed only at self-defense. But that was by no means the case. Not only did the majority declare that they deemed this opinion just and Catholic, and conformable to the Gospel, but they also demanded that the Protestant minority erase the disputed articles from their Confession and return to a unity of faith with the universal orthodox Church. No attention was paid to their agreement in what was essential, ancient, and original, so long as the slightest difference, though merely in acci-dental and unessential particulars, was discernible. Whatever had been altered, whether by the inevitable pressure of circumstances, or in consequence of the legal enactments of a former Diet, was to be re-stored to its original state. The emperor declared himself entirely of this mind. At the end of the confutation, which was published in his name, he admonished the evangelical party to return immediately to obedience to the Roman and Catholic Church. If not, he must proceed against them as became a Roman emperor, the protector and steward of the Church.

The time for mildness was over; the time for severity seemed to have arrived.

The pope had already spoken.

At the very beginning of the meeting, the emperor had de-manded a short statement of the most important demands of the Protestants, drawn up by Melanchthon, which he communicated to the legate, who forwarded it to Rome. As far as we are able to ascertain, the following points were mentioned as indispensable: the Sacrament under both species; the marriage of priests; the elimination of the Canon from the Mass; the cession of the secularized Church properties;

and, finally, the discussion of the other contested questions at an ecumenical council. The document was laid before a consistory of cardinals on July 6. What an opportunity this would have been if they had but entered on the consideration of it in a conciliatory spirit! But they at once declared these articles at variance with faith and discipline, as well as with the interests, of the Church; they decided to reject the petition, and simply to thank the emperor for his zeal.

The assembly of the empire itself had exhorted the emperor to act as became the steward of the Church.

Urged on by both sides, bound by his treaties, and totally surrounded by persons who either had no idea of the real character and views of the Protestants or had long been their enemies, Charles assumed the sternest deportment. Not content with his general declarations, he showed his sentiments by his ungracious behavior to individuals; to the Elector John, especially, he expressed his displeasure that he had separated himself from the emperor, the defender of the faith, introduced innovations, and sought to form confederations. "His majesty also had a soul and a conscience, and would do nothing contrary to God's word." If the Elector would not return to the faith which their forefathers had held for centuries, his majesty, for his part, would not be disposed to grant him infeudation or any of the other favors which he craved.

## RESISTANCE

The might and energy of Latin Christendom was once more exhibited to the world in the person of the emperor. By his brilliant victories he had secured universal peace; even from the Ottoman power he had nothing to dread during the present, or probably the coming, year. The papal authority, as well as the collective power of the states of the empire, was on his side. The Protestants, on the other hand, had no religious or political support in any quarter, or even that internal strength which a firm bond of union would have given them.

It might indeed be doubted whether German princes and lords, trained in the chivalrous life of courts, and converted to the new doctrines in mature age by the arguments and instructions of strangers, to whom a good understanding with their neighbors, and, in their more important affairs, the favor of the emperor, were indispensable, would

have a sufficient constancy to maintain their opinions in defiance
of his express displeasure and of the power concentrated in his person.

The immediate decision of this question depended on the most eminent and powerful among them, to whom the others looked up, and
against whom the emperor chiefly directed his attacks: the Elector
John of Saxony.

Elector John of Saxony, the last of the four excellent sons of Elector
Ernest—educated with the greatest care, at Grimma, to qualify him
for either the spiritual or the temporal dignities of the empire; the
progenitor of the Ernestine House, which now has such numerous and
flourishing branches—possessed neither the political genius nor the
acute and penetrating mind of his brother Frederick. On the other
hand, he was remarkable from his childhood for good nature and
frankness—"without guile and without bile," as Luther said; yet he
was full of that moral earnestness which gives weight and dignity to
simplicity of character. He is believed to have lived to his thirty-
second year, when he married, in perfect chastity; there is at least no
trace of evidence to the contrary. The brilliant and tumultuous knightly
festivals in which he sometimes took part at the court of Maximilian
afforded him no satisfaction, although he always made a distinguished
figure at them; he once said, at a later period in his life, that not one of
these days had passed without a sorrow. He was not born for the amuse-
ments and dissipations of the world; the disgust which inevitably at-
tends them made too deep an impression on him, and gave him more
pain than their frivolous enjoyments gave him pleasure. With his
brother, who was his co-regent, he never had a difference; never did
the one engage a person in his service without the full consent of the
other. From the first appearance of Luther in the world, John embraced his doctrines with the most joyful sympathy; his serious and
profoundly religious mind was gradually but completely imbued with
them. His greatest enjoyment was to have the Scriptures, which he
now heard for the first time, read aloud to him on an evening; sometimes he fell asleep—for he was already far advanced in years—but
he awoke repeating the last verse which he had dwelt upon in his
memory. He occasionally wrote down Luther's sermons, and there is
extant a copy of the lesser catechism in his handwriting. Examples are
not wanting, both before and since his time, of princes whose powers of

action have been paralyzed by absorption in religious contemplation; but with him this was not the case. The extreme simplicity of his character, notwithstanding, he was no less conspicuous for the elevation and force of his will. When, during the Peasants' War, the cause of the princes was in so tottering a state, he did not disguise from himself that a terrible convulsion might ensue; he was prepared for reverses, and he was heard to say that he would content himself with a horse or two, and be a man like other men. But this sentiment did not prevent his defending his good right as bravely as any of his brother princes; only he used his victory with greater clemency. It would be difficult to point out a moment in the subsequent years of his reign in which he could have indulged in a merely contemplative piety. We know of no prince to whom a larger portion of the merit of the establishment of the Protestant church can justly be ascribed. His brother and predecessor had merely not suffered the new doctrines to be crushed; he had taken them under his protection in his own dominions, and, as far as it was possible, in the empire. But when John assumed the government, there were rocks on both sides, on which the whole cause might have gone to wreck, and which could have been avoided only by a policy founded on those lofty convictions which never for a moment failed or wavered. The Peasants' War was followed by violent reactionary tendencies, and as urgently as the adoption of these was pressed upon him by his worldly-wise and experienced cousin, John did not allow himself to be mastered by them. On the contrary, the course which he took at the ensuing Diet contributed to the passing of that Recess on which the entire subsequent legal structure of Protestantism was reared. It soon appeared indeed as if the impetuosity of the Hessian ally would hurry the Elector into a series of political perplexities of which nobody could foresee the end; but his calmer and better judgment saved him in time, and he returned to that defensive position which was natural to him and which he was able to maintain. His sole object and endeavor was to give to the new doctrines an utterance and a recognized existence in his dominions. He introduced into Germany the first evangelical form of church government, which, to a greater or lesser degree, served as model for all the others. He speedily put a stop to the arbitrary acts of his nobles; mild and sweet-tempered as he was, he was not to be induced to grant any unjust favor, and he

censured his son for listening more than was prudent to those about
him. In all these respects Luther had the greatest influence over him:
Luther knew how to set the secret springs of this pure and noble soul
in motion at the proper time and to keep this upright conscience constantly alert. Thus, it was John of Saxony who took the lead in that
Protest which gave its name and position to the entire party. For when
justice and religion were on his side, he knew not hesitation; he sometimes quoted the proverb "Straight forward makes a good runner"
["*Gradaus giebt einen guten Renner*"]. He was by nature retiring,
peaceful, unpretending; but he was raised to such a pitch of resolution
and energy by the greatness of his purposes that he showed himself
fully equal to their accomplishment.

Here, in Augsburg, Elector John had to stand the test whether his
intentions were unadulterated gold or whether they were mixed with
any baser matter.

He felt the reverence to the emperor natural to a prince of the empire, and at first he had no doubt that he would easily be able to reconcile that sentiment with his religious convictions. But it very soon became obvious that this would be impossible; and in order to avert the
danger from the head of their prince, some of his learned men reverted
to the old idea that he should not espouse their cause, but leave it to
stand or fall by itself. They were prepared to deliver the Confession
solely in their own names. The Elector replied, "I too will confess my
Christ" ["*Ich will meinen Christus auch mit bekennen*"].

From that time on, the emperor evinced more and more alienation
from him. "We have implored his imperial majesty," says the Elector
in one of his letters, "to invest us with the electoral dignity according
to the feudal forms; this has been refused. We stand at a great cost
here, having just been obliged to borrow 12,000 gulden; his imperial
majesty has, as yet, given us no word of promise. We cannot think
otherwise than that we have been sorely slandered to his imperial
majesty, and that this has befallen us through our own kinsfolk."

We see the state of mind to which he already had been brought;
and now followed the confutation and the threatening declaration
annexed to it.

That he, with his narrow strip of land on the Elbe and his little
Thuringia—without any allies on whom he could rely—could offer re-

sistance to the emperor, who had just achieved so exalted and commanding a station and was enabled to enforce the ancient ordinances of Latin Christendom, was too wild a thought to be entertained seriously for a moment. Moreover, he was paralyzed by the doubt, whether he had a right to resist, and inclined rather to the opinion that it could in no case be justifiable.

Care was taken to let him know clearly what awaited him. A prince greatly in the confidence of the court told him one day that if he would not submit, the emperor would attack him with an armed force, drive him from his country and his people, and execute the extremest rigors of the law on his person.

The Elector doubted not that it might come even to this. He came home greatly moved, and expressed his consternation that he was required to deny what he had acknowledged to be the truth, or to plunge, with all belonging to him, into irretrievable ruin.

Luther affirms that, had John wavered, not one of his council would have stood firm.

But his simple and straightforward mind viewed the question laid before him in so clear and direct a light that his decision was inevitable. "Either deny God or deny the world," said he; "who can doubt which is better? God has made me an Elector of the empire, a dignity of which I never was worthy; let Him do with me further according to His good pleasure."

A dream which he had about this time affords a curious proof of what was passing in his mind. He was seized with that sort of stifling oppression in which the sleeper feels as if he were expiring under a crushing weight. He dreamed that he lay under a mountain, on the summit of which stood his cousin George; toward morning the mountain crumbled away, and his hostile kinsman fell down by his side.

In short, the aged prince neither quailed nor wavered. Great events rarely come to pass without those great moral efforts which are the necessary, though hidden, germs of new social and political institutions. Elector John continued to declare that the emperor should find him a loyal and peaceful prince in every respect, but that he would never be able to induce him to regard the eternal truth as not the truth or the imperishable word of God as not God's word.

The man who had the greatest influence in keeping him steadfast in this determination was unquestionably Luther, though he was not with him.

Luther's sentence of ban was not yet revoked, and though he remained secure in spite of it, the Elector could not bring him to the Diet. He left him at Coburg, on the frontier of his territory.

It was a great advantage to Luther that he was not involved in the turmoil of affairs and the incidents of the day; he could thus take a more comprehensive view of what was happening.

He was struck with surprise that the emperor appeared so intimately connected with the pope, and so secure of the French; and that the states of the empire had again espoused the pope's party. He treated these things with a sort of irony. "Monsieur Par-ma-foi," as he called the king of France, would, he thought, never forget the disgrace of the battle of Pavia: "Master In nomine Domini" (the pope) would not be much delighted with the devastation of Rome; their amity with the emperor belonged to the chapter "Non credimus." He could not understand how the princes took it so easily that the pope had crowned the emperor without their presence. He compared their assembly with the conclave of jackdaws before his window; there he witnessed the same journeying to and fro, the clamors and pratings of the whole flock, the monotonous preaching of the sophists. "A right useful folk to consume all that the earth brings forth, and to while away the heavy time with chattering." It struck him in particular that the state of things when he first rose to prominence seemed to be entirely forgotten; he reminded his friends that, at that time, the sale of indulgences and the doctrine that God might be satisfied by pious works were universally prevalent; that new services, pilgrimages, relics, and, to crown all, the fable of the garment of Christ, were daily brought forward; that Masses were bargained for and sold for a few pence, more or less, and held to be a sacrifice well-pleasing to God. He called to remembrance that the most effectual weapons for putting down the Peasants' War (at least those of a literary kind) had been used by the Protestants, as a requital for which their enemies were now laboring for their destruction. For he had never for a moment doubted how this matter would end: from the time the emperor had prohibited the preaching, he had ceased to have the slightest hope of reconciliation; he saw that Charles would urge all the subordinate princes to renounce their opinions. Not that he thought the emperor himself was disposed to violence; on the contrary, he never spoke of "the noble blood of emperor Charles" without reverence; but he knew in what hands their good lord was; he beheld in him only the mask behind which their old enemies were concealed; and these, he was persuaded, meditated nothing but force, and trusted to their superior numbers. He thought that the Florentine who now occupied the papal chair would find some opportunity to cause streams of German blood to flow.

But these prospects did not disturb him. "Let them do as they list," he said; "they are not at the end yet."

He could not think of retreating one step farther. "Day and night," he said, "I live in these things. I search the Scriptures, I reflect, I discuss; every day I feel increasing certainty; I will not allow more to be taken from me, let what God wills befall me in consequence." He laughed at the demands of the Catholics for restitution. "Let them first," he exclaimed, "restore the blood of Leonhard Kaiser and of so many other innocent men whom they have murdered!"

His intrepidity was solely the result of his persuasion that his cause is the cause of God. "Some are sorrowful," he said, "as if God had forgotten us; but He cannot forget us, our doctrine, or His work. If Christ is not with us, where then is He in the world? If we do not have God's word, then who has it?" He consoled himself with the words:

> Trust to me, I have overcome the world.
> The Lord dwelleth in the mist; He hath His dwelling place in the darkness. Man seeth not what He is; but He will be the Lord, and we shall see it.
> And if we are not worthy, it will be brought to pass by others. Have our forefathers made us to be what we are? God alone, who will be the Creator after us, as He was before us, causes it to be with us even as it is. If the enemy put me to death, I shall be better avenged than I could desire: there will be one who will say, "Where is thy brother Abel?"

In this temper of mind all his letters of that time are written. Never was a man more intensely penetrated with the immediate presence of the Divine Being. He knew the eternal, all conquering powers in whose service he was engaged; he knew them, such as they had revealed themselves, and he called upon them by their names. He rested with dauntless courage on the promises which they had given to the human race, in the Psalms or in the Gospel.

He spoke with God as with a present Lord and Father. His amanuensis in Coburg once heard him praying to himself: "I know that Thou art our God," he exclaimed; "that Thou will destroy them that persecute Thy people; didst Thou not thus, Thou wouldst abandon Thine own cause; it is not our cause, we have been compelled to embrace it; Thou therefore must defend it." He prayed with the manly courage which feels its right to the protection of the divine power to whom it has devoted itself; his prayer plunges into the depths of the Godhead, without losing the sense of its personality; he does not desist until he has the feeling of being heard—the greatest feeling of which the human heart, raised above all delusion, is in its holiest moments susceptible. "I have prayed for thee," he writes to Melanchthon, "I have felt the Amen in my heart."

A genuine expression of this frame of mind is the hymn "Ein' feste Burg ist unser Gott" ("A Mighty Fortress Is Our God"), the composition of which is justly attributed to this period. It professes to be a paraphrase of Psalm 16, but is in fact merely suggested by it. It is completely the product of the moment in which Luther, engaged in a conflict with a world of foes, sought strength in the consciousness that he was defending a divine cause which could never perish. He seems to lay down his arms, but it was in fact the manliest renunciation of a momentary success, with the certainty of a success which is eternal. How triumphant and elevated is the melody! How simple and steady, how devout and elevated! It is identical with the words; they arose together in those stormy days.

Such was his temper of mind, when he exhorted not only his nearest friends, but the Elector and his council, to be of good courage.

He told his prince to take comfort, that no other crime was imputed to him than the defense of the pure and living word of God. Therein indeed consisted all his honor. In his land he had the best preachers; childhood and youth grew up in the knowledge of the catechism and the word of God, so that it was a joy to see them; this was the paradise over which God had set him as guardian; he not only protected the word, but maintained and nourished it, and therefore it came to his aid. "Oh!" exclaims he, "the young will be your helpers, who with their innocent tongues call so heartily on Heaven."

"I have lately seen two wonders," he wrote to Chancellor Bruck;

> The first: I looked out the window at the stars of heaven, and at the whole beautiful vaulted roof of God, and could nowhere see a pillar upon which the Master had placed His roof; and yet it stands fast. The other: I saw thick clouds hanging over us, and yet no ground upon which they rested, no vessel in which they were contained; yet they fell not, but greeted us with a gloomy countenance and passed on—for God's thoughts are far above our thoughts; if we are only certain that our cause is His cause, then our prayer is already heard and our help already at hand: if the emperor granted us peace, as we wish, the emperor would have the honor; but God Himself will give us peace, that He alone may have the honor.

A determined will always has the power of carrying others along with it. How resistless must it then be in one so filled with the Spirit of God! Luther exercised perhaps a greater influence over his followers from a distance than his continual presence could have given them.

All the other princes vied with Elector John in firmness.

It was on this occasion that Duke Ernest of Lüneburg won the name of the Confessor. Instead of retreating a single step, he received into his intimacy Urbanus Rhegius, the chief promoter of the reformation in his duchy, and took him home from Augsburg, as the most precious treasure which he could bring his people.

The emperor and the king had promised Margrave George of Brandenburg to favor his interests if he would renounce the new doctrine, a consideration which carried all the more weight since Brandenburg even then had claims on certain possessions in Silesia; but the margrave rejected every proposal of the kind. Nor was this all; his powerful and zealously Catholic cousin, Elector Joachim, was no less insistent that he quit the evangelical party, and bitter altercations took place between them. The margrave declared his conviction that the doctrine could not be called an error so long as Christ was really Christ: it taught a man to turn himself to Christ alone; of this he had full experience. Without entering seriously on the discussion of this point, the Elector mainly insisted on the emperor's determination to restore everything to its former state. The margrave replied that the emperor might abolish what he chose; that he himself must submit, but that he would not assist in the work. The Elector asked whether the margrave remembered what he had at stake. He replied, "They say I am to be driven out of my country. I must commit the matter into God's hands."

Wolfgang of Anhalt was by no means a powerful prince; he nevertheless said with the greatest calmness, "Many a time have I taken horse in the cause of my good masters and friends, and my lord Christ deserves that I should venture something for His sake also." "Master Doctor," said he to Eck, "if you are thinking of war, you will find people ready on this side as well."

This being the disposition of the other reformers, it was not likely that the high-spirited landgrave would be brought to concede anything. The Hessian chronicler Lauze relates that, after the Confession had been delivered, certain men took the landgrave to the top of a high mountain and showed him all the good things of the world—that is, held out to him hopes of favor in the affairs of Nassau and Württemberg—but that he refused them all. One day he heard that the emperor intended to reprove him; instantly, accoutered as he was, he hurried to court and begged the emperor to state the acts by which he had incurred his displeasure. The emperor enumerated some, whereupon the landgrave gave an explanation which Charles accepted as satisfactory. But the grand difficulty was yet to come; the emperor required him to show himself a dutiful subject in the matter of the faith, and added, that otherwise he would take the course which befitted him as Roman emperor. But threats were vainer than promises. Philip, moreover, was growing more impatient every day with an assembly in which, in keeping with the hierarchical rules of the empire, he held a position which, in no way, corresponded with his power. He begged the emperor to dismiss him; and when the emperor refused, he rode away one evening without leave. He wrote from a distance to the Elector of Saxony to assure him that he would stake body and goods, land and people, with him and with God's word. "Bid the cities," he wrote his council, "that they be, not women, but men. There is no fear; God is on our side."

And in fact the cities proved themselves not unworthy of the princes.

"Our intention is," the Nuremberg delegates said, "not to yield, for by so doing we should put the emperor's favor above that of God; God, we doubt not, will grant us steadfastness." The burgomaster and council were of the same mind as their delegates.

Others at a distance took part in these events in a similar spirit. "Your Grace," the councilors of Magdeburg wrote to the elector of Saxony, "stands carrying on a perilous struggle in the affairs of all Christendom under the banner of our Saviour: we pray to God daily to grant you patience and strength."

Things had thus already assumed a distinct shape in Germany. On the one side, there was a majority claiming all the rights and privileges of the empire, united with the emperor, and allied with the powers of ancient Europe; on the other, a minority struggling for its existence, isolated and formless, but full of religious fortitude and constancy. The majority, with the emperor at their head, considered using force; steps were already taken to raise troops in Italy. The minority had as yet no plan; they knew only that they were determined not to yield.

But, it might be asked, was not every violent measure full of danger to the majority of the states as well? They were not sure of their own subjects; the suggestion of the Elector of Mainz about the danger with which both parties were threatened in case of a well-timed invasion by the Turks made a deep impression. From these considerations the original proposal of the pacific party, incorporated in the resolutions of the Diet, was adopted, and an attempt at mediation was resolved on.

## ATTEMPT OF THE STATES TO MEDIATE

On August 16 a conference was opened, in which two princes, two doctors of canon law, and three theologians of each party took part, and which soon appeared to promise great results.

The points of dogma at issue presented no insuperable difficulties. On the article of Original Sin, Eck gave way as soon as Melanchthon proved to him that an expression objected to in his definition was in fact merely a popular explanation of an ancient Scholastic one. As far as the article on justification "through faith alone" was concerned,

Wimpina expressly declared that no work was meritorious if performed without grace; he required the union of love with faith; and only to that extent did he object to the word "alone." In this sense, however, the Protestants had no desire to retain it, and they consented to its erasure; their meaning had always been merely that a reconciliation with God must be effected by inward devotion, not by outward acts. On the other hand, Eck declared, the satisfaction which the Catholic Church required to be made through penitence was nothing other than reformation, an explanation which certainly left nothing further to be objected to in the doctrine of the necessity of satisfaction. Even on the difficult point of the Sacrifice of the Mass, there was a great approximation. Eck explained the sacrifice as merely a sacramental sign, in remembrance of the sacrifice which was offered up on the cross. The presence of Christ in the Eucharist was not debated. The Protestants were easily persuaded to acknowledge not only a true, but also a real, presence. This addition is actually inserted in the Ansbach copy of the Confession.

It was certainly not the difference in the fundamental concepts of the Christian dogma which perpetuated the contest. Luther had done nothing more than to revive and re-establish the primitive doctrines of the Latin Church, which had been buried under both the hierarchical systems of later times and an ever-increasing load of abuses. Such diversities as those which we have just mentioned might be reciprocally tolerated; and indeed different opinions had always co-existed. The real cause of the rupture lay in the constitution and practices of the Church.

And with respect to these the Protestants yielded as much as possible. They were persuaded that the division was an obstacle to good discipline in Church and school; and that the government of the Church would be both ill conducted and costly in the hands of temporal sovereigns. The Protestant princes and theologians declared themselves ready to restore to the bishops their jurisdiction, right of anathema, and control over benefices, provided no attempt be made to abridge the liberty of the reading and expounding of the Gospel. They were even disposed to observe fasts, not as an ordinance of God, but for the sake of good order; and, in regard to confession, to admonish the people to confess all matters in which they felt a want of advice and consolation—concessions which, in fact, included a restoration of the externals of the Church to an extent no longer to be expected.

Nor is there any ground for the assertion that the refusal of the Protestants to restore the property of the suppressed convents was the obstacle to a reconciliation. Though the Protestants retorted upon their antagonists the charge of worse acts of spoliation—such as the seizure of the bishopric of Utrecht by the emperor, an event of far greater importance than the suppression of a few convents, since the constitution of the Church was founded on bishops, not on monks—the Elector of Saxony at last agreed to place all the suppressed convents under sequestration; the sequestrators, honorable men chosen from among the nobility of the land, were to pledge themselves to the emperor to allow nothing to be abstracted from the property until a council should decide on its application.

Such were the advances once more made by the Protestants to the Church of Rome and to the majority in the empire. It is difficult to understand why the majority did not meet them with eagerness.

On one point the committee of the majority made a great concession to the Protestants. It expressed the hope of obtaining, at the ensuing council, the general admission of married priests, according to the example of the primitive church. It also offered no objection to the Sacrament under both species.

After so near an approximation, how important were a few differences in practice? Was it necessary to sacrifice to them the unity of the empire and of the nation and the blessings of peace?

That such was the lamentable result may be ascribed mainly to the inability of the Catholic leaders to act as they perhaps would have wished. We know that the affair had already been discussed and decided at the papal court. The papal legate, Campeggio, did not neglect to visit the emperor at the critical moment in order to arouse his Catholic zeal and to bring him back to the views of the Curia. He maintained that all the ordinances of the Church were immediately dictated by the Holy Ghost. He worked on the minds of the states with similar arguments, and at length they demanded that, until the decision of the council, the Protestants should appoint no more married priests to benefices; they persisted in compulsory confession; they would consent neither to the elimination of the Canon from the Mass nor the abolition

of private Masses in Protestant countries; and, lastly, they required that
the reception of Holy Communion under one species be declared no
less valid than under both.

But these were concessions which would have as completely destroyed the infant work of Protestant organization as those demanded
in 1529. Half-formed convictions would thus have been shaken to
their very foundations. The Protestants were prepared not to condemn
the Sacrament under one species; but it was impossible for them to
resolve to declare it equally comfortable with Scripture as their own
form "since," as they affirmed, "Christ instituted the Sacrament under
both species." Nor could they be expected to reintroduce the private
Masses which they had so vehemently denounced as utterly at variance
with the idea of the Sacrament. This would have been to destroy their
own work, their conviction that they had undertaken it on just grounds
notwithstanding.

As the negotiations advanced, too, every step revealed a greater
difference of fundamental principles than the parties had admitted to
themselves. The Catholics regarded the ordinances of ecclesiastical
authority as the rule which admitted, at the utmost, of rare exceptions.
But the Protestants saw the rule of faith and life in Scripture alone;
they would admit the peculiar institutions of the Roman Church only
conditionally, and insofar as doing so was wholly unavoidable. The
former derived all the ordinances of the Church from divine right;
the latter saw in them only human and revocable institutions. But
little was gained as long as the Protestants were unanimously inclined
to regard the papacy as an earthly and human institution, and therefore
one needing limitations; and the religious ideas of the opposite party
were entirely founded on the divine right of the Catholic Church, and
the character of its head as vicar of Christ.

And even had they come to some sort of understanding, and agreed
on some terms of compromise, it would have been almost impossible
to put them into execution. What difficulties, for example, the re-estab-
lishment of bishoprics would have created! The character of the new
church rested mainly on the independence of the lower clergy, and its
immediate connection with the territorial power. The old antipathy of
the cities was already aroused by the suggestion; the Nurembergers
declared they would never again submit to the domination of a bishop.

Another and a less numerous meeting, consisting of only three members on both sides, was convened toward the end of August, after the first negotiations were suspended; but on following their discussions with attention, we find that they never approached the point which the former assembly had reached.

Some isolated attempts at conciliation were afterward made. Duke Henry of Brunswick conferred with the son of the Elector John Frederick, in the garden of a citizen of Augsburg. In the church of St. Maurice, the chancellor of Baden made certain proposals to the chancellor of Saxony, who was accompanied by Melanchthon: these were discussed for a time, but could lead to no results.

The Protestant party had conceded as much as they could and still remain consistent with their religious convictions; they had reached the farthest limits of compliance. Murmurs were already being heard in their own body against the concessions which had been made; it was impossible to induce them to advance a single step farther. During these negotiations Elector John exhorted the theologians only to look at the cause and to take no thought for him or his land.

Nor was any farther concession to be extorted from the other side, fettered as it was by the pope.

## THE EMPEROR'S NEGOTIATIONS

It was impossible that the emperor should be inclined to acquiesce in such a termination of the Diet or to allow it to disperse thus. He was, on the contrary, all the more convinced that an interminable train of still greater evils and troubles must then ensue.

At the very beginning of the deliberations, the Catholic majority had repeated the demand for a council, and Charles, who had already contemplated an ecclesiastical assembly from his own peculiar point of view as emperor, had written about it to the pope. Clement VII laid the demand before a congregation which he had appointed to settle matters of faith. Many declared themselves against it, especially on the two following grounds: (*a*) that those who had rejected the former councils would not consent to a new one: and (*b*) that any attack by the Turks would be far more dangerous while the public attention was absorbed by these internal affairs. But the pope was bound by the promises which he had made during his captivity in the Castel Sant' Angelo, and by expressions which he had let slip in conversation at Bologna. He therefore entreated the emperor once more to weigh the thing maturely; but if his majesty, who was on the spot, and whose zeal for the Catholic religion was undoubted, held it to be absolutely necessary, he also would consent—but only under the condition laid down by the emperor and the states themselves: that the Protestants must, until then, dutifully return to the rite and the doctrines of Holy Mother Church. He proposed Rome as the most suitable place for the meeting.

It was in consequence of this correspondence that, on September 7, the emperor sent a message to the Protestants, in which he announced the council, adding "that they must in the interval conform to the faith and practices of the emperor, the states, and the universal Christian Church."

Did Charles really believe, after all that had happened, that a command of this nature would be obeyed? Such an expectation would only prove that the temper and modes of thinking of the Protestants were forever closed and unintelligible to him. They had already heard of the intended proposal and were prepared. They replied that to comply with such a demand would be to run counter to God and their consciences; moreover, that they were not legally bound to do so; and that the council granted was a consequence of previous decrees of the empire, but that no condition like that now attached to it had ever been so much as discussed. No resolutions which the majority might recently have passed in Speyer to this effect could possibly bind those who had solemnly protested against the whole proceedings there. In the oral communication the emperor had described them as a sect; against this they entered an immediate and solemn protest.

We are in possession of the letter which the emperor thereupon sent to the pope; it proves that he was no less mortified than incensed. "They have answered me," he said, "in the stubbornness of their error, whereupon I am reflecting on what to do."

Since the necessity of resorting to force already arose in prospect before him, he thought that, although the mediation of the states had so utterly failed, he might be able to effect something by his personal intervention. "In order that all our measures may be more completely justified," he continues, "it seems good to me that I should speak with them myself, both jointly and severally, which I think immediately to proceed in." Not, therefore, without giving notice to the court of Rome, he offered the Protestants his personal endeavors to discover means of restoring unity before the meeting of the council.

But he deceived himself greatly if he hoped to accomplish anything with the Protestants through such a missive as he now addressed to them. In it he maintained the nullity of the Protest, without going into the grounds on which it rested, and solely because it was reasonable and expedient that so insignificant a number should yield to the majority; he likewise expressed his astonishment that the Catholic deputies had carried their concessions so far. Since the Protestants had already expressed their final decision, they could not do otherwise than to reject a negotiation founded on such assumptions as these. They entered into no discussion of the religious questions in their answer; they sought only to make the legality of their proceedings clear to the emperor. They replied that they were determined to take their stand on the Recesses of the Diets of 1524 and 1526—a position from which no majority could remove them—and asked for nothing save external peace.

Inevitable as such an answer was, it deeply offended the emperor, and he gave the Protestants to understand that he had received it "with notable displeasure." He said in one of his letters that he could not describe the vexation which this affair caused him. Clinging tenaciously to the idea of the Latin Church and animated by a chivalrous sort of ambition, he had hoped to triumph over all his enemies. Instead, he saw himself involved in a dispute, the very grounds of which were unintelligible to him.

In fact, he now thought that all peaceful means were exhausted and that he must resort to arms. In the letter to the pope which we have just mentioned, he said, "Force is what now would bring the most fruit"; and he was restrained only by the consideration that he was not sufficiently prepared. After the second answer of the Protestants had been received, he declared to the majority of the states that, since he could consent to nothing prejudicial to the faith, and since all conciliatory measures had been of no avail, he was ready to risk his possessions and his person in the cause, and with the aid and counsel of the states, to do whatever might be necessary. He would likewise seek assistance from the pope and other sovereigns.

This thought had been entertained in his privy council from the very beginning of the Diet. Should the Protestants remain obstinate, and, as their enemies wished, refuse to submit either to the judgment of the emperor or to the council, the legate was to be consulted as to the kind of force to be employed.

The emperor appeared disposed to treat the Protestants as he had the Moors in Spain. Had he been fully prepared with munitions of war, and had he not been bound by the resolutions of the majority, he would probably, in spite of his natural mildness, have been led by his consistent adherence to engagements to proceed immediately in this work.

It is, however, not surprising that the majority in the Diet had some hesitation in assenting to such a course. Certain interests had been agitated (as we have already mentioned), about which the states were not fully agreed with the emperor; they were not disposed to follow him implicitly in a crusade. The old sentiment of members of the empire had not yet so entirely given place to religious hatred. On the contrary, at this moment the project of electing a king of the Romans (to which we shall shortly recur) excited fresh dissatisfaction among them.

The states submitted a project of a Recess, which held out, indeed, a menace of war, but at a distance; the Protestants were to be allowed time for repentance until the following May 5 in order to explain themselves on the articles on which it had been found impossible to come to an agreement.

But unfortunately this project, too, was conceived in terms which wounded the feelings of the Protestants. It was said that they must compel no one to join their sect; the word and the thing were equally odious to them, and contained ordinances to which they did not think themselves at liberty to submit: for example, not to allow anything relating to matters of faith to be printed within the period assigned and to allow monks to confess and say Mass; and, lastly, it was expressly asserted that the Confession had been confuted with arguments drawn from the holy Scripture. By accepting and subscribing this Recess, they would have signed the condemnation of their own cause. They rejected it without a moment's hesitation. They not only explicitly stated the grounds for their refusal, but seized the opportunity offered them by the assertion that the Confession had been confuted to lay before the emperor an apology for it. On all main points the apology is like the Confession; but, if I am not mistaken, the nature and style of the former recede still more widely from Catholicism.

This brought down upon them another storm. Elector Joachim of Brandenburg announced to them that if they refused to accept the Recess, the emperor and states were determined to venture person and property, land and people, in order to put an end to the matter. The emperor declared that he would consent to no further alterations. If the Protestant party would accept the Recess, there it was; if not, he, the emperor, in concert with all the other Estates, must take immediate measures for the extirpation of their sect.

But if former threats had been unavailing, these were not likely to make any impression. The religious spirit which, in the rigor of its conscience, had scorned every alliance not founded on perfect uniformity of belief now showed itself no less inflexible toward the system from which it had seceded.

Such was the end of every attempt at approximation. The minority were determined to maintain their position in all its integrity and calmly to await whatever their enemies might undertake against them.

Thus the parties separated.

It would be a complete mistake to imagine that the Elector of Saxony had any political schemes of opposition to the emperor. On the contrary, it was a sincere affliction to him to be forced to sever himself thus from his emperor and lord; but he could not do otherwise. The moment had arrived when, being about to depart, he went to take his leave. "Uncle, uncle," the emperor said, "I did not look for this from your dear person." The Elector made no answer; his eyes filled with tears, but he could find no words; so he left the palace and, immediately after, the city.

A complete separation had taken place among the princes of the empire. In Speyer this had extended to the princes alone; now the emperor was not only present but implicated.

The rupture, which hitherto had been concealed beneath the hope of a reconciliation, was now laid bare. . . .

The most important question was the attitude which the emperor and the majority would assume in their relations with the states which had rejected their Recess.

From all I have been able to discover, it appears that the emperor was more in favor of an immediate resort to force, while the majority were inclined to defer taking up arms.

After being asked repeatedly, they gave in their opinion that the emperor should issue a new religious mandate on the basis of the Edict of Worms. If Saxony with his followers should refuse obedience to it, the emperor should summon them to appear before him, pronounce the due punishment, and proceed to its execution.

The Recess was conceived in the same spirit.

The emperor therein proclaimed his serious determination to enforce his Edict of Worms; he specified a number of infringements of it, all of which he condemned, whether they be called Lutheran, Zwinglian, or Anabaptist; he insisted on the maintenance of every point of the disputed usages or doctrines, and re-established the jurisdiction of the spiritual princes. The imperial fiscal was immediately to proceed judicially against the recusants, even to the punishment of the ban of the empire, which should be executed according to the ordinances of the public peace.

A main point, and one to which we shall shortly have occasion to return, is that the Imperial Chamber was immediately reconstituted and bound to enforce this Recess.

But an appeal to arms remained, as we see from this document, always in reserve; it was an idea to which the emperor incessantly recurred.

In a letter of October 4 to the pope, he expressed himself with great vivacity on the subject; he informed him that the negotiations were broken off and their adversaries more obstinate than ever, but that he was determined to apply all his force to subdue them. He wished the pope to exhort the other princes of Christendom to espouse this cause.

We have another letter, dated October 25, from Charles to the cardinals, in which he earnestly entreated them to promote the convocation of a council. Meanwhile, he wished to consult with them on how he should act toward the Lutherans in the interval in order to avoid further danger; and, in particular, on how he ought to fulfill the functions of an emperor, which had devolved upon him. "We declare to you," he added, "that for the termination of this affair we will spare neither kingdoms nor dominions; nay, that we will devote to it body and soul, which we have wholly dedicated to the service of Almighty God."

On October 30 he sent his major domo, Pedro de la Cueva, to Rome to inform the pope that the Catholic princes were indeed of the opinion that the year was too far advanced to undertake any immediate measures against the Lutherans; but to exhort him (the pope) by no means to desist from preparations for such an enterprise. The emperor, on his side, however desirable it might be for him to go to Spain, would postpone everything in order to put into execution immediately whatever in the pope's opinion might be conducive to the service of God and of His Holiness.

In Rome the question had long been decided. Campeggio had told the emperor that, without some strong measure, he would arrive at no result. He had reminded him of Maximilian, who had never been able to obtain obedience until he took up arms, and used them successfully against the House of the Palatinate.

In short, since the Protestants were not to be brought to conform by mild measures, Western Christendom and the German empire, represented by the pope, the emperor, and the assembly of the empire, appeared resolved to put them down either by law or by force.

It remained to be seen whether the recusants would have the physical and moral strength necessary to make effective resistance.

# CARDINAL RICHELIEU

Ranke's treatment of Cardinal Richelieu is not only a masterful sketch, but the keystone to his description of French history in the early-seventeenth century. In it we can discern clearly the disparate political and social elements of that period, embodied to a striking degree in the person of the cardinal; the struggle for power in the state, dynastic rivalry among the aristocracy, the interplay of Church and state, and the fine threads connecting power with culture. These were the historical themes which most attracted Ranke himself, and he rose to the occasion. Assessing Ranke's portrait of the cardinal, Lord Acton paid him a half-compliment: "Richelieu . . . is a man after his own heart, and his history of Richelieu is the masterpiece of his historical art, though he has lost sight of Richelieu the churchman." A more modern biographer of the cardinal, Willy Andreas, praised Ranke's work for having a moderate understanding of Richelieu "remarkable even from the standpoint of recent research. . . . the historical portrait of the cardinal-minister is of an unusual psychological depth and sharpness, even for Ranke, and one of the most colorful and rich in nuances of his art." This brief picture of Richelieu is taken from Book X, chapter 7, of Ranke's *History of France in the Seventeenth Century*, reprinted in SW 9:399–410. Harper's published only the first two volumes of this work in English translation in 1853; the rest, beyond 1593, remains untranslated.

HIS REAL GREATNESS lay in his ability to raise himself above the regions of private life, above the internal and external enmity always directed against him personally. He at least was convinced that the early misunderstandings with England were aroused by his enemies in order to depose him; the later ones we can connect with the resistance which the queen offered him, under the influence of a personal enemy of the cardinal's. From the very first moment, all the efforts of the Spanish were directed toward his dismissal: they stood in close alliance with Montmorency and the Duke of Orléans, finally with Soissons and Effiat. These efforts drew the whole of Europe into these conflicts. To maintain himself in France, he had to strike an alliance with Sweden, and to protect himself against the continual danger of hostile actions and the melancholy temperament of the king, he had to declare war on the Spaniards. Every military reverse brought concern for himself; every success strengthened his security.

I find it recorded that the cardinal's niece, the Duchess of Aiguillon, had sleepless nights during the siege of Hesdin; for if it failed, her uncle's position would have been threatened. The conquest of Perpignan was supposed to be the price for which the king would have banished Cinq-Mars, had his banishment not come about by news of his participation in a conspiracy. The quarrels and conflicts in France's internal politics affected her neighbors, insofar as they sought to take advantage of them and draw France into ruin. There were persons who aroused such great hate against themselves that it was exceeded only by the hatred which they directed against their opponents.

Richelieu had a streak of amiability in him; he could be irresistible when he wanted to be. But this cultured and delicate spirit was at the same time bitter and prejudiced, and had a hardness and sharpness which would have sufficed for a grand inquisitor. No minister was ever better informed about secrets. Once the papal nuncio wanted to give him information about certain proposals which the Duke of Orléans had made to the vice legate in Avignon. Richelieu returned his confidence by giving him the answers which the vice legate had made to the proposals. When one of the notables of the kingdom came to him to inform him about politically dangerous accustations, the cardinal drew out a paper which already listed the allegations point by point. It was said that all the fathers-confessor were in his service, but that indicates only the astonishment his kind of political omniscience caused, and how much it was generally believed. His ability to gather secret information allowed him to repel all attacks directed against him. He looked with pleasure on his enemies, as they were caught in their own snares and entangled, just as a hunter pursues his game. He reckoned account of their most secret statements and totaled the sum of their sins with unmerciful strictness. Though political trials of questionable justice had been a characteristic throughout French history, they were never more frequent, never of such surprising extent, never of such predictable result, as under Richelieu. He used his social position to carry them out. One day the Count of Cramail drove to the cardinal's for an audience. As he left, a stranger took the reins of his coach and drove him at once to the Bastille. Cramail was the

best-liked cavalier of the court, but he was blamed for having made
the king unnecessarily concerned about the military situation. The
cardinal was able to dine with the Marquis of Fargis before having
him arrested. While he conversed with Puylaurens, the preparations
for his imprisonment were being arranged. Marillac was condemned
in the cardinal's house at Ruel. Popular legend about his violence,
mythically exaggerated in the popular mind, but gladly repeated by
historians, has centered on this residence of his.

One of the cardinal's basic rules when deciding whether reward or
punishment would be more vital to the state was to choose punishment. It was a crime against the public interest to ignore any actions
by those who injured that interest. Conscience must have courage; a
timid conscience only favored evil. He acted to produce the greatest
amount of terror. In cases of treason, the proceedings began with an
execution, to avoid any danger of a lesser sentence of imprisonment or
exile. One could hardly speak of procedures to protect the innocent:
the concept of an unapproachable, powerful state hung like a sword
over all opponents.

How many of them perished! Others, like the marshals Bassom-
pierre and Vitry, lived in the Bastille; still others fled into exile, like
Vendôme in England, awaiting the changes which time must bring.
Most of the great officials were dismissed. Epernon, who had maintained himself for so long, was finally banished to one of his castles.
The old republican custom of sending members of the opposition, out
of favor, to a fixed and distant place of residence was often used. In
all the circle surrounding the supreme state power the dominating
idea was exclusively: how could one exercise influence over this power?

It would be a misunderstanding to assume that Richelieu wanted
to reduce everyone in the land to an equal level. Rather, it was more
his personal ambition to elevate his own family to higher rank under
the aegis of royal favor, surpassing notables of equal birth. Though he
fought with the great governors for the royal prerogative to change
the provincial administration whenever he saw fit, he made no concession to the popular desire that they be changed at regular intervals.
He maintained, rather, that the most notable men, who had connection
with the country as landowners, should be in charge of the provinces.
In entrusting military commands, he selected men of highborn origin.

It almost seemed to him that royal authority was not strong enough in itself to enforce orders unconditionally. And, similarly, the lower nobility, deprived by the changes in the military organization of that unruly military service and feudal privilege which had caused Henry IV so often to complain, eagerly joined the regular military units which the new century required. This brought them to a new vocation and way of life, but it also gave the service a certain brilliance as well.

We have seen how Richelieu restrained the political ambitions of the *parlements*; he generally took the side of the clergy in their disputes with these bodies. But far from encroaching upon their traditional position, he even contributed to strengthening it. After hesitating for some time in the matter, he finally confirmed the inheritability of office through new decrees, and the concept of the nobility of the robe continued decisively to establish itself from that time.

Richelieu sought to rule chiefly with his friends, relatives, and those who joined with him, whom he called his alliance. His family played an important part in the government and in war. The Marquis de Pontcourlay, the son of his oldest sister, whose children continued the name of Richelieu, was general of the galleys. He was the one who defeated the Spanish before Genoa. His brother-in-law, the husband of his younger sister, Urbain Marquis de Brezé, commanded the army, not without distinction. He became vice regent of Catalonia; his son Fronsac excelled at sea. A nephew of the cardinal's mother, the Duke of Meilleraye, commanded before Perpignan, and held the post of Grand Master of Artillery. There were still Swiss soldiers in French service, and when in 1635 four infantry regiments were recruited, another cousin of Richelieu's, Caesar de Cambout, received appointment as colonel of these troops, with the right to grant patents to the officers. Harcourt, who reconquered Savoy, was married to a sister of this Cambout. But Richelieu arranged the most brilliant marriage for his niece, the daughter of Brezé: she married Condé's eldest son, Enghien, later called "the Great Condé." What a triumph, according to the ideas of the time, to join the most able young heir of the two great families of Lorraine and Bourbon in such close alliance with the cardinal!

Nothing was more useful to him than the good relationship with the Duke of Condé which this alliance brought. Both Condé's prominence

and his loyalty to the cardinal caused everyone to regard it as a high
favor for Richelieu to become related to the pair.

And how many others were there whom the course of events had
placed in higher or lower office who attached themselves to the cardinal with equal devotion!

Richelieu's closest ally was François Le Clerq du Tremblay, known
in the Capuchin order as Father Joseph. The latter had already seen
military service when he entered the order. He was uncommonly effective as a preacher, missionary, and professor, an eager persecutor of
any deviation in and out of Catholicism. With a great reputation for
spirituality, coupled with an adroitness in foreign affairs, he established
a strong influence on the most important persons at court. Richelieu's
rise to power was partly due to him. The two became acquainted at
first in religious transactions, and became allies. Later the priest aided
the cardinal in secular matters. For this purpose he secured dispensations from the general of his order and the pope. With four other
Capuchins, who were supported by the king, he formed a sort of min-
isterial bureau for secret business of a diplomatic, religious, or even
military nature. Here such matters were prepared for the information
and decision of the cardinal. Often Father Joseph would work together
with him. At Ruel, a residence was always kept in readiness for him.
The same was true of the royal palaces of St. Germain, Fontainebleau,
and even the Louvre. He used his influence on the king in full support
of the cardinal, and shared his opinions. With regard to Duke Bernard, whose best and most useful friend he appeared to be, he said:
"We must support our friends, for they are the ones who will maintain
us." Once he had been seen with knapsack on his back, a poor monk
wandering along the highways. Now he rode in a royal coach from
palace to palace. Representatives of foreign powers paid court to him,
if they were fortunate enough to be able to find him.

Father Joseph was not creative in discovering new expedients or
remedies; nor did he have that pertinent grasp of the possible which
characterizes a great statesman, and which the cardinal so outstandingly
possessed. But working together, they developed the greatest political
intelligence of their age. The priest had not only the head but the nerve
for everything; nothing disconcerted him. He could excuse anything;
he accepted responsibility for the most odious things without hesita-

tion. He opened the way to a politics of dark power which was appalled at nothing. He, even more than the cardinal, abandoned all scruples. In all heaven and earth, he was concerned with nothing but the politics of the moment. It was in the midst of a conversation with a Spanish secret agent that he suffered the stroke which led to his death. On his deathbed he saw the fall of Breisach as in a vision—not because of inspiration, as has been assumed. But he had lived and worked for no other goal. Knowing that things there had reached a state of desperation, he told the papal nuncio that the event had occurred and that it would advance the peace settlement. The cardinal declared that he had lost the man on whom he most depended and who had most satisfied him, and in his family, Father Joseph was mourned.

In Richelieu's ministry there occasionally were disturbances: thus Bouillon and Chavigny once allied to oust Servien, who disagreed with them. But this was not the cardinal's doing. Noyers, who undertook the burden of preparing political business after Father Joseph's death, working day and night over the documents, was more of a sharp thinking assistant than an original mind. "Under the cardinal," the Venetian ambassador reported of these ministers, "they carry on the work; the cardinal informs them of his inclinations and intentions; they are tools in his hand."

If we wish to know how things were managed, we should study the instructions which Bouillon received upon taking charge of finances. The cardinal reminded him that he ought thenceforth to show the same concern for the public wealth as he had previously shown in increasing his own; that from then on he must content himself with the salary which the king awarded; that he was to devote all his thoughts to the reform of finances and the relief of the people; and that he must renounce the feelings which he had held against others, and decide all matters according to reasonable grounds. Bouillon promised him, on his honor, to follow each point exactly. Richelieu warned the archbishop of Sourdis—in order to refute imputations that the cardinal could not get along with anyone—that he was a man of deeds, not merely of words; and that the slightest mishap by the bishop would be sufficient for the cardinal to banish him. Pontcourlay, who justly deserved blame for extravagant living above his means, and who did not amend his ways, lost his position despite the most brilliant victory.

Richelieu allowed those who served the state also to take care of themselves. He once reminded the king of the saying of an ancient emperor: that he might not neglect the business of those who directed his own. But, he continued, if anyone should use the public business as an excuse for accomplishing his own personal profit, he would become a plague to the state. Richelieu tolerated no mistakes, even in his personal entourage, which damaged the state.

Richelieu was like a second king in the land. As early as in 1629, it was remarked how the climbing and ambitious crowd filled his houses and the doors of his apartments. When he was carried out in his sedan chair, they greeted him with deep respect. One knelt down; another tendered him a petition; a third sought to kiss his robe; every man counted himself fortunate who could boast of having received a favorable glance. For the sum of the business of state was already in his hands; and he held the highest honors which a subject could enjoy. He was regarded even more highly for possessing at the same time the crimson robes of a cardinal. Even Condé, the leading prince of the blood royal, gave him precedence.

Afterward, he became still more powerful and especially more frightening. He lived in deep seclusion at Ruel, in a park somewhat sheltered from the north wind. Here even today, in the ruins left by the French Revolution, can be found a few traces of the artisans' skill, a few remains of the art of fountain building which was transplanted here from its native Italy. He was scarcely accessible—foreign ambassadors had to have something essential to present if they wished to speak to him—but he was the real center of the government. The king often came over from St. Germain to meetings of the state council. If the cardinal went to the king, he went surrounded by his own bodyguard, who were sworn to loyalty and whom he himself paid, for even in the royal household he wished to have no fear of his enemies. There were large numbers of young nobles from the most distinguished families who joined his service and supplied his personal needs. He established a school for them. He maintained a completely equipped stable, a brilliant array of servants, a more expensively provided table than the king's; he lived better. In Paris, he owned the lesser Luxembourg and built for himself the Palais Royal, which at that time bore in large letters the inscription Palais Cardinal, as well as Hôtel Richelieu. He had there a golden chapel, the church fixtures of which were made of the most precious metals and jewels, as well as a glorious collection of well-selected art works, a library, and his own theater. He invited the famous Italian singer Signora Leonora to his own country house. He had a warm interest in the developing French drama. Whatever caused him pleasure, such as the little Jacqueline Pascal, earned his favor. Even his friends thought it seemed that the cardinal was paying too exacting an attention to the plays which he had presented. He found it essential to surround himself with clever and pleasant friends. Their society was once prescribed for him by the physicians as a proper medicine. He also had a natural liking and inclination for literature. We are still struck by the forceful and productive minds he had surrounding him. Along with the rise of the monarchy came the rise of the literary movement which was to glorify it. Richelieu's primary intent was directed toward purifying the French language. In his public pronouncements he displays the contemporary exaggerated idiom; but in his private letters, his style is pure and correct. The words are carefully chosen and pertinent; in the style of his sentences we can catch the changing of his moods. His chief thought when founding the Académie Française was to cleanse the French language of all the deformities which it had acquired from capricious or unstructured usage. He wanted to raise it forever from the status of a barbaric tongue, to attain, as the third in the series, the rank which Greek, then Latin, had formerly held. The concept of a modern classicism, which he consciously encouraged, also had a political significance. Like the newspaper which he had published, it was a monarchical institution.

As Richelieu brought literature into close connection with contemporary life, he always kept posterity and its judgment in mind. On his orders, numerous collections of official documents were made, of which the most important appeared in connection with a book which he himself undertook, a history of his times. These contain, although unspecified, many traces of his revision. They include also the most remarkable of all the productions associated with him: the countless memoranda which he presented to the king at important moments. These memoranda can be compared to Machiavelli's for the sharpness of their insights, and to those of the Spanish State Council for the detailed argumentation of motives. They have no equal in their boldness, greatness of historical view, direct presentation of goals, and effect on world history.

They are doubtless one-sided. Richelieu recognized no law but his own. He persecuted the enemies of France with no less hatred than he persecuted his own. The documents display no spiritual tendencies directed toward the highest goals of human existence; they are wholly bounded by the horizon of the state. But they testify to an acuteness which perceived the results of an action into the farthest distance, could discern the most feasible of possible alternatives, and determine among several goods the best and better courses of action. It was Richelieu's ambition to lead the king by convincing him, rather than by his authority. His detailed expositions and strong conclusions sought to hold the king to the advice which he offered. All these memoranda are filled with a single thought, which develops with increasing breadth of perspective and goal: to raise the monarchy above the will of every single person in France and to extend the authority of France over Europe. Never was a policy accorded a more brilliant success.

He had become master of all his enemies.

Where was Count Olivares with his threats, his personal as well as his national enmity? The Spanish monarchy was thrown back on all its frontiers and internally ruined. Buckingham aside, where was the resistance which even the king and queen of England offered him? Charles I withdrew to York; his wife left the country. The alliance with Spain, which had given increased power to the Holy Roman Emperors in previous decades, now became ruinous for them; Richelieu could have a party in Germany and in Europe which would not recognize Emperor Ferdinand III in his office.

And whatever happened to those who had so often led the internal storms of France, had gathered themselves up against Richelieu? From the moment of her banishment from France Queen Marie de Medicis never enjoyed an instant of contentment or satisfaction. She fled from country to country, never welcomed. When she once brought herself to petition for permission to return to France, the council met and denied it. While the prince whom she had brought into the world conquered new provinces, she died in a private house. It was the same house in Cologne in which the painter Rubens is said to have been born, the person who, as the inscription there states, represented the "zenith of her life in gorgeous painting" in the happier days of her changing fate. The demons whose conquest the artist had then celebrated now gathered against her, joining with another opponent and changing her fortune. The man for whom she had done the most, and whom she had raised to his position, had become her most dangerous enemy.

The Duke of Orléans, who took part in still another conspiracy, that of Cinq-Mars, went to Savoy. In order to be allowed to return, he had to promise to live only as a private person without military or governmental office, and to live wherever the king pleased.

Richelieu made arrangements in the royal household itself which displeased the king, but which he did not dare to countermand.

For this, in sum, was the character of his life: every step he took bore traces of reckless violence; and no mortal was ever so favored by fortune. Or was his success due to an insistent search for knowledge of every detail, correct and infallible calculation? His admirers assure us that he wrenched good fortune itself from fate.

Yet while Richelieu ruled so great a part of the earth with a hint of his will, he himself was crippled in all his limbs and suffered from the most painful and dangerous illness. He could no longer bring his hand to sign his name or mount a carriage to transport himself from place to place. A sedan chair was built for him containing a bed, a table, and a chair for those with whom he wished to converse. This was carried by his bodyguard who would allow no one else to do it, two teams of eighteen men each, who would change positions with one another, from Narbonne to Paris. Here and there the walls of the cities were broken through or their moats covered with bridges, to prepare for him a less unpleasant path.

Still he thought himself far from his goals, whether for himself, for France, or the world; he still grasped the rudder of the ship with searching glance and his usual security when in December 1642 he suffered a renewed attack of his illness. Dying, he declared that he had never had a single enemy who was not the enemy of the state. The identification of his personal interests with those of the state, which was his undeniable strength throughout life, accompanied him to his death.

"A great politician has died," Louis XIII remarked upon hearing of his death. Nothing could be heard of personal grief. But in these words lay the explanation and justification of the cardinal's entire life.

Whatever contemporaries and posterity have judged concerning Richelieu, be it admiration or hatred, revulsion or respect, this was a man who bore the stamp of his century upon his countenance. He gave the Bourbon monarchy its powerful position in the world. The epoch of Spain was over; the epoch of France, about to begin.

# VI

# Personal Reflections
## on History

Those students such as Heinrich von Sybel or Wilhelm Dilthey who sat through Ranke's lectures commented on the lively digressions which frequently interrupted the set presentations of his thoughts. However learned his preparation—and we know from surviving lecture notes that they were voluminous and often reworked—Ranke could not resist spontaneous utterances, frequently on the craft of history. His private notes and letters abound with them, and we even find such short dissertations inserted in the introductions and narrative of his formally composed histories. Unlike that of Droysen, who summed up his conception of history in his *Historik*, Ranke's legacy is scattered. Although no collection of fragments can wholly recapture the coherence of his original thoughts, I have tried in the following pages to give examples of Ranke's ideas on the personal meaning of history, on its demands as art and science, and on the role of the historian.

The first selection captures something of the excitement of the young *Gymnasium* teacher about to launch his career, while a few of the latter documents picture the reflections of an old man on his life's work. The priestly office of the historian which appears in his letter to his brother in 1820 is still in his mind as he writes to his son in 1873. The intervening selections focus on the mind of a working historian. They deal with such topics as the nature and method of historical research, the relationship of history and biography, the understanding of universal history, of freedom and necessity in history, of power and the state. Finally, the section concludes with two aspects of Ranke's legacy, as teacher, and as writing historian.

# THE HOLY HIEROGLYPH

*To* his brother Heinrich

Frankfurt on Oder, End of March 1820
...I had a wonderful hour with Heydler.* I find, as you said, that he tried not to offend me, and I will also make the effort. We sat with our wine. The newspapers lay on the table with the campaign of Riego and the stories about Corunna and Navarre. We looked through them, reading: "Cadiz, Cadiz, Arise!" In happy intoxication we strolled home. "But I cannot," he said, "convince myself to die for this freedom." We spoke together about the different manifestations of God, and how this sanctifying belief has been held in all ages and centuries, and of how we are all destined for death, so that God might be free. I stood by the stove, much moved; he paced back and forth about the room. I stopped talking; "continue, continue," he said. Finally, we both stopped and parted with triple good-nights.

Heydler feels himself limited by the school. I believe that the faithfulness to detail which he exercises will raise him above others, better and faster than two or three books about Greek theater.

How very sweet it is to gorge ourselves with the riches of all the centuries, to see the heroes face to face, almost more impressive and vital, to live again with them all, how very sweet, and how very enticing!

Now comes my vacation, and there awaits for me a capital piece of work. I want to learn something about the life of the nations in the fifteenth century, of the renewed germination of all the seeds sown by antiquity—as if the old blooms had been blighted, and the long planted seed sprouted high. I still know nothing about it. But at least I foresee that these strivings, formations, desires were a thing not only of the literate nobility but in a certain form of the people. I know this from the Reformation. Even though the Gospel was revealed by God's grace

* Ferdinand Heydler (1793–1859) had been a student at Pforte and Leipzig with Ranke and was a colleague at the Frankfurt on Oder *Gymnasium.*

originally to Luther, the success of the message was based on completely different grounds. Only dry wood quickly catches the flame.

And so I hope I shall learn, or surmise, the way in which empire and papacy died and gave forth a new breath of a new life, passing on vitality with the same certainty and universality with which infected air produces contagion.

Fichte, I think, once said that his love of the living past, of its idea, this inner drive to acquaintance with antiquity in its depth, leads to God. I cannot forget the saying: "Who takes the Lord's Body and does not believe does it to his judgment." But is it not thus: that those who only shallowly and superficially grasp the past sinfully also do it to their own judgment? Their sorrow deepens; their life becomes more shallow; their thinking, more congealed. What once occurred in Italy now happens to so many, as if the indwelling spirit revenges itself for being mocked.

In all of history God dwells, lives, is to be found. Every deed testifies to Him; every instant preaches His name, but above all, I think, the great interactions of history. He stands there like a holy hieroglyph, perceived only in its outline and preserved lest it be lost from the sight of future centuries.

Boldly then! Let things happen as they may; only, for our part, let us try to unveil this holy hieroglyph. And so shall we serve God; so are we also priests, also teachers.

God be with you, my brother. You are constantly in my mind. I clasp your hand.

L.

(SW 53/54:88).

# THE STATE OF
# HISTORICAL RESEARCH

In our times historical studies have turned more than ever toward the original remains of the past from all the centuries. The deciphering of the Assyrian and Egyptian monuments, the collection of Greek and Roman inscriptions, the editing of documents and literature from the Middle Ages, the scholarly search through modern archives—all, despite differences in object, methods of study, and intellectual abilities, have the same end: to go beyond inherited tradition, to establish mastery over the lives of former times through direct participants or those related to them, and to see the past like the present before one's own eyes.

The modern centuries have also produced in more than one nation historians of real talent who are perhaps equal to the masters of antiquity. But they stand in a far different—and indeed disadvantageous—relation to present studies than do the earlier writers. Archaeological discoveries scarcely touch the area of political events with which the historical accounts are concerned. The archival research of modern times is directed primarily to this topic. The ancients stand alone and great over a dead world, and are hardly vulnerable to criticism based on other information. The moderns, in contrast, can receive such criticism in its fullest extent. The materials still exist from which they composed their works. And beyond these are countless other witnesses to the forces, drawn from the course and interaction of affairs, which affect every historical event. I would surprise you if I asserted that archival study of periods slightly removed from our times has an advantage over a view of the present. But it allows us to recognize more completely and clearly the relationship of events than we can surrounded by contemporary passions and interests. How much in every period remains necessarily secret, and even intentionally falsified! The inner circumstances of events first come to light with their results. While still engaged in struggle, the conflicting intentions cannot possibly be given justice. It is precisely this conflict of contemporaries which gives rise to most historical works of a period, and which determines the historical tradition. These have in themselves an invaluable worth; but in order not to be directly dependent upon them or their errors, and to avoid continuing unintended or intentional distortions and bias, it is necessary to seek a broader basis for our portrayal. This can be gained only through a study of the original documents of the period and through the light which subsequent time has cast upon it. This is, I think, particularly suited to the progress of German historical scholarship, which expresses the genius of the nation in attempting to comprehend the history of all other peoples with the same trouble and effort as its own. One should not allow oneself to be bound and determined by the one-sided conceptions which necessarily form in every nation, in every age, as a reaction to political tendencies. Otherwise, a universal history of objective value would be unthinkable.

Everything hangs together: critical study of authentic sources, impartial understanding, objective narration—the goal is to bring to life the whole truth.

I advance an ideal which people will say is unrealizable. The facts are thus: the idea is infinite; the achievement by its very nature, limited. Fortunate enough, when one sets forth on the correct path and attains a result which can withstand further research and criticism.

from the *History of England* (SW 21/22:113).

# HISTORICAL RESEARCH

## (From His Notes of the 1840s)

In General: Historical Research

It is necessary to strip away the phraseology from the account, to restore it to its original essence and content. Is a completely true history possible?

1. Exact knowledge of the particular moments.

2. Their personal motivations.

3. Their cooperation, the active movements of their personalities, their changing reactions to one another.

4. The universal interrelationships.

The final result is a sympathetic comprehension of the universe.

(SW 53/54:569).

History will always be rewritten, as has often been remarked. Every age, with its main tendencies, makes history its own, and has its own ideas of it. Thus praise and blame are distributed. So the process slowly continues, until we can hardly recognize the event itself. Then nothing can help but a return to the original sources. But would these ever be studied, without the impulses generated by the present? Granting this, we must always strive to obtain a clearer view of the events. This exalted goal is to be shared by philosophy and human history.

(SW 53/54:569).

# HISTORY AND BIOGRAPHY

Plutarch once reminded us that he wrote, not history, but biography. In this remark, he touched upon one of the principal difficulties of general historical as well as biographical presentation. In portraying a living personality, we must not forget the conditions in which he appeared and was active. In sketching the great course of world historical events, we must always be aware of the personalities from which they derive their impetus.

How much more powerful, deeper, and all-embracing is the general course of life which fills the centuries in unbroken flow than the personal life, allotted but a span of time, which appears only to begin things, never to end them. Human decisions proceed from the possibilities offered by the general situation. Meaningful successes occur only in collaboration with the homogeneous world-elements. Each person appears only as the child of his age, the expression of a general tendency which also exists outside him.

But personalities also belong to a moral world order in which they are completely themselves: they have an independent life of original strength. If, as we like to say, they represent their age, they also draw upon their inborn inner force and affect their times decisively.

A man can mature only in continuing participation in public affairs, which then earns him a place in the memory of posterity. In times of great crisis, in which personalities develop most their inborn nature and power to strive for their aims, conditions also change the most rapidly. Each change of conditions dominates the world or seems to do so. Each stage of the development of the world offers the enterprising spirit new tasks and new viewpoints. The general and the particular alike must be presented to our eyes if we are to understand either: the effect which the one exercises, and the reaction which it then experiences from the other.

Events develop in an interaction of individual forces with the objective world situation. Success is the measure of these forces.

The rich variety of history consists in its assimilation of the biographic impulses. But biography can also, at certain times, broaden into history.

from the Introduction to his biography of Wallenstein (SW 23:v–vi).

# ON UNIVERSAL HISTORY

## I

Great peoples and states have a double character—one national, and the other belonging to the destinies of the world. Their history, in a similar manner, presents a twofold aspect. Insofar as it forms an essential feature in the development of humanity in general, or records a prevailing influence exercised upon that development, it awakens a curiosity which extends far beyond the limits of nationality; it attracts the attention of and becomes an object of study for even those who are not natives of the lands whose story is narrated.

Perhaps the difference between the Greek authors who treated the history of ancient Rome in its flourishing period, and the Romans themselves, consists in the fact that the Greeks regarded the subject as it affected the entire world, while the Romans looked at it nationally. The object is the same: the writers differ in the positions from which they view it, but together they inform posterity.

Introduction to the *History of France* (SW 8:v).

## II

When we contemplate the framework of the earth, those heights which testify to the inherent energy of the original and active elements attract our special notice; we admire the massive mountains which overhang and dominate the lowlands covered with the settlements of man. So also in the domain of history we are attracted by epochs in which the elemental forces, whose joint action or tempered antagonism has produced states and kingdoms, rise in sudden war against each other, and amidst the surging sea of troubles upheave into the light new formations, which give to subsequent ages their special character. Such an historic region, dominating the world, is formed by that epoch of [seventeenth-century] English history to which the studies, whose results I venture to publish in the present work, have been devoted: its importance is as great where it directly touches on the universal interests of humanity as where, on its own special ground, it develops itself apart in obedience to its inner impulses. To comprehend this period we must approach it as closely as possible: it is everywhere instinct with collective as well as individual life. We discern how great antagonistic principles sprang almost unavoidably out of earlier times, how they came into conflict, where the strength of each side lay, what caused the alternations of success, and how the final decisions were brought about; but at the same time we perceived how much, for themselves, for the great interests which they represented, and for the enemies which they subdued, depended on the character, the energy, and the conduct of individuals. Were the men equal to the emergency, or were circumstances not stronger than they?

From the conflict of the universal with the particular the great catastrophes of history arise, yet it sometimes happens that the efforts which seem to perish with their authors exercise a more lasting influence on the progress of events than does the power of the conqueror. In the agonizing struggles of men's minds ideas and designs appear which pass beyond what is feasible in that land and at that time, perhaps even beyond what is desirable; these find a place and a future in the colonies, the settlement of which is closely connected with the struggle at home. We are far from intending to involve ourselves in juridical and constitutional controversies, or from regulating the distribution of praise and blame by the opinions which have gained the day at a later time, or which prevail at the moment; still less shall be guided by our own sympathies: our only concern is to become acquainted with the great motive powers and their results. And yet how can we help recognizing manifold coincidences with that conflict of opinions and tendencies in which we are involved at the present day? But it is no part of our plan to follow these out. Momentary resemblances often mislead the politician who seeks a sure foothold in the past, as well as the historian who seeks it in the present. The Muse of History has the widest intellectual horizon and the full courage of her convictions; but in forming them she is thoroughly conscientious, and, we might say, jealously bent on her duty.

Introduction to the *History of England* (SW 14:ix–x).

# III

. . . In the sense in which I use it, universal history encompasses the events of all nations and periods, with this limitation: that they be possible subjects for scholarly work. For a long time, the view of universal history drawn from the prophetic Biblical books, of the four universal monarchies, was accepted as satisfactory. This view persisted even into the seventeenth century, but in the eighteenth it was replaced by that of the progress of the modern world. Under the influence of the revolution in ideas, universal history was secularized. The previous concept became untenable after the publication of the voluminous history of nations published in England under the title *History of the World.* This found a corresponding response from German historians, and stimulated them to similar efforts.

But a history of the several nations is not sufficient. A collection of the history of different peoples in narrower or broader framework is still not a universal history. The interrelationships of things is lost from sight. This is precisely the task of the study of universal history: to recognize these interrelationships, to indicate the course of large-scale events, which bind all the peoples together and dominate their history. Even a glance teaches us that such a relationship exists.

The origins of culture belong to an epoch whose secrets we cannot decipher. But its further development forms the most powerful manifestation in the centuries for which we have a reliable tradition. No single word can completely describe its nature. It includes both the religious and the political, the foundations of law and of human society. Sometimes the ancient, inherited condition of one or another Asiatic people is regarded as the basis of all history. But it is impossible to proceed from a people of perpetual unchangingness to grasp the inner dynamics of universal history. The nations can come under consideration only insofar as they react upon one another and with each other form a living unity.

What we call culture, or civilization, contains one of the most powerful motives for its own inner evolution. Were we to ascribe to this process a specific goal, then we would only obscure the future and miss the boundless breadth of the historical process. Within the limitations of historical research, we encounter only the most varied forms in which this civilization appears, while at the same time it is resisted by the indigenous forms and customs of the different peoples and races. These too have their own original justification, and cannot be coerced. But history does not consist solely in cultural development. It arises still more from impulses of a completely different sort, the antagonism between nations, which fight over territory and predominance with one another. In these battles, which always also include the domain of cultural life, the great powers of history are formed, which continue without respite contending for leadership; thereby the particular is transformed by the universal, at the same time defending itself against the latter and reacting toward it.

World history would become fantasy and philosophic dream if it were to cut itself off from the sound foundation of national history; but neither can it remain upon that plane. In the nations themselves the history of humanity appears. There is an historical life which passes progressively from one nation to another, from one group of peoples to another. In the battles of individual groups of peoples universal history arises, and the nationalities themselves are brought to self-awareness. The nations themselves are not entirely natural creations. Nationalities of such great power and unique cultural form as the English or the Italian are not so much the products of their own land and race as results of great changes in events.

How then are we to investigate and understand the general life of humanity and at least that of the foremost nations? We dare not ignore the laws of historical criticism, as they apply to every research into particular events. For only critically researched history can be regarded as history. Our eyes must always be directed toward the universal. But false premisses can lead only to false conclusions. Critical research, on the one hand, and comprehensive understanding, on the other, will reinforce one another.

In discussions with trusted friends, I have often raised the question, whether it would be at all possible to compose a universal history in this sense. The conclusion was that it is not possible to satisfy these most stringent standards, but it is necessary to try.

*Weltgeschichte* I, pp. vi–ix.

# SPIRIT AND THE STATE
# IN HISTORY

KARL: But you will not deny that these distinctions [in the abstract types of the monarchy, aristocracy, and democracy] are important. You will not disagree that the different states have something in common?

FRIEDRICH: It seems to me, however, that we must distinguish between the real and the formal elements. The formal is the universal; the real, the particular, the living, element. Certain forms of constitution—namely, those which are intended to limit personal power or the relationship of the classes—may be necessary for all states. But these are not the original source of life, which alone can give content to the forms. There is something which makes every state not merely a compartment of general reality, but a living individual, a unique self.

KARL: If I understand you correctly, your opinion differs from others in that one usually begins with the different political forms, and proceeds from them to present the particular examples of the types described. You, on the other hand, regard these forms only as a secondary, subordinate element. For you the original fact is the unique spiritual existence of the individual state, its principle.

FRIEDRICH: Let me explain with an example from the study of language. The forms by which grammar operates are generally applicable. They repeat themselves universally in a certain way. But the spirit of each particular language creates an infinite variety of modifications. By the principle of the state we should understand, not an abstraction, but its inner life. This principle gives to these forms of human society what is undeniably essential: their own specific modification, their own reality.

KARL: You maintain that there are different spiritual essences, then, which alone bring to life all the various constitutions and societies. . . .

FRIEDRICH: All the states which count in the world and are significant are motivated by a particular tendency of their own. It would be ridiculous to describe them as so many police departments for the benefit of individuals who have compacted together to protect their property. These tendencies are, rather, of a spiritual nature, which determines the character of their citizens, and indissolubly marks them. Out of the differences which arise from these tendencies come the modifications in constitutional forms everywhere, although these modifications also derive from common necessity. Everything depends upon the higher idea. This remains so even if we say that the states also derive their origin from God. For the idea is of divine origin. Every independent state has its own independent life, which, like any living thing, can, of course, perish. But while it lives it fills its whole environment and dominates it; it is identical with no other state.

KARL: In this sense, you take the states to be individuals?

FRIEDRICH: Individualities, each analogous to one another but essentially independent. Instead of these temporary conglomerations which the contract theory of the state presents, like cloud formations, I see them as spiritual substances, original creations of the human mind—one could say, thoughts of God. . . .

KARL: In this regard it would be possible for the state always to become more perfect. This would admit of progress.

FRIEDRICH: Only admit? The state is a living being whose every nature requires that it develop unceasingly, and progress irresistibly.

KARL: After what model, what ideal?

FRIEDRICH: All life bears its ideal within itself. The innermost drive of spiritual life is movement toward its idea, toward greater perfection. This drive is inborn, implanted in its origins.

KARL: You will not deny that there are often obstacles, failures, or even, let us say, relapses?

FRIEDRICH: When are they ever lacking in human affairs? But we should not lose courage for this reason. When we are otherwise healthy, these are only passing illnesses.

KARL: I still cannot see how these can be made harmless, for your government has no formal counterweight.

FRIEDRICH: Nonetheless, there is a spirit of the community which is not so easy to overcome. It can be obscured, but as long as some vital energy remains, it will reappear, gain the upper hand, and, in the end, dominate affairs and move them in its direction. It is, moreover, a great thing how the common interest becomes personified in the prince and necessarily appears as his own interest in his self-awareness.

KARL: But then why don't you allow the spirit of the community to come to its full awareness and expression? Why do you avoid representative bodies?

FRIEDRICH: Heraclitus tells us that the hidden harmony is often better than the obvious one. You must not misunderstand me. I do not condemn these forms of government. I wish that, wherever they do exist, they would develop in as salutary and brilliant a manner as possible. But I do not regard them at all as being indispensable. I am of the opinion that the public spirit has still other organs which often serve it even better.

KARL: Do you mean that this inner relationship is better than all forms of social contract?

FRIEDRICH: What naturally belongs together does not need it. No treaty is required between parents and children, between brothers and other members of the family.

KARL: I have one more thing on my mind. You give to the state so many attributes of spiritual unity, and the submission you demand to it is so complete, that I am afraid that you encroach upon the territory of the church.

FRIEDRICH: I should think not. Church and state are perpetually separate. The church links mankind in the highest, most supreme, society. She establishes an unchangeable rule of conduct, the rule of this mysterious society, that of religion. She tries to ward off everything which might damage it. But here is also the limit of her effectiveness. In a positive way, she does not have any influence upon human affairs. Whatever she claims in secular power she loses in spiritual force. She has, as I have said, nothing direct to do with the institutions of the state.

KARL: But both of these possess a spiritual nature. Where would you draw the boundaries between them?

FRIEDRICH: The spirit of the church is applicable to all humanity, is universal. By nature, each church asserts its universality. The idea of the state, on the other hand, would be destroyed if it were to include the entire world, for there are many states. The spirit of the state is truly touched with the divine, but rests upon human efforts. The state is a society of limited nature; above it there soars a higher society more freed from practical affairs.

KARL: Now I believe I grasp your thought as a whole: the states are spiritual entities, distinguished from one another by necessity and by their idea. Forms of constitution and the particular institutions necessitated by the general requirements of human existence are modified by this idea, which first fills them with reality and necessarily makes them into something different. Private and public life are up to a certain point identical. Private life is also dependent upon the idea which animates the state. These manifold creations of spiritual life are subordinated to the highest society, that of the church.

FRIEDRICH: But only come to see these entities in their full significance! So many separate, earthly-spiritual communities, called forth by genius and by moral energy, caught up in never-ending development, each in its own way progressing toward the ideal with its own inner drive, through the disturbances of the world! Behold them, these heavenly bodies in their orbits, their mutual attraction, their systems!

from the "Political Dialogue" (SW 49/50:323–24, 328–29, 337–39).

# FREEDOM AND NECESSITY

In history, too, freedom and necessity contend with and infuse each other. Freedom appears more in personalities; necessity, in the life of common humanity. But is the first really ever complete, or the second ever absolute?

(SW 40/41:v).

# THE GREAT
# COMBINATIONS

Out of the distance of the centuries we come to know the great combinations which lie within things. But the real activity of any contemporary present cannot be dependent upon these combinations. It arises from a proper conduct of the matters immediately at hand, on the good cause which one supports, on the moral energy which one applies. The forces which determine the progress of world history are, I might say, a divine mystery; the worth of a man consists in his own self-determination and activity.

from the *History of the Reformation in Germany* (SW 4:46).

History is no criminal court.

from his biography of Wallenstein (SW 23/24:513).

# POWER, MORALITY, AND THE
# PRIMACY OF FOREIGN AFFAIRS

KARL: In your political philosophy, it seems that foreign relations would play a great part.

FRIEDRICH: The world, as they say, has all been occupied by someone. To be something, you have to rise through your own efforts, and develop true independence. The rights which will not be conceded to us must be fought for.

KARL: But won't everything then be decided by brute force?

FRIEDRICH: Not so much as the word "fight" might seem to indicate. When the basis is at hand to form a community, it will still require moral energy above all else, if it is to raise itself to universal significance. This alone can enable it to overcome its competitors and enemies.

KARL: Then you consider the bloodiest warfare to be a contest of moral energies! Beware, lest you become too sublime!

FRIEDRICH: You know very well, that our ancestors, who certainly were not sublime, also thought of things that way. Thus those Tenctarians, those Amivarians, offered the Romans combat over the possession of vacant territory. But, in point of fact, you would be able to name very few significant wars in which it could not be shown that true moral energy achieved the final victory.

KARL: And from these battles and victories you will now derive the forms of internal political organization?

FRIEDRICH: Not completely, not originally, but certainly their modifications. The degree of its independence determines a state's position in the world, and requires that the state mobilize all its inner resources for the goal of self-preservation. This is its supreme law.

from the "Political Dialogue" (SW 49:327–28).

# POWER AND SPIRITUAL
# FORCE IN HISTORY

Victory falls wherever the greatest energy, the most vital concentration of forces, lies. What we often describe as material force has in itself a higher significance, for the greatest possible unfolding of the rule of the spirit reveals itself among the most resolute.

Every century has the tendency to consider itself the most progressive, and to measure all others according to its own ideas.

That is why we study history. An age must always be brought to a realization of its own image and of how it came to be.

But how and when was this concept itself fashioned?

Only the outbreak of conflict reveals which historical forces are the strongest. If we could calculate these, then history would become predictable.

from Ranke's notes; Fuchs dates it "1846?" (SW 53/54:570).

# THE HISTORIAN'S TASK

The task of the historian: Everyone is satisfied when a poetic work combines spiritual content and pure form. When a scholarly book thoroughly works over its material and explains it anew, we expect no more. The task of the historian is at once both learned and literary, for history is at once both art and science. It must fulfill the same demands of criticism and learning as a philological study, yet offer the educated reader the same pleasure as the most accomplished literary production. One might perhaps incline to the belief that beauty of form can be attained only by a sacrifice of the truth. Were this so, then we would have to give up the ideal of joining art and scholarship, and condemn it as false.

But I am convinced of the contrary. I think that the effort to improve the form also improves the investigation. On what should we base our narrative if not on living knowledge? But this is not to be achieved without penetrating and creative research. A free and great form can be the result only of something most fully understood and apprehended.

This is truly an ideal, which will never be attained, and which is unendingly difficult to strive toward. Successful poetic creations are undying; historical works of great reputation and usefulness become obsolete. This is especially true of modern history, where the nature of the subject makes it inevitable that much will remain hidden for a long time, and where an author will have no means other than his suspicion with which to discover (or perhaps conceal) events which he will nonetheless present as recognized truth. Facts which later come to light reveal the attempted reconstruction as erroneous. The chief requirement for an historical work remains always that it be true; that events actually happened as they are described. The scholarly service performed by the work is by far the most important. In order for us to put together a work which does not bear the imprint of the past, our research must proceed to a stage at which the whole truth in its full extent can be safely determined.

from the *History of France* (SW 12:5).

# THE HISTORIAN'S IDEAL

To look at the world, past and present, to absorb it into my being as far as my powers will enable me; to draw out and appropriate all that is beautiful and great, to see with unbiased eyes the progress of universal history, and in this spirit to produce beautiful and noble works; imagine what happiness it would be for me if I could realize this ideal, even in a small degree.

(SW 53/54:261).


# THE HISTORIAN'S OFFICE

*To* his son Otto

May 25, 1873

I was overjoyed by the hearty reception which you have accorded the Correspondence [of Friedrich Wilhelm IV with Bunsen]. One requires an inner sympathetic understanding which can arise only from conviction to appreciate the book. Had I felt duty bound to public opinion or anxious to win its applause, I would never have written it. But that was never my intention. Historical scholarship and writing is an office which can be compared only with the priest's, no matter how secular the objects with which it is concerned.

For the running current seeks to dominate the past and force it into its course. The historian exists to understand and to learn to understand the significance of every epoch in and for itself. He must impartially keep in view only the object itself and nothing more. Over everything hovers the divine order of things, which, though it cannot be directly proven, can be intuited. In this divine order, which is identical with the succession of the ages, significant individuals have their place; and in such a way must the historian comprehend them. The historical method, which seeks only the genuine and the true, thus enters into an immediate relationship with the highest questions of humanity. . . .

from "Erinnerungen an Leopold von Ranke mit bisher
ungedruckten Aufzeichnungen desselben . . ."
(*Gartlenlaube*, 51 [1895], 874).

# AN HISTORIAN
# MUST BE OLD

The proverb tells us that poets are born. Not only in the arts, but even in some scholarly fields, young men develop into full bloom, or at least show their original energy. Musicians and mathematicians have the expectation of attaining eminence in early years. But an historian must be old, not only because of the immeasurable extent of his field of study, but because of the insight into the historical process which a long life gives, especially under changing conditions. The great writers of antiquity lived among the movements of republican politics: the most read and perhaps the best of all historians, on the very threshold of the republic and the monarchy, nourished by the first and not hindered by the second, at the moment when the latter gathered into itself all the strands of civilization.

It is fortunate for a modern historian to belong to a monarchical state, especially in an age which does not limit his genius. But it would hardly be bearable for him to have only a short span of experience. For his personal development requires that great events complete their course before his eyes, that others collapse, that new forms be attempted. It is often said that an historian must be active in public affairs. This may well be true, if one is thinking of an account of the particulars of government. But this experience is not universally required of all historians. What is necessary is that they have a vital participation in the events of the time, that where possible they make intimate acquaintance with the principal leading personalities, so that the changing pattern of events appears before their eyes as it occurs. My own sympathies belong to a monarchy, which offers a secure basis for cultural life, and acts independently in world affairs. But I have never felt allegiance to any particular or narrowly restrictive form of monarchy.

a diary entry (SW 53/54:613).

# THOUGHTS
# AT EIGHTY

November 1875

Old age in and of itself is loneliness.

For the aging body loses its ability to react meaningfully; the soul is turned back in upon itself. Just as the life of society withdraws itself from us, so we ourselves withdraw from society. As the infirmities of the body increase, can the spirit maintain itself? I find that the spirit exercises a great influence on the whole person, even the life of the body. Nothing is more important for this than to fix my thoughts on my studies, which are at once productive and regenerative. In the world of thought, loneliness is even useful; I am less disturbed by the trifles of the situation or by daily events. I am afraid sometimes of how little attention I am able to pay to them these days.

Is this not egoism? But, I think, not only a permitted form, but a necessary one, for one's inner existence depends upon it.

a diary entry (SW 53/54:604).

# HIS OLD STUDENTS

April 6, 1884
The presence of the once young but now graying members of my historical seminar brings to my memory the studies we long ago began in German history. A lengthy series of the Yearbooks of the German Empire lies before my eyes, and I am aware of the still greater picture of historical and diplomatic studies carried out in all directions. What we then so quietly began, the seed we planted, has now become a mighty tree in which the birds of heaven nest.

The historical seminar connected my thoughts with the earlier studies I had carried on while I was in Frankfurt. Even then I had begun to peruse the old collections of various documents, albeit with incompletely authentic texts. My memory returned still further to Stenzel, who was tutor for a preacher in Leipzig, though a trained historian by profession. Under his direction, I saw the first collection of *Scriptores*, and began to read them in his house. This I continued in Frankfurt, where I attempted a work about the old emperors in preparing my lessons. Since then, the first volumes of Pertz appeared, but they continued down only to Carolingian times, not really into German history.

We therefore had to begin by revising the old editions. I am still amazed at the talent and effort of those young men who gathered around me. They were: Giesebrecht, who visited me today; Köpke, Wilmans, and Waitz. Of the last I said even at the time—for he made such an impression on me—that he was destined to become the Muratori of German history. Giesebrecht had poetic talent; even at that early date he knew how to write. Köpke was full of wisdom, with the gifts of a scholar; Dönniges, enterprising, full of practical intentions. Among this group the work prospered. We took up the job of the chronicle of Corvey, whose falsehood I first recognized, but was unable to prove. The members of our group carried out the research which proved it counterfeit. At the time Waitz was absent; he had gone to Copenhagen, and when he returned, he tried to attack our thesis, but was finally convinced. Along with Hirsch, another of our able colleagues, he then completed the editing of the work in a way which convinced everyone. Hirsch was the youngest of them all, very well prepared, and zealous.

We then agreed to edit the Yearbooks of the Saxon Dynasty. What brought about my determination to undertake this was primarily the example of Räumer's Hohenstaufen and Stenzel's Salian emperors. While I was traveling through the Harz mountains and visiting Quedlinburg, the remains of this era made a great impression on me. Perhaps, too, I was influenced by my earliest childhood memories of the monastery at Memleben, and the valley of the Unstrut, where my family lived.

We could hardly compete with the two works mentioned, with so many and such different persons working together. We resolved upon partial publication of our work, in volumes for which we expected no financial return. My introductions set the direction of our labor. I should include them in my collected works, just as they were. The blessing of Heaven guided these beginnings. The men I mentioned have made fine careers for themselves, and they all remain friends— insofar as they still live—with each other and with me. It is a sort of family founded in literature. May no ill wind destroy this friendship!

a diary entry (SW 53/54:649ff.).

# THE LEGACY

. . . For, in fact, knowledge is a possession; one could say a great entailed estate. It is an acquisition in the realm of spirit. One generation passes it on to the next; and eternal blame belongs to those who let it be destroyed, for they are bound to deliver it, no less than the soil we cultivate or the cities we inhabit, as an inheritance from the generations which preceded us to those which follow. . . . But it is not sufficient to maintain it in lifeless books and libraries. It lives only in the spirit. The true transmission occurs only in living persons, withdrawn from the world in lonely pondering, who have mastered knowledge and filled their souls with it. The state must take care that such persons live, and live in honor, as befits those who practice one of the noblest professions—I except the armed defense of the fatherland— which humanity can practice, and see that they are able to develop their gifts in freedom.

from "Über die Wechselwirkungen zwischen Staat, Publikum,
Lehrern, und Schülern in Beziehung auf ein Gymnasium,"
(*Frühe Schriften*, pp. 619–20).

# Annotated Bibliography

FOR THE ENGLISH-SPEAKING READER, there is at once too much and too little available on Ranke. The German literature is enormous, comprising, in addition to Ranke's own voluminous writings, a very large number of specialized studies, dissertations, articles in journals, and *Festschriften*. To a large extent, subsequent German historiography has been a dialogue with Ranke, and there are many superb insights into his work in this literature.

Ranke's own works may be found in these collected editions: Sämtliche Werke, 54 vols. (1868–1890); and *Weltgeschichte*, 9 vols. (1881–1888). Supplementing the Collected Works are the critically edited re-editions of Ranke's *Deutsche Geschichte im Zeitalter der Reformation*, ed. J. Joachimsen, 6 vols. (1925–1926); and *Zwölf Bücher preussischer Geschichte*, ed. G. Küntzel, 3 vols. (1930) from the incompleted effort of the German Academy of Sciences to public critical editions of all Ranke's works. Later reissues of Ranke's main works are reprints of these earlier texts. Supplementing the personal letters and notes in Volume 53/54 of the Collected Works are *Das Briefwerk*, ed. Walther Peter Fuchs (Hamburg, 1949) and *Neue Briefe*, edd. Bernard Hoeft and Hans Herzfeld (Hamburg, 1949). The Historical Commission of the Bavarian Academy of Sciences (of which Ranke was a founding member) is now publishing a series of excerpts from Ranke's surviving unpublished manuscripts. So far Volume one, *Tagebücher*, ed. Walther Peter Fuchs (1964) and Volume two, *Über die Epochen der neueren Geschichte*, edd. Theodor Schieder and Helmut Berding (1971) have appeared under the general title *Aus Werk und Nachlass*. Volume three, *Frühe Schriften*, covering Ranke's activities to 1824, appeared in 1973. Volume four, *Vorlesungseinleitungen* (1975), contains excerpts from his lectures.

English editions of Ranke's writings include:

*History of the Latin and Teutonic Nations, 1494–1514*, trans. P. A. Ashworth (London, 1887); and G. R. Dennis (London, 1909); both omit the Introduction and the critical appendix, *Zur Kritik neuerer Geschichtsschreiber*.

*The Ottoman and Spanish Monarchies in the Sixteenth and Seventeenth Centuries*, trans. Walter K. Kelly (London, 1843; Philadelphia, 1845).

*The Popes of Rome: Their Ecclesiastical and Political History During the Sixteenth and Seventeenth Centuries,* trans. Sarah Austin (London, 1840). Other translations of the *Popes* were done by Elizabeth Foster (London, 1845), available in a revised three-volume edition by G. R. Dennis (London, 1907); by D. D. Scott, with an introduction by J. H. Merle D'Aubigne (Glasgow, 1846–1847); and by Walter K. Kelly (London, 1842; Philadelphia, 1844). This was Ranke's most popular work, and there have been several editions of the above.

*History of the Reformation in Germany,* trans. Sarah Austin (London, 1845–1847; Philadelphia, 1844). A 1905 re-edition is now available as a reprint (New York, 1966).

*Memoirs of the House of Brandenburg and History of Prussia During the Seventeenth and Eighteenth Centuries,* trans. Sir Alexander and Lady Duff Gordon, 3 vols. (London, 1849). Another translation, of only Volume I, by a Professor Demmler appeared in London in 1847–1848. This is a translation of Ranke's nine books of Prussian history rather than of the later, expanded version containing twelve books.

*Civil Wars and Monarchy in France in the Sixteenth and Seventeenth Centuries: A History of France,* trans. M. A. Garvey, 2 vols. (London, 1852; New York, 1853; repr. New York, 1973). This includes just a part of Ranke's French history, extending only to 1593.

*History of England Principally in the Seventeenth Century,* 6 vols. (Oxford, 1875; repr. New York, 1966).

*Universal History. I. The Oldest Historical Group of Nations and the Greeks,* trans. G. W. Prothero (London, 1884; New York, 1885).

*Ferdinand I and Maximilian of Austria: An Essay on the Political and Religious State of Germany Immediately after the Reformation,* trans. Lady Lucie Duff Gordon (London, 1853).

In addition, there are modern translations of a few Ranke pieces: the Introduction to the *History of the Latin and Teutonic Nations* by Fritz Stern in his collection *The Varieties of History* (New York, 1956); the essay on "The Great Powers" and the "Political Dialogue" of 1836 are both sensitively translated by Hildegard Hunt von Laue in Theodor H. von Laue, *Leopold Ranke: The Formative Years* (Princeton, N.J., 1950). Georg Iggers and Konrad von Moltke have edited an excellent anthology of Ranke pieces which complements the present volume, with translations by Wilma A. Iggers and Konrad von Moltke: Leopold von Ranke, *The Theory and Practice of History* (Indianapolis & New York, 1973).

The best general study of Ranke's life and work is that of Leonard Krieger, *Ranke: The Meaning of History* (Chicago, 1977). Von Laue's perceptive study of Ranke's earlier development, mentioned above, ends with 1836. Briefer surveys of Ranke's entire career can be found in: G. P. Gooch, *History and Historians in the Nineteenth Century*, rev. ed. (Boston, 1959); Hans Liebeschütz, *Ranke* (Historical Association Pamphlet; London, 1954); and Georg G. Iggers, *The German Conception of History: The National Tradition of Historical Thought from Herder to the Present* (Middletown, Conn., 1968). The last has the special virtue of placing Ranke within the complex tradition of German historicism, and showing some of the implications which his work had for his pupils and successors. Peter Gay's *Style in History* (New York, 1974) has a useful interpretative chapter on Ranke.

Some accounts by contemporaries throw light on Ranke's international significance for nineteenth-century historians: Herbert Baxter Adams, "Leopold von Ranke," *American Historical Association Papers* III (New York, 1888), pp. 101–20; Edward G. Bourne, "Leopold von Ranke," *Annual Report of the American Historical Association* (Washington, 1896), pp. 67–81. Lord Acton treats him not only in book reviews, but in two essays: "Inaugural Lecture on the Study of History" (in *Essays on Freedom and Power*, ed. Gertrude Himmelfarb [Boston, 1948], pp. 3–29) and "German Schools of History" (in *Historical Essays and Studies*, edd. John Neville Figgis and Reginald Vere Laurence [London, 1926], pp. 344–92). Acton's own attitude toward Ranke and Ranke's contribution are discussed in Herbert Butterfield's *Man on His Past* (Cambridge, 1955; repr. Boston, 1960).

See also Helen Liebel, "Ranke's Fragments on Universal History," *Clio*, 2, No. 2 (February 1973), pp. 145–59. Ranke's relationship to classical history is explored in Hajo Holborn's "Thucydides and Ranke," in *The Interpretation of History*, ed. J. R. Strayer (Princeton, N.J., 1943). Also useful for this topic is Helen Liebel's "The Place of Antiquity in Ranke's Philosophy of History," *Clio*, 5, No. 2 (Winter 1976), 211–31.

The effects of Ranke on later historians and the public are treated critically by Pieter Geyl, "Ranke in the Light of the Catastrophe," in Geyl's *Debates with Historians* (Cleveland & New York, 1958). Contrasting with Geyl's negative assessment of Ranke's influence upon German politics, Friedrich Meinecke tried to weigh the relative contributions of "Ranke and Burckhardt" in his address of that title to the German Academy of

Sciences in Berlin in 1948, concluding in favor of the latter, after having spent his whole life's work in the tradition of Ranke. A translation, by Karl W. Deutsch, is available in *German History: Some New German Views*, ed. Hans Kohn (Boston, 1954).

Finally, the subsequent influence of Ranke on history in Germany and America is traced in articles by Georg Iggers, "The Image of Ranke in American and German Historical Thought," *History and Theory*, 2 (1962), 17–40; and Ferdinand Schevill, "Ranke, Rise, Decline and Persistence of a Reputation," *Journal of Modern History*, 24 (1952), 219–34.

Readers seeking to explore the extensive German literature should begin with the bibliography in the newest edition of Dahlmann-Waitz, *Quellenkunde der deutschen Geschichte* (Stuttgart, 1965— ), Section 7, and Günter Johannes Herz, *Leopold Ranke: Leben, Denken, Wort, 1795–1814* (Cologne, 1968), which updates the earlier *Ranke Bibliographie* edited by Hans F. Helmholt (Leipzig, 1910). Helmholt's biography, *Leopold Rankes Leben und Wirken* (Leipzig, 1921) is valuable, as are the essay by Alfred Dove in the *Allgemeine Deutsche Biographie* (XXVII 258–59) and Eugen Guglia's *Leopold von Rankes Leben und Werke* (Leipzig, 1893). Friedrich Meinecke dealt with Ranke frequently in his own work, as a disciple in the Idealist tradition. Aside from the above-mentioned "Ranke and Burckhardt," see his 1936 memorial address "Leopold v. Ranke," appended to his *Die Entstehung des Historismus*, reprinted as *Werke* III (Munich, 1959). An English translation, *Historicism* (London, 1971), contains an introduction by Isaiah Berlin. There is another brief sketch of Ranke, in Meinecke's *Zur Theorie und Philosophie der Geschichte*, ed. Eberhard Kessel, *Werke* IV (Stuttgart, 1965), pp. 254–63.

Finally, the reader is referred to a number of specialized studies which give further bibliography and suggestions for understanding Ranke. For analysis of his relation to other thinkers of the Romantic era, see Carl Hinrichs, *Ranke und die Geschichtstheologie der Goethezeit* (Göttingen, 1954); and Theodor Schieder, "Ranke und Goethe," and "Das historische Weltbild Leopold von Ranke's" both in Schieder's *Begegnungen mit der Geschichte* (Göttingen, 1962). Ranke's historical logic is carefully related to the Romantic and to Droysen in Hellmut Diwald's *Das historische Erkennen* (Leiden, 1955). His political significance is treated in Wilhelm Mommsen, *Stein, Ranke, Bismarck* (Munich, 1954), and Otto Vossler, *Ranke und die Politik* (Wiesbaden, 1961). A critical view of Ranke's neglect of social factors and conservatism is given in Gerhard Schilfert, "Leopold von Ranke," in *Studien über die deutsche Geschichtswissenschaft*

I, ed. Joachim Streisand (East Berlin, 1963), pp. 241–70. Rudolf Vierhaus presents a more balanced approach in his *Ranke und die soziale Welt* (Münster, 1957).

Ranke's appreciation of universal history is explored by Ernst Schulin, *Die weltgeschichtliche Erfassung des Orients bei Hegel und Ranke* (Göttingen, 1958); his founding of an historical school is treated in Günter Berg, *Leopold von Ranke als akademischer Lehrer* (Göttingen, 1968). Both these books draw extensively upon the unpublished notes of Ranke's lectures at Berlin, and reveal many insights complementary to his printed works on modern history. Some of these notes and fragments will appear in the series edited by Walther Peter Fuchs, *Aus Werk und Nachlass*, still in progress. A guide to some of the insights which these manuscripts can provide is offered in Herz's *Leopold Ranke: Leben, Denken, Wort, 1795–1814*, mentioned earlier. Some of Herz's interpretations of Ranke's work differ from those of Fuchs and his staff of co-workers, primarily over readings of the nearly impossible handwriting of the great historian. If the shade of Ranke no longer dominates German historical scholarship, a lively interest in him continues, and further studies may be expected.

# INDEX